Korean American Evangelicals

Korean American Evangelicals

New Models for Civic Life

ELAINE HOWARD ECKLUND

UNIVERSITY PRESS

2006

UNIVERSITY PRESS

Oxford University Press, Inc., publishes works that further
Oxford University's objective of excellence
in research, scholarship, and education.

Oxford   New York
Auckland   Cape Town   Dar es Salaam   Hong Kong   Karachi
Kuala Lumpur   Madrid   Melbourne   Mexico City   Nairobi
New Delhi   Shanghai   Taipei   Toronto

With offices in
Argentina   Austria   Brazil   Chile   Czech Republic   France   Greece
Guatemala   Hungary   Italy   Japan   Poland   Portugal   Singapore
South Korea   Switzerland   Thailand   Turkey   Ukraine   Vietnam

Copyright © 2006 by Oxford University Press, Inc.

Published by Oxford University Press, Inc.
198 Madison Avenue, New York, New York 10016

www.oup.com

Oxford is a registered trademark of Oxford University Press

All rights reserved. No part of this publication may be reproduced,
stored in a retrieval system, or transmitted, in any form or by any means,
electronic, mechanical, photocopying, recording, or otherwise,
without the prior permission of Oxford University Press.

Library of Congress Cataloging-in-Publication Data
Ecklund, Elaine Howard.
Korean American evangelicals : new models for civic life / Elaine Howard Ecklund.
p. cm.
Includes bibliographical references and index.
ISBN-13 978-0-19-537259-5

1. Korean Americans—Religion.   2. Christianity and politics—United States.   3. Church work
with immigrants—United States.   4. Evangelicalism—United States.   I. Title.
BR563.K67E35   2006
280'.4089957073—dc22   2006005349

Printed in the United States of America
on acid-free paper

Preface

On a warm summer day while attending a wedding in northern California, I spoke with Scott, the pastor of a small, largely white, evangelical Christian church. During our conversation, I asked Scott what he thought are some of the most pressing issues currently facing Christian churches. I was surprised when he responded by talking about the increasing racial and ethnic diversity in American Christianity. In an animated fashion, he went on to discuss how he learned through a regional meeting of his denomination that the most influential church in his area is a 2,000-member multiethnic congregation with a large number of Asian members. Scott told me specifically about this church's Korean American leaders, who he said are bringing novel issues to the fore at regional denomination meetings. He told me these pastors have helped him realize that the Christian message necessitates that churches increase their abilities to reach out to diverse ethnic and racial groups and advocate for social justice on behalf of poor ethnic minorities. Scott said he wonders how this will happen in his particular congregation.

Two years after that initial conversation, I saw Scott again and he told me that an Asian American congregation now uses his church's fellowship hall for its services. Initially a small group, the Asian American congregation quickly outgrew the membership of his own church and is now rejuvenating some of his congregation's programs. He and other leaders of his church are thinking about letting the Asian American congregation take over the sanctuary and moving their church into the smaller fellowship hall, or even trying to join the two congregations together.

At its most encompassing, this book addresses the issues brought to light in my discussions with Scott. It provides a window into the influence that Korean Americans and other nonwhite evangelicals are having and will likely continue to have on American evangelicalism, particularly on evangelical attitudes toward race, ethnicity, and social justice. I initiated a study of religion and civic integration because I wanted to know whether new Americans are using religion to become involved in American civic life and to what extent their civic involvement will look like that of other groups of religious Americans. Through talking with various white evangelical pastors around the country, I quickly realized that Asian Americans are growing rapidly within American evangelicalism. I developed a growing interest in how faith influences the lives of Asian American evangelicals generally, and how it influences their civic involvement specifically. I was especially curious about how this happens for members of the second generation, who often have the citizenship and U.S. cultural background their parents lacked at their age. I decided to investigate this set of issues by looking at second-generation Korean American evangelicals, a growing part of this influx.

Against the backdrop of the broad changes that growing ethnic diversity is bringing to American evangelicalism, I take an in-depth look at two different types of evangelical congregations attended by Korean Americans. I tell the stories of Korean Americans in these churches who are struggling with issues of what it means to be an American and how their identities as Christians shape their concepts of race, ethnicity, and the consequent frameworks of caring for a local community. I show that their churches help Korean Americans look outward to consider the different ways Christians ought to care for a broader American society. And I argue that, particularly for other groups, who, like the Korean Americans I studied, already have educational and financial resources, the kinds of moral frameworks their churches provide for interpreting race and ethnicity may be *more* important for civic life than their role in providing skills for civic participation. In the end, Korean Americans' religious communities may help them order and shape their own racial and ethnic identities and the way these inform civic identities. It is from these case studies that I draw broader implications about the influence Korean Americans and other nonwhite evangelicals are having on American evangelicalism. Some of the Korean Americans I studied view themselves as part of a Christian ethnic minority—the kind of civic identification that may lead them to join with other nonwhite Americans in bringing changes to the relationship American evangelicalism has with civic life.

When I first began this book, I imagined what it would be like to write about the process that brought it into being. Social scientists have a unique vantage point, in that they study the world of which they are very much a part. As a result, many research endeavors germinate from personal life experiences. This book really began through my experiences at college, where, in the midst of a faith community, I began to reflect on what my upbringing as part of a racially diverse (black and white) family might mean. Since I came from a largely white, rural town in upstate New York, it was only during college that I developed friendships with those who were the children of immigrants. The second-generation immigrants, and particularly the Korean Americans who were part of this faith community, pushed me to think about the racial space I occupied as a white person in American society. They also shared openly about their own struggles of what it meant for them to come to terms with issues of race. In particular, they wondered, as those with the resources of education from an elite private university and, for some, with wealth, how they would give back to American society and what kind of impediments they might face as those who are sometimes seen as racial outsiders when trying to do community service. These personal experiences resurfaced again in graduate school and formed part of the motivation to do a more formal study of religion and civic life among a second-generation immigrant group, and particularly among Korean Americans.

Those who made this research possible by letting me into their churches, homes, and, in many cases, their lives, so that I might tell their stories here, deserve my sincere thanks. The leadership of "Grace" and "Manna," who became the subjects of the two central case studies for this research, deserves special gratitude, and I am grateful to them as well for allowing me to spend extended time in their congregations. I am thankful also to Oxford University Press for supporting this work, and particularly to my editors, Cynthia Read and Julia TerMaat.

Several small grants supported this research. Support for data collection came from the Religious Research Association and the Society for the Scientific Study of Religion. In addition, I received a grant for data analysis from the Graduate School at Cornell University. I presented portions of this research at the University of Southern California, Princeton University, and Cornell University and at meetings of the Society for the Scientific Study of Religion, the American Sociological Association, and the Religious Research Association. Conversations following these presentations provided valuable insight at various stages of this research. Several individuals provided useful feedback through lengthy discussions at various phases of the research and on portions of the manuscript. Special thanks go to Nancy Tatom Ammerman, Karen Chai Kim, Derek Chang, R. Stephen Warner, Pyong Gap Min, Helen Rose Ebaugh, Rhys H. Williams, Paul Lichterman, and Richard Alba. Pastors Dave Jones, Chuck Tompkins, Harry Heinz, Kate Kotfila, John Lee, Christine Lee, and Peter T. Cha all provided useful insights about American evangelicalism or Korean American evangelicals. In particular, Michael O. Emerson has provided valuable support and feedback during various stages of research and writing.

I spent a year at Princeton University as a visiting graduate student during the time I did background work for this study. I met several individuals there who gave of their time (sometimes extensively) to help me with this research. Thank you to Patricia Fernández-Kelly, Michèle Lamont, Margarita Mooney, Joan Walling, Becky Y. Hsu, Conrad Hackett, Jennifer Wiley Legath, and Tisa Wenger for discussions and helpful insights. Thank you to Robert and Margaret Slighton, who provided a place to live during that year.

During the data collection and editing of the manuscript, several individuals provided research support and valuable assistance with editing and formatting the manuscript. These include Emily Levitt, Satina Smith, Leslie Smith, Aggie Steele, and Melanie L. Daglian.

The bulk of revision on the manuscript was completed during a postdoctoral fellowship at Rice University. I am thankful to my colleagues at Rice, who have provided the ideal scholarly community in which to write a first book. Elizabeth Long, in particular, provided guidance during the process of publication. Anne Lincoln has been a helpful sounding board throughout this process.

Several friends read early, middle, and final drafts of this work. These include Kristen Schultz Lee, Kelly Dietz, Wendy Cadge, Jerry Park, and D. Michael Lindsay. Beyond their help with ideas and advice on writing, these friends deserve my gratitude for tireless encouragement. During my time at Cornell University, I received helpful guidance in and strong support of this research from Victor Nee and David Strang. Also at Cornell, Diana Hernandez, Evelyn Bush, Pawan Dhingra, and Keith Hjortshoj and other members of the Cornell University interdisciplinary writing group provided helpful insights that strengthened research and writing.

Thank you to Penny Edgell and Robert Wuthnow. I hope to repay you by providing the kind of academic mentoring to others that you have provided to me.

My personal community outside the academy provides a constant reminder that there is much more to life than the scholarship that occupies so much of my time. Thank you, in particular, to my parents, Robert and Betty Howard, Bonnie Howell, Fern Vaughn, and Stan and Marian Ecklund. I have received no end of encouragement from each of you. I thank my siblings Carolyn August, Kate Howell, Ellamay Vaughn Reyes, Anthony, Aaron, Elissa, Amy, Andrew, and Adam Vaughn, Kier and Hung Ecklund, and Karen and Kreig Ecklund. Several friends provided particular support during crucial parts of this research. These include Shanna, Stephen, Emma, Elizabeth, and Peter Jesch, Barbara Westin, Jim and Jill McCullough, Jimmy and Christine Lee, and others who are part of my larger church community.

Finally, my deepest gratitude goes to my husband, Karl. Your intellectual and emotional support of me during this research has far surpassed anything for which I could have hoped.

Contents

1. Religion and Civic Life for Korean Americans, 3
2. Theoretical Interlude: A Cultural Approach to Connecting Institutions and Identities, 17
3. Religion, Race, and Ethnicity in Two Churches, 29
4. Models of Civic Responsibility, 51
5. Civic Identities, 73
6. Civic Models and Community Service, 95
7. Evangelicalism and Politics for Korean Americans, 119
8. Implications for Institutional Change, 139

   Appendix A: Data and Methods, 159
   Appendix B: Interview and Survey Guides, 165
   Notes, 173
   References, 189
   Index, 199

Korean American Evangelicals

I

Religion and Civic Life for Korean Americans

Bill is a second-generation Korean American in his midtwenties who works as an engineer.[1] As I sat across from him in a noisy coffee shop in Old Town, a small city in the Northeast, I asked Bill where he fits in American society and what difference attending a church with only other Korean Americans makes in his life. Bill told me he does not see himself as being very Korean: "I guess at times I think of myself as a Korean American, but I mostly think of myself as a U.S. citizen." Later Bill explained that he is primarily a "Christian" and an "American." He said being a Christian means believing that "Jesus Christ came to save my sins and that I must share my faith with others," a definition that aligns well with that given by many white evangelicals.[2]

The relationship between religion and civic life for Bill would not easily be captured by a survey of civic practices. Bill does not vote regularly. He does not participate actively in campaigns or donate much to nonreligious charities, either financially or through time. During my extended conversation with Bill I discovered, however, that in another sense he is very civic-minded. Church is a big part of Bill's life and much of his time outside of work is spent in church activities. Because it is a topic brought up in his church, Bill thinks often about the kinds of responsibilities to American society he has as a Christian. One of these is community service. Through church, Bill participates quite a lot in Old Town, often putting in overtime at work so that he can have the weekends free to help at a local community shelter for disadvantaged teens. Although his church motivates Bill to provide more help to the needy in his local community, he also finds it difficult because many of those in his community are black Americans living in poverty, a group to whom he finds it difficult to relate.

At a different coffee shop in Old Town, I spoke with Jim, also a second-generation Korean American in his midtwenties. Jim works as the director of youth ministry at a multiethnic church. Unlike those in Bill's church, Jim's congregation attracts individuals from various ethnic backgrounds, including some white and black Americans, as well as members of many non–Korean Asian ethnic groups. Jim has a more complicated interpretation of ethnic identity than Bill, and one that also influences the way he thinks about civic responsibility. Jim told me it is not easy for him to separate being American from being Korean and explained that he is inseparably "Korean American." According to Jim, "I go to Korea and I am American. And if I am here, well, then I am Korean... You can't really separate them because it is so intertwined."

It is easy for him to explain what it means to be a Christian, however, and Jim provides a definition that is similar to Bill's. Importantly, he also uses Christianity to interpret his sense of identity, in particular how he thinks about race and ethnicity. At Jim's church they talk a lot about race and ethnicity and their relationship to being a Christian. Being part of his church challenges Jim to break down racial and ethnic barriers—particularly those with black Americans—and to carefully consider how he might be an agent for social justice in his local community. The mandate to help in the local community that Jim hears in his church pushes him to think about how he might help others in a variety of contexts—it doesn't matter whether that helping occurs through the church or some other nonreligious community organization. According to Jim, his church helps him to "just [be] involved in the community... pouring resources back in to Old Town." Jim ended our discussion by posing a series of self-reflective questions: "Where do you see the Korean American community ten or fifteen years from now? How much will we have assimilated or kept to ourselves? As a group in America what will we look like collectively? What kind of contribution will we make?"

The stories of the Korean American evangelicals I present on these pages provide insight into broader issues of how religious participation guides the ways that children of new Americans are becoming involved in American civic life. It is clear that in some sense being a Christian means the same things to Bill and Jim. Both also think it is important to reach out to their local community. Each attends a church that reinforces this idea and provides different resources for community involvement. So, in a narrowly defined way, each experiences a form of civic assimilation, meaning that Bill and Jim both value caring for those outside their own ethnic community and outside their church.

But their churches play different roles in helping Bill and Jim develop civic identities and practices. For Bill, his church provides civic resources to help him think about what it means to be a good American, as well as church-sponsored programs to do actual community service. For Jim, a church-based model of civic life means the more individualized notion of simply using Christianity to break down barriers with others. His church helps Jim devise a personal ethic for civic participation, one that involves using Christianity to reinterpret his ideas about race, ethnicity, and class, and learn to think about caring for the poor and needy at all times, rather than be involved only in church-based programs.

Their discourse also provides insight into more complicated questions than whether or not assimilation occurs, bringing understanding of the kinds of cultural resources (specifically, interpretive frameworks) that different church contexts provide for developing ideas, identities, and, ultimately, practices related to civic life. Attention to their discourse also tells us how the different models of civic life Bill and Jim found in their churches compare to other evangelical Christian models for civic life.

In the pages ahead, I'll compare the cultural resources—in particular, the cultural schemas, or interpretive frameworks—that Korean American and mixed ethnic churches provide Korean American evangelicals for understanding racial and ethnic identities and the consequences such interpretations have for civic responsibility.[3]

Religious and Ethnic Diversity Influence American Civic Life

The American racial, ethnic, and religious landscapes are diversifying. Korean Americans like Bill and Jim are part of the growing number of nonwhite Americans. This group, census estimates tell us, resulted largely from post-1965 immigration and will grow to over 50 percent of the population by the middle of this century.[4] Most Korean Americans came to the United States during this large immigration influx, one that was due largely to reforms that ended many national-origin quotas.[5] These legal changes meant that immigrants from Asia, Latin America, and the Caribbean Basin replaced earlier waves of Europeans.[6] Korean Americans belong to the 10 percent and growing group of Americans who are *second-generation* immigrants, those born in the United States to immigrant parents, who will continue to reshape American institutions for years to come.[7] They are also part of the increasing number of Asian immigrants and their children. According to the 2000 Census, Asian immigrants accounted for over 40 percent of immigration between 1990 and 1999, and the Asian American population grew 43 percent nationwide to 10.8 million. Asian Americans currently constitute between 4 and 6 percent of the U.S. population and are one of the fastest growing immigrant groups in the United States.[8]

The increasing diversity of the American ethnic landscape has also meant changes to the religious landscape. While some bring non-Western religions, increasing the visibility of Buddhism, Hinduism, and Islam, the largest change to American religion is occurring as new immigrants restructure the racial and ethnic composition of American Christianity and, in particular, American evangelicalism.[9] Asian Americans, and Korean Americans specifically, are the largest nonwhite group in American evangelical seminaries, meaning that they stand poised to contribute significantly to this publicly influential tradition.[10]

In the age of what many call a declining civil society, it is centrally important to ask how changes in the racial, ethnic, and religious composition of the United States will influence how we live together as American citizens and how we experience civic life. American civic life incorporates all of the ways in which citizens realize their duties, rights, and responsibilities. It includes the kinds of choices we make as citizens about how to participate in American society—participation that can range from volunteering in a local soup kitchen to campaigning for politicians or causes. Civic actions are often borne out of our identities as citizens—they are generally voluntary, not aimed at reaping an economic profit, and are often concerned with improving some version of the common good.[11] American citizens all wrestle with the meaning of civic identity—the extent to which we see ourselves as being part of the United States. The content of civic identity consists of decisions about which groups we are part of and for whom we have a responsibility to provide care.

Religious communities are among the most central places where Americans form civic identities. Religion is an undeniably important facet of the American tapestry, and participation in religious communities is a way that many Americans link with one another. About 90 percent of Americans believe in God, and 40 percent say that they attend a congregation (place of worship) weekly.[12] Through their religious communities, Americans also link with nonreligious American civic life. Congregational attendance provides participants with religious teachings that justify community participation, networks of like-minded individuals (who ask them to participate), and an awareness of needs in their communities.[13] Alexis de Tocqueville, the early nineteenth-century French social observer, wrote that for Americans, "religious communities impart visions of the common good that support democratic participation."[14]

By far the largest percent of religiously involved Korean Americans are evangelicals. Since between 20 and 40 percent of all Americans identify themselves as evangelicals, Korean Americans are part of the largest religious movement in American society.[15] Evangelicals share certain core beliefs, including the Bible as trustworthy, human nature as sinful, hope for salvation in God's son, Jesus, absolute moral standards, a personal knowledge of God, and a mandate to share one's faith with others. We need only read a local newspaper to see that American evangelicals appear to be a religious group that is focused outwardly. They currently have a felt public presence at all levels of society: local, state, and national.[16] The most public model of evangelicalism is the "Religious Right," those who connect conservative Christianity with conservative political views on abortion, homosexuality, education, and other issues. Yet there are also other models of political participation among evangelicals.[17] A less public model is that among black churches. Although not always identifying as evangelicals, many black Americans are conservative as Christians and politically liberal on multiple social issues.[18] In addition, there is a small "Christian Left" among American evangelicals who connect Christianity to a more liberal social justice political framework, and there are a variety of other subgroups within the evangelical movement who combine various political views across a broader spectrum.[19]

Scholars of American religion have different interpretations of the extent to which being part of an evangelical church motivates local community participation and giving to the poor. Some argue that evangelicals are often more concerned about those in their own church communities than about wider societal participation. Because evangelicals stress listening to the individual conscience, developed from a relationship with God, over following the mandates of a religious tradition, evangelicalism may foster less care for the poor than religions that make such service a greater constituent of their tradition.[20] Others argue, however, that evangelicals are becoming increasingly aware of needs in their communities and, in some measures of volunteerism and financial contributions, actually surpass other groups of religious Americans.[21]

Scholars of late nineteenth- and early twentieth-century European immigration have seen religious participation as an important part of adjusting to civic life for new Americans. To these theorists, "cultural assimilation" has meant adopting the cultural patterns of the host society, including its religious beliefs.[22] In addition, high levels of cultural and religious assimilation were expected to foster large-scale inclusion into the networks and institutions of American society, including adaptation to mainstream American civic life. Those who study the religious participation of recent immigrants, however, largely focus on the ways religion fosters retention of ethnic networks and identities and provides functional resources for adaptation. Religious organizations offer places for immigrants to gain access to job networks, a social community in a new environment, and English language classes.[23] For the second generation, they provide reinforcement of an ethnic language and a means of learning practices that facilitate retention of ethnic identity.[24]

But what these studies largely have neglected is religion's power to bring broader civic integration, both the desire of new Americans to participate in American civic life and the desire of other Americans to accept new peoples.[25] Little work has focused outwardly—on how religious participation might guide new Americans toward caring for those in local communities outside their religious organizations, forming coalitions with diverse ethnic and racial groups, or getting involved in American politics. In the midst of growing concern about the influence of immigrant religion on the public arena, researchers need to focus outwardly and thoroughly examine the connection of religion to civic life for new Americans.

As this work examines religion and civic life for one group of new Americans, it will ask what kind of resources local congregations provide them with for developing civic identities. Scholars of early immigration note that part of becoming involved in American civil society has included integration into the Protestant, Catholic, or Jewish faith traditions.[26] Indeed, we need to ask, as Korean Americans and other new Americans become part of the dominant American religious movement known as evangelicalism, how they will adapt to broader evangelical models of civic responsibility.[27] We also need to ask to what extent new groups will *influence* and *change* American evangelicalism, particularly to reshape how evangelicals view the intersection between Christianity, race, and ethnicity, and their relationship to American civic life.

The Case of Korean American Evangelicals

Though Korean Americans are not the most populous second-generation immigrant group, several factors make them ideal for a study of evangelical Christianity's influence on civic life among new Americans.[28] They are Asian Americans, one of the two fastest growing racially defined groups of new immigrants.[29] Demographically, Korean Americans form a cohort older than some other groups of second-generation immigrants. Because there was a large wave of Korean immigration in the 1970s, there is a growing group of second-generation Korean Americans. Decisions about civic participation, whether to become politically active or volunteer in a local community, are more relevant to this group than they might be to a younger cohort; second-generation immigrants of middle-school age, for example, would have little opportunity to make independent decisions about civic involvement.[30] Korean Americans are also very likely to achieve economic and professional success in the United States, factors that often foster civic participation among other groups of Americans.[31] Therefore, in one sense Korean Americans are a group of new Americans that scholars would expect to easily become involved in American civic life. However, even though they are economically successful, as nonwhite Americans they also face significant barriers and discrimination in the course of their daily lives, with other Americans continuing to view them as "perpetual foreigners."[32] Because of discrimination and this sense of "otherness," it is not obvious that Korean Americans will be motivated to show concern for racial and ethnic groups outside their own.

Most Korean immigrants are Christians. There is a prevalent saying in the Korean community: "The Chinese come and they open a restaurant, and the Koreans come and they open a church."[33] South Koreans come from a nation that is heavily populated by Christians. Indeed, many of my respondents told me that their parents did not even know there were white Christians before coming to the United States. Since Christianity is such a central part of the Korean culture, their familiarity with this religion may mean Korean Americans have more freedom than other groups of immigrants to assert a particular approach to Christianity and civic life in American society.

Christianity in Korea and Korean American Christianity

To adequately understand religion in the U.S. Korean immigrant community, it is necessary to step back and briefly look at Christianity in Korea. The most rapid growth of Asian Christianity in the last century occurred in South Korea.[34] According to Korean studies specialist Andrew Kim, "by 1989, nearly one fourth of South Korea's 40 million people were Protestant Christians.... Moreover, by 1989, there were 29,820 Protestant churches and 55,989 pastors, making the Protestant Church in South Korea one of the most vital and dynamic in the world."[35] Much of what is distinctive about contemporary Korean Christianity can be traced to the influence of early twentieth-century Protestant missionaries. They imported what modern scholars think of as a fairly fundamentalist form of Christianity, which stressed the inerrant character of the Bible and firm ideas about morality.[36] However, Korean Christians made Christianity distinctively their own. They emphasized the Korean Confucian tradition of hierarchical relationships and the shamanist tradition of religious emotionalism. The rapid Christian expansion in Korea occurred in a period of Japanese occupation, which provided a unique subversive and political context in which Christianity thrived.[37]

While Buddhism and other religions are popular in the rural areas of Korea, Christians often inhabit cities. Those who live in the more prosperous Korean cities are also the most likely to emigrate. Most post-1965 Korean immigrants came to fill professional worker shortages in the United States, and many of these immigrants are Christians.[38] Korean immigrants quickly set up Christian churches after immigrating, importing pastors from Korea to lead these fledgling congregations. By 1990 there were about 2,000 Korean churches in the United States, with one church for every 300–350 Korean immigrants.[39] Although there are no recent studies, there are undoubtedly many more Korean churches today. As practitioners of conservative Protestant Christianity, Korean immigrants practice a religious tradition that is understood, is culturally accepted, and has an existing institutional infrastructure in American society. They become part of American denominations familiar to them from Korea, such as Methodism and Presbyterianism, and form separate Korean-speaking congregational associations affiliated with these larger bodies.[40]

Beyond spiritual fulfillment and maintenance of religious practices, churches provide a number of largely nonreligious functions for Korean immigrants.[41] For those who lose status in the migration process, churches are places where immigrants (particularly men) can retain positions of respect as leaders in their congregations. Through their churches, Korean immigrants find social services, education in American customs and ways of life, and help with locating jobs and navigating the American immigration system. Even those who are not Christians often attend church to obtain these social services.[42]

Much is known about religion for first-generation Korean immigrants, but less is known about their American-born children.[43] Although church leaders decry the "silent exodus" of the second generation from Korean churches, many second-generation Koreans are religiously involved.[44] One study of Korean Americans in the New York metropolitan area, for example, reveals that over 50 percent of Korean Americans there are involved in Protestant churches, many of which are evangelical.[45] Korean Americans most commonly attend all-Korean second-generation churches, similar to the church Bill attends.[46] These congregations are generally affiliated with and supported by first-generation churches. Increasingly, however, more Korean Americans are becoming part of pan-Asian or multiethnic churches, like the one Jim attends, a congregational form that is also growing in American society in general.[47] The small body of existing research on religion and the second generation generally focuses on the internal and functional roles of religion, such as its ability to help members of the second generation retain ethnic identities and offer safe places from the larger society where Asian Americans are marginalized.[48]

Asking only what functional benefits (such as job networks and English training programs) these churches give Korean Americans neglects examination of the ways churches might also be providing broader cultural resources that motivate Korean Americans to serve the wider American society. Unlike their parents, members of the second generation are native English speakers and match or surpass other American evangelicals in terms of education and wealth. They do not attend church to develop job networks or learn English language skills. They are also American citizens by birth and consequently have the right to vote and participate in all other spheres of American political life. Because of these factors, they are more likely than their parents to make changes to American civil society, specifically the religious institutions in which they are involved. If the second generation continues to participate in the mainstream institutions of American evangelicalism (as they are currently doing), they have the potential to join with other groups of nonwhite Christians to bring noticeable changes to the political and civic outlook of American Christianity.

Korean American Evangelicals in Local Congregations

To explore the relationship between evangelical religious participation and civic life for Korean Americans, I spent nine months attending two different evangelical churches. One, Grace Church, was a second-generation Korean congregation, and the other, Manna Fellowship, was a multiethnic congregation with Korean American participation. I chose to study two congregations that were adjacent to the same urban community in the Northeast, which I call Old Town. I primarily compared these two congregations and the Korean Americans in them. Choosing churches in the same geographic area allows insight into how two congregations might respond to the same community in different ways.[49]

Data about the churches came from the nine months I spent in each and the interviews recorded with leaders and members. I also conducted a survey at Grace and Manna, with a total of 225 respondents. To provide a national context, I also attended the services of and interviewed Korean Americans in seven other congregations (multiethnic and ethnic only). Overall, I completed 92 interviews with second-generation Korean American evangelicals and 11 interviews with Korean American leaders in other contexts, and with non-Korean members of multiethnic churches, for a total of 103 interviews. In appendix A I provide further explanation of the issues surrounding access to these religious centers and analysis of the data.

Answering the questions that are at the core of this book required that I study the Korean Americans in these churches in ways that would allow me to gain a broad understanding of the kinds of resources for civic life these church contexts provide Korean Americans. Specifically, it was important to analyze the different cultural understandings Korean Americans in these religious bodies have about what it means to be a "good" citizen.[50] Insight into such understandings came from talking with Korean Americans in the churches about how they view the relationship of their faith to civic participation. I also went with them to participate in local community volunteer activities, observing how they practiced their beliefs. This approach was important in capturing the relationship between construction of civic identities and actual civic practices.

Using Christianity to Interpret Race and Ethnicity and Create Civic Identities

Initially, I thought Korean Americans might move from second-generation to multiethnic churches as they gain distance from the ethnic culture of their parents and assimilate into mainstream American religion. I wondered how this move based on ethnic identification would influence the connection of evangelicalism to civic life for Korean Americans in these two kinds of congregational contexts. Korean immigrant churches often place a priority on serving the needs of their own members, helping immigrants adapt to American society.[51] Therefore, I thought Korean Americans in ethnic-specific churches might be less likely than those in diverse churches to prioritize caring for individuals outside the Korean community. I reasoned that Korean Americans who attend multiethnic churches might be more assimilated to American society and place more emphasis on serving the needs of diverse groups of individuals outside their churches.

Instead, I quickly realized that Korean Americans in both church types thought being an evangelical was at its core about reaching outward. These Korean Americans all used Christianity to justify broad civic participation. The more significant question to ask about Korean American evangelicals in these churches is not *whether* they are becoming part of American civic life but *how* they are doing so. The central question of this book became: How do multiethnic and ethnic-specific churches, and the Korean Americans in these churches, connect religion and civic life? I found that while each church was outward-looking, each had a different discourse about reaching out. Korean Americans with the same basic structural locations, meaning those demographically similar in terms of race, ethnicity, and class, came to very different understandings of Christianity's relationship to these categories and consequent models of civic responsibility.

Congregations provide their members with religious moral schemas—ways of justifying certain actions as more in keeping with their religious teachings than others. Often congregation-specific, these schemas structure legitimate ways of interacting with the world, ways that are stated in doctrines and enacted in the practices of congregation members. They provide a means of developing a "moral self," a framework for determining what it means to be a good person and a good citizen both inside and outside of specifically religious settings.[52] Both second-generation and multiethnic churches provide Korean Americans with different and distinctively evangelical frameworks for interpreting race, ethnicity, and their location as second-generation Koreans.

Specifically, a church's *interpretation* of race and ethnicity, regardless of the actual demographic makeup of the congregation, was a factor of organizational moral schemas that largely determined different approaches to civic life between these two types of churches in the same tradition.[53] Identities among the Korean Americans in these two church types did not reflect a straightforward model of assimilation. They reflected, instead, diverse ways of using evangelical Christianity to form patterned and overlapping constructs of ethnicity, race, and class in developing civic identities.

As evangelical Christians, Korean Americans use religious resources in very conscious ways to create civic identities. Yet the specific cultural schemas in their churches (in this case, referring to uses of Christianity to interpret race, ethnicity, and class) also structure the range of acceptable civic identities. For example, because the churches are evangelical, even when ethnic diversity is a spiritual value, it is not legitimate for Korean Americans to prioritize a racial identity as an American minority over an identity as an evangelical Christian. This discovery broadens understanding of religion's role in civic life. For these Korean Americans, Christian identities do more than sit alongside other identities; they actually have the ability to reorder racial and ethnic identities and consequent approaches to civic life. If found among other Korean Americans and other nonwhite American evangelicals, such identity constructs may influence how American evangelicals view the racial, ethnic, and class context of civic life.

My research uncovered diverse expressions of Korean American evangelicalism. In particular, I discovered that an individualistic ethic of civic responsibility, such as that found at Manna and the other multiethnic churches, actually has the ability to promote more volunteering than a collectivist ethic toward volunteering, such as that found at Grace and the other Korean Americans congregations. By way of implication, this work also examines the potential for evangelical racial minorities to reshape the conservative Protestant landscape.

The Plan of This Book

To develop my central arguments this book is organized as follows. In chapter 2, I draw on insights from the sociology of culture to explain how organizations and institutions have the ability to structure the development of religious, racial, and civic identities. I also explain how individuals (in this case Korean Americans in ethnic-specific and multiethnic churches) use the cultural schemas from their particular congregations and those from broader American evangelicalism to construct identities with the potential to change the broader institutions they inhabit. In chapter 3, I discuss Grace, the second-generation church, and Manna, the multiethnic church, as cases of congregations with different approaches to ethnicity. I specifically examine the people and their approaches to Christianity and ethnicity within each church. In chapter 4, I discuss the organizational differences in how Grace, Manna, and other second-generation and multiethnic churches view the relationship between ethnicity, religion, and civic responsibility. I argue there are two distinct models of civic responsibility found between ethnic only and multiethnic churches. In chapter 5, I show that the two congregational models developed in ethnic-specific and multiethnic churches provide Korean Americans with different resources to create identities. Korean Americans use these different interpretations of Christianity to create civic identities with overlapping religious, class, and ethnic components. Such perspectives structure how Korean

Americans view their relationship with other ethnic groups, particularly with black Americans. Chapter 6 explores volunteerism among Korean Americans. Korean Americans at both Grace and Manna see their churches as places to get involved with community service, and look to them for models of how to interact with their local community. Chapter 7 examines how Korean Americans view themselves vis-à-vis larger American evangelical attitudes toward politics. In particular, I show that some Korean Americans borrow models of politics from black Christians. Chapter 8 argues that diverse approaches to Christianity among Korean Americans and other new nonwhite Americans have the potential to reshape race relations within evangelicalism and their impact on wider American civic life by bringing a diverse racial consciousness to a primarily white evangelical leadership.

Broader Issues of American Civic Life

There is a practical message on these pages that is relevant to all concerned citizens. Many of us are asking what it will take for Americans to care more about their neighbors. At its core, the question is also a very religious one—and one with which Korean American evangelicals grapple: "Who is my neighbor?"[54] It is important to note that the form of religion in each of these churches motivates Korean Americans to consider providing care for a variety of "neighbors" outside their own ethnic and religious groups. In different ways, the particular models these churches foster for relating Christianity to civic life are successful.

Such findings also speak directly to the current discourse on a declining civil society. Scholars and public commentators often argue that increases in diversity will result in polarization and further erosion of civic participation. "If I am not like those in my community," this argument goes, "then why should I care for them?" Contrary to this argument, the religiously motivated model of civic life in each of these churches reorders how Korean Americans think about race and ethnicity and justifies caring for diverse groups of people. Second-generation Korean American evangelicals are trying to create identities that are different from those of their immigrant parents, identities that fully incorporate being a Korean and an American in the context of being a Christian. One way they do this is through being *distinctively* evangelical—but in a way that sometimes puts more emphasis on race and ethnicity than other American evangelicals do, and stresses one's commitment to care for those who are most different.

Finally, understanding religion and civic life for Korean Americans provides a window into the larger American story. Korean American civic identities, and the consequences these identities have for civic practices, helps us see how demographic changes may influence the relationship religion has to social and political systems in the United States. By using Christianity to interpret unique immigrant histories and present ethnic minority experience, nonwhite evangelicals may create new religiously based categories for civic life, changing the taken-for-granted ideas of what it means to be a "good" American.

In the next chapter, I pull the lens back further from the specific lives of Korean Americans and turn to a broader discussion of the theoretical work in the sociology of culture that informs the interpretation of findings presented in subsequent chapters. In doing this, chapter 2 highlights a core contribution of this book: to bring the diverse theoretical lenses of institutional approaches to culture and identity formation to bear on the research topic of how Korean Americans use religion to construct racial and civic identities. This and subsequent chapters couple insights from the sociology of culture with those in the sociology of religion and the sociology of race and ethnicity to provide a multidimensional interpretive lens.

2

Theoretical Interlude

A Cultural Approach to Connecting Institutions and Identities

Growing migration, in particular of Asian and Latino Christians, to the United States is changing the racial character of American evangelicalism beyond a black and white demographic. These new nonwhite *and* nonblack Christians, and particularly their children, are grappling with what it means to be U.S. citizens, religious people, and nonwhites within the broader context of American evangelicalism and American society. Sociologists of culture, scholars of religion, and those who study race and ethnicity are rarely in dialogue with one another about how the different cultural frames formed by religion and other sources inform individual identity construction. Within this chapter and the book as a whole, I bring together these bodies of literature to examine how the various levels of analysis at which culture operates—individual, organizational, and institutional—fit together with the diverse and patterned interpretations of religious culture at these different levels. I accomplish this through examining how Korean-only and multiethnic congregations develop varying interpretations—cultural schemas—of American evangelicalism, which individuals then use to create civic identities. Such a theoretical framework opens empirical understanding of how new Americans are more broadly changing approaches to race, ethnicity, and civic life within American evangelicalism.

I ask how culture operates at different levels of analysis as a way of gaining access to the various ways individuals and organizations draw on institutions to construct identities that may change the very institutions that constrain them. In this specific study, I uncover the kinds of models (schemas) of civic responsibility that ethnic-specific (Korean) and multiethnic congregations develop. I ask how Korean Americans in these churches respond to such different models. By way of implication, I also ask how Korean Americans and other nonwhite newcomers to the United States might change the relationship between evangelical identity and civic practices such as volunteering and political participation.

The chapter proceeds as follows. First, I provide an overview of my approach to culture and the utility of using a cultural analysis in this specific research. Second, I give a description of cultural schemas, the interpretive frameworks generated and used by individuals and organizations in the construction of identities. Third, I provide an explanation of how cultural schemas operate within American evangelicalism and specific evangelical congregations. Fourth, I discuss how understanding the development of schemas within organizations provides insight to the different kinds of civic, racial, and ethnic identities developed by Korean Americans in ethnic-specific and multiethnic churches.

Approach to Culture

Rather than a coherent system of symbols, as earlier theorists of culture have argued, culture is better described as a collection of resources.[1] In this work, I see culture broadly as the range of meanings and resources that individuals and organizations use to make sense of their lives, as well as the links these meanings and resources have to specific strategies of action.[2] Theorists generally think of resources in nonhuman terms such as money, education, houses, or military arms. This work joins with that of other sociologists who bring the importance of nonmaterial resources to the surface, revealing the ways resources can also be human, including certain kinds of emotions or propensities to act in clearly defined ways in specific arenas.[3]

Several debates in the study of culture are particularly germane to this work. These include the degree of agency that individuals have in constructing culture. For example, do cultures act on individuals or do individuals create and change culture?[4] In this work, I show that individuals both act on and are acted upon by culture. Theorists of culture have recently been interested in the ways culture is constraining, or the way culture limits the possibilities for action in a given situation.[5] Here, by broadening our understanding of the abilities individuals have to shape culture, I argue that we must also examine the conditions under which culture enables or empowers individuals to bring about change.[6]

My empirical observations led me to a view of culture that is neither completely coherent—as some early theorists have argued[7]—nor totally malleable and context-dependent, as some present-day theorists argue.[8] Understanding the different contexts in which culture is malleable—through examining different forms of Korean American religion and civic life—helps us see how individuals in two types of churches within the same religious tradition might develop very different ways of using culture to create racial, ethnic, and civic identities.

Through examining the diverse interpretations of civic life developed by Korean Americans in churches with different ethnic compositions, I became more convinced that individuals are not passive in the interpretation of institutions and the development of organizational cultures. They bring interpretations from nonreligious social locations with them into religious settings. These social locations, which might include class, racial, or gender experiences, encounter existing religious interpretations of other constructs, for example, what it means to be a good American citizen. These extrareligious social locations have the potential, under the right conditions, to inform religious ways of interpreting and acting in the world.

Cultural Schemas

I join with cultural sociologists who increasingly talk about culture as having levels of analysis.[9] The way I understand the levels of analysis of individuals, organizations, and institutions to interact with one another is through cultural schemas or interpretive frameworks. Individuals within organizations create interpretive frameworks through drawing on extraorganizational institutions, whose meanings are then funneled to individuals in organization-specific ways. These individuals may then use such organizational interpretations to actually change the institutions by which they are constrained.

Schemas are a key part of understanding this sort of back-and-forth exchange between institutions, organizations, and individuals. Sociologist Paul DiMaggio defines schemas as "knowledge structures that represent objects or events and provide default assumptions about their characteristics, relationships, and entailments under conditions of incomplete information."[10] Individuals have access to different schemas, in part, on the basis of experiences as a result of social locations such as career, gender, age, and income levels. Schemas reveal organizational and individual differences in institutionally based cultural repertoires that have implications for social practices, such as how best to serve one's local community or choices about the types of volunteer organizations in which to participate.[11]

In this set of cases, I examine how different religious organizations and the individual Korean Americans who are part of these organizations appropriate American evangelicalism. I show that they create specific schemas for evangelicalism that indicate ways of understanding and acting in American civic life. For example, the religious institution of evangelicalism provides adherents a specific description of what it means to be a "good" religious person or what good religious people do to participate in broader society. Such existing frameworks may stress that members of a religious community ought to be especially concerned about helping the poor because particular teachings of their religion motivate them to do so. The way evangelical civic responsibility is enacted, however, will vary among organizations and individuals that call themselves evangelical. For example, in the ethnic-specific churches I studied, a more privatized view of American evangelicalism was promulgated; the only public responsibility of members involved personal evangelism. Although they also had an individualized view of religion (each person decides what God is telling him or her to do), in the multiethnic churches, individuals actually had a more public view of civic life. This stressed the necessity of each individual choosing some sort of public role for community service. These different congregation-specific schemas for the meaning of civic responsibility within evangelicalism had implications for specific sets of practices. In most of the multiethnic churches, for example, individual parishioners were encouraged to take some active role in community service, whereas in the second-generation Korean churches, individuals only had to participate in community service *if* such participation directly resulted in evangelism.

An Example of Schemas

Stepping outside the realm of religion for a moment, consider how cultural schemas might operate in the life of one physician. Individual physicians inhabit a specific social location in American society. The physician social location generates certain cultural schemas. However, inhabiting a social location does not always determine which schemas will be enacted or how they will be enacted in a specific context. In this case, our physician might also be a mother and a member of a traditional Buddhist temple with specific gender boundaries—other social locations with different attendant cultural schemas than those gained from being part of the medical profession. Generally, preference for a specific cultural schema flows from a social context, like being inside a certain kind of organization. If our physician is in a hospital, for example, there are clear ways, as a doctor, that she will interpret the world. Yet, in certain contexts, individuals might switch from one interpretive framework to another, even if this seems to violate the preconditions of the social context. If our doctor is in a temple and a man begins to have a heart attack (a medical situation enters the religious context), she may choose to preference aspects of a professional schema over her traditional religious schema and the gender boundaries that flow from it by beginning to take on a leadership position in this situation and directing others in the temple to help her in specific ways.

This transference of cultural schemas may occur the other way around, with our doctor bringing schemas generated from a religious membership or her role as a parent into a medical organization. For example, the doctor may encounter a fellow traditional Buddhist or another mother who comes into her practice, and may bring to these situations specific schemas resulting more from her position as a mother or religious affiliate. Institutional constraints may tell us which identity and attendant interpretive framework to preference in a given social situation, but these constraints do not absolutely dictate which interpretive frameworks we actually preference.

Giving preference to alternative frameworks outside the norms of a given institution may be a mechanism for actual institutional changes. In her medical practice, the same doctor may very well bring her Buddhist tradition into consideration as she asks patients about their religious background in the course of gathering a patient history. In essence, while schemas are often institution-specific, they also have—through conditioning identity formation that transcends institutional domains—the potential even to transform the institutions that have acted as a resource for their development. In the example, the fact that a woman who is both a mother and a member of a Buddhist temple is currently fulfilling a role as a doctor does not mean that she leaves her other identities at the hospital door. Rather, her different identities as mother, religious adherent, and doctor overlap, providing her with aspects of diverse interpretive frameworks. When she is at the hospital, while she may draw most heavily on her identity as a doctor, she may also draw on aspects of her identities gained from other institutional spheres. For example, in the course of taking a patient history, she might ask a patient about his religious background and how he uses faith to interpret his illness. If this doctor has power within her particular office and makes it known that she asks patients questions about their religious background in the medical context, this may further influence accepted institutional practices for religion entering medicine. Depending on the doctor's clout, this could change the institution of medicine, beyond simply the office of this specific physician.

Cultural Schemas within Institutional Evangelicalism

Sociologists John Meyer and Brian Rowan apply cultural analysis to the understanding of institutions, describing institutions themselves as a form of culture. According to Meyer and Rowan, institutions are the "social processes, obligations or actualities that take on a rule-like status in social thought and action."[12] They stress that institutions are a kind of cultural resource that provide organizations with ways of interacting with their environment.

As an American religious institution, evangelicalism is a patterned set of elements that express something about the moral order. Those who are evangelicals see certain actions as being more or less right, in keeping with the doctrines of their faith. American evangelicalism is also a system of symbols, such as the cross, the symbol of the person Jesus Christ. American evangelicalism contains material resources as well—all of the congregations and all of the denominations that are evangelical. Indeed, to sustain themselves, institutions need both material and ideational resources. Evangelicalism, as an institution, influences the distribution of cultural resources like legitimacy. For example, congregations that have active programs of sharing the Christian message are more likely to be called a part of American evangelicalism by other religious organizations than those that do not make these actions part of their focus.[13]

As an institution, American evangelicalism generates different possibilities for developing cultural schemas or ways of interpreting the world and attendant strategies of action. Institutions are both constraining and enabling to organizations. For example, evangelicalism as an institution dictates that organizations that call themselves "evangelical" should be universally concerned with "sharing the gospel," defined here as telling others about one's faith with the hope of persuading them to convert.

Theorists who stress an institutional approach to understanding organizations generally emphasize the ways that institutions constrain organizations. Here I hold open the possibility that organizations also have the ability to change the institutions they inhabit.[14] One way change might occur is when organizations develop different understandings of their larger institutions. For example, even though institutional evangelicalism dictates that evangelical churches be concerned about "sharing the gospel," it is clear that ideas about how evangelism is best practiced differ radically among churches that all consider themselves evangelical. Evangelism could mean the classic stereotype of standing on a street corner actively telling individuals that they will go to hell if they do not repent and follow Christ. It could also mean just "being Christ in the world," through giving a homeless person one's spare change, without ever mentioning the connection of one's actions to specific Christian tenets.

Possibilities for Change within Evangelicalism

In some ways, my data reflect the top-down approach to institutions I have just described. Institutional evangelicalism is indeed constraining. However, there are several things about evangelicalism as a religious institution that also make it more malleable, more open to change, than other institutions and, specifically, other American religious institutions. Evangelicalism is not as highly codified or structured as many other religious institutions. This means that organizations and individuals have considerable agency to determine how they might share their faith differently in diverse kinds of contexts. As a religious institution, American evangelicalism has more potential to change than other religious institutions, such as American Catholicism, which would need to obtain approval from Rome in order to bring change at the institutional level.[15]

Similarly, there are a variety of different programs and organizational forms that might all be considered legitimately evangelical. There is no mandate about what kind of ministry programs congregations must adopt. Race, for example, can shape the entire vision of ministry for a specific congregation or be something that is hardly mentioned at all.[16] As long as there is some evangelical component to the ministry, then the church will be considered evangelical by other churches and leaders within the institution.

Despite famous faces on television that appear to be speaking for all American evangelicals, the leadership of evangelicalism is actually quite local. The religion, therefore, exhibits greater flexibility in the hands of individual adherents, meaning that personal agency is easier to observe in this particular religious institution. As mentioned before, bona fide evangelicals can appropriate evangelicalism differently: from the highly public method of street-corner evangelizing to the more private "living the gospel through one's life" approach. That both can be understood as valid ways of "sharing the gospel" is representative of evangelicalism's elasticity as an institution.

Institutional American evangelicalism acts as one resource that congregations use to develop cultural schema, in particular ideas about and practices of civic responsibility. This book examines this particular role of institutional evangelicalism. Because of their location within evangelical Christianity, both ethnic-specific and multiethnic churches adopt evangelism as an organizational priority, but they have the freedom to do so in different ways. Through studying these individual congregations, I have been able to see in what ways leaders and participants in these churches think they are invoking evangelical ideals and practices, and in what ways they see themselves departing from them.

Congregations also have resources outside the institution of evangelicalism that are used in the creation of schema. These include additional social locations, like experiences with gender, ethnicity, and class, that provide compatible and competing frameworks for the churches. These frameworks influence action. For example, in addition to being evangelicals, my respondents are also ethnic (Korean American), as well as racial (nonwhite) minorities in the United States. Such social locations sometimes give them access to alternative schemas for understanding the world, schemas they bring with them to their congregations. Analyzing frameworks for civic life developed by multi-ethnic and ethnic-specific congregations helped me to understand how two types of congregations, both of which were evangelical, could adopt different ideas about and strategies of action for civic life.

Cultural Schemas and Individual Identities

While researchers generally talk about the relationship of institutions to organizations, institutions can also be important in the formation of individual identities. Diverse schema gained from religious institutions, organizations, and nonreligious social locations are all possible resources in the construction of identities. One of the ways we have access to the construction of identities—both the ways individuals have agency in identity construction and the ways they have identities constructed for them—is through understanding these schema.

There are multiple arenas where identity construction is done for and by the individual; in this book, I specifically discuss the arenas of racial, ethnic, class, and civic identities within the context of multiethnic and Korean-only congregations. Identity is best defined according to three categories.[17] Individuals have personal, social, and collective identities. Social locations determine aspects of identities at all three of these levels. The social psychologist Timothy Owens describes *personal* identity as "identities attached to individuals."[18] Personal identities are characterized by membership in specific social networks, such as being a member of the First Presbyterian Church in Rochester, New York. *Social* identities tend to attach to groups and do not need to be internalized by individuals. They reflect larger social categorizations than personal identities do; examples include being a Catholic or an Asian American. According to Owens, social identities are the "groups, statuses, and categories to which individuals are socially recognized as belonging."[19] While individuals are categorized by others as falling into specific social groups, at the same time they have the possibility of rejecting social identities that are applied to them.

Part of social or group identity construction has to do with what sociologist Michèle Lamont calls "boundary work"—the act of generating categories of difference between one's group and other groups. Lamont brings the concept of "morality" to the construction of identities, explaining that identities are often created by boundaries that have moral dimensions.[20] Here I see the kind of boundary work Lamont is discussing as one aspect of individual-level cultural schema. Individuals use moral frameworks that define which people and actions are "good" or "bad" to interpret their social distance from other groups. Such boundaries help one to distinguish between members of one's own group and members of what one perceives as "other" groups.[21] Identities also have the potential to be *collective,* forming the basis for political mobilization. We might think of social movements as resulting from collective identities, where individuals share a common consciousness that is oriented toward action.[22] Although this book is primarily concerned with social identity formation rather than collective identities, changes in social identities can ultimately contribute to the restructuring of collectives that bring changes to institutions.[23]

Analyzing cultural schemas brings to the discussion of identities an emphasis on agency; here I argue that social identities are constructed both for *and by* the individual. For example, one's income automatically places one in a specific class location in the United States. Two individuals might earn exactly the same income, say at the level of the top third of U.S. citizens. Yet these two persons may each use a different schema to interpret what it means to be in the *social* location of those who earn at that income level, as a result of their participation in different social contexts that provide diverse ways of viewing income. For example, does an individual interpret her social location as meaning she is "wealthy"? And if she is wealthy, does she think her wealth is as a result of "blessing from God" or from her own hard work? Although an individual is automatically placed in an income group by census categories of wealth, one's cultural schema for wealth, one's understanding of the source and meaning of a specific level of income will indicate the extent to which one feels a sense of belonging with those at one's similar wealth level, and will also have implications for specific practices surrounding how one uses one's money.

Subcultural Identities

The Korean Americans in the congregations I studied developed frameworks for interpreting the interconnected aspects of religious, racial, class, and civic identities at both the personal and social level. Part of identity construction relates to Korean Americans' perceptions of themselves as part of institutional evangelicalism. In his work on American evangelicalism, sociologist Christian Smith provides extensive evidence to argue that the religious identities individuals develop within the institution of American evangelicalism are best described as "subcultural identities," identities that are characterized by distinctiveness from the American mainstream in ways motivated by evangelicalism. Rather than forming a separate enclave that has little intersection with the rest of the world, or developing cultures and practices that are not different from the larger American culture, Smith argues that American evangelicalism generates what I would call a specific kind of "schema" for identity formation. According to Smith, the evangelical subcultural identity is best described as both remaining engaged in the surrounding culture and remaining distinctive. Smith writes:

> Religion survives and can thrive in a pluralistic, modern society by embedding itself in subcultures that offer satisfying morally orienting collective identities which provide adherents meaning and belonging.... In a pluralistic society, those religious groups will be relatively stronger which better possess and employ the cultural tools needed to create both clear distinction from and significant engagement and tension with other relevant out-groups, short of becoming genuinely countercultural.[24]

For evangelicals, symbolic conflicts with "out-groups" actually strengthen the tradition's own in-group identity.

Racial and Religious Identities

Although Smith's theory of subcultural identity has been appropriated to the realm of gender, sociologists have done little to export this framework to the realm of race and ethnicity.[25] As I explained earlier in this chapter, I see racial location as one of the social locations that individuals inhabit, and the experiences of racial location often provide a particular cultural schema for interpreting one's own racial identity and one's proximity to other racially defined groups. Smith implicitly assumes that subcultural identities will be the same for all evangelicals, regardless of race or ethnicity. It is possible, however, that certain subgroups within American evangelicalism may also have a modified out-group relationship with other evangelicals, based specifically on differing Christian understandings of race and ethnicity. In subsequent chapters, I will argue that there might be diverse and patterned types of subcultural identities developed by different groups of evangelicals, in part dependent on the interpretation of race and ethnicity and its connection to Christianity as promulgated at the organizational level.

Researchers need to ask whether nonwhite evangelicals, particularly those for whom immigrant and racial identities overlap, will develop the same kind of subcultural identities as white evangelicals. I argue here that new Americans bring more than a new demographic to American evangelicalism—they bring new interpretations or cultural schemas for race and ethnicity and its relationship to civic life. Yet the literature on American evangelicalism assumes a "whiteness" framework—if not explicitly, at least implicitly. By not directly confronting race in discussions of evangelicalism, researchers are tacitly assuming that all American evangelicals are white.[26]

An exception to this implicit whiteness framework is a work by sociologists Michael Emerson and Christian Smith, *Divided by Faith*.[27] Comparing white and black Christian approaches to racism, Emerson and Smith argue that white evangelicals have an individualized approach to racism in American society because they have largely bought into the ideal of "American individualism." The emphasis by white evangelical Christians on the concept of accountable individuals has taken blame away from structural issues as central factors in current U.S. race relations. In contrast, Emerson and Smith find, black Christians are more structural in their explanation of race relations—more likely to see economic inequality between black and white Americans as resulting from systemic historical inequalities between blacks and whites. Structural factors would include the historical, legal, and educational inequalities that in the modern climate have brought about an unequal playing field for black Americans.

It is important to note that even in this rare treatment of race in the context of evangelicalism, Emerson and Smith focus exclusively on the experiences of white and black Christians. My research adds a new facet to Christian Smith's theory of subcultural identity through a cultural analysis of frameworks for race and ethnicity among nonwhite and nonblack Americans. Here I ask what cultural schemas will be developed for the relationship between race, religion, and civic responsibility by Korean Americans, how such conceptions will influence their religious identity construction, and how differing identities might bring potential changes to institutional approaches to race in broader American evangelicalism.

Summary

I have argued here that cultural approaches to understanding institutions need to move in the direction of asking how institutions change, rather than seeing them largely as constraining. Understanding the institution of American evangelicalism as being malleable substantively helps us see how two congregation types, ethnic and multiethnic, could develop very different approaches to interpreting what it means to be a Christian and the consequences such meanings have for civic life. Understanding the various resources, particularly cultural schemas, that individuals and organizations use to develop identities also pushes forward a theory of how individuals in the same institution, class, and ethnic group could develop very different ways of viewing their race/ethnic and class locations and the implications these have for civic life. Finally, attention to cultural schemas brings to light the connection between individuals and institutions, particularly the conditions under which individuals have the possibility to bring changes to the very institutions that constrain them.

I now switch from a discussion of larger theoretical issues to an intimate look at Grace and Manna, the two churches where I spent the most time. These churches are the particular religious communities of Bill and Jim, the Korean Americans I introduced in chapter 1. I explore how these two church communities are organized. I examine their different approaches to what it means to be a Christian and consequent interpretations of race, ethnicity, and gender. Chapter 3 provides building blocks for understanding differences in the church-based models of civic responsibility that Korean Americans use in forming civic identities.

3

Religion, Race, and Ethnicity in Two Churches

Grace, a second-generation Korean congregation, is located on a secluded tree-lined street with modest one- and two-story homes that sit close together in a suburb of Old Town. Entering the parking lot, you will immediately notice three signs: one reads, "Community Lutheran Church"; the second is written in Korean and reads "Bu-Hual," meaning "Resurrection"; and the last reads "Grace Church."[1] This building, used for all three congregations, is a substantial space, with a high ceiling and a sanctuary capable of seating about 150 people. The first thing that might catch your attention when you enter the sanctuary is a large wooden cross at the front. The cross sits behind the altar, and to its left stands a substantial American flag on a moveable pedestal. Next to the flag are a set of drums, speakers, and a microphone. The drums and sound system belong to Grace; the crucifix and American flag belong to Community Lutheran Church, the largely white church that owns the building.

Every Sunday, during the early afternoon, between 85 and 100 second-generation Korean Americans meet at Grace for a worship service. They are mainly young adults, and they are always well-dressed: the women wear dresses or dressy pants suits, and many of the men wear ties with dress shirts and slacks. As newcomers walk toward the sanctuary, they are handed a visitor's card.

I described the beginning of one Sunday service in my field notes:

> When I first enter the building, there are people standing and singing, swaying to the music. Some clap their hands.

The songs are upbeat praise choruses projected on a screen at the front of the room. People continue trickling in to the service until about 20 minutes or so after it officially begins. These latecomers move immediately to a seat, sit briefly and bow their heads, move their lips silently in prayer, and then stand and join in the singing. After a few more songs led by the worship leader, another man dressed in a suit comes to the front of the room. The upbeat music then stops abruptly, and he proceeds to tell the group to look at their bulletins, where a portion of the Westminster Confession of Faith is printed.[2] We repeat the confession in unison. Then Pastor Joseph, the head pastor, comes to the pulpit. After praying that his sermon will be pleasing to God, he begins speaking.... The congregation members sit quietly and listen, and most look intently at Pastor Joseph as he speaks. The entire service lasts almost an hour.

The building where Manna, a multiethnic church, meets is also near a street lined with modest homes. On the days when the weather is nice, boys in their early teens ride skateboards up and down the sidewalk outside the building. At the edge of the parking lot there is a sign that reads "First Baptist Church." First Baptist Church is a largely African American church. There is no sign indicating that late every Sunday afternoon, Manna also meets in the building. The sanctuary of First Baptist, which owns the building, is somewhat formal. Purple stained-glass windows and a wreath decorate the front of the church. An American flag also sits on one side of the sanctuary and a Christian flag on the other.[3] About 150 people usually attend Manna's Sunday service. Members include those from several different Asian ethnic groups, as well as numerous white and black persons and several Latinos. The group is young; few are over 40. People dress casually. Some wear sport pants and sneakers; a few of the men sometimes wear baseball caps.

I wrote the following in my field notes after one Sunday service:

Mainly young adults are standing in the sanctuary. At the front, a young Asian American woman is playing bongo drums, and an Asian American man plays the guitar. There are no bulletins because things proceed freely with no apparent need for an order of worship. Someone at the front of the room works on a laptop throughout the service to project words for songs on a screen. Even without this assistance, the verses are repeated often enough that a newcomer could easily follow along. The music is lively, and people sway to the songs and clap their hands. After a few songs, Pastor Simeon, the main church pastor, goes to the front of the congregation, and after standing near the worship team for a moment, whispers something to the guitar player, who immediately starts playing more softly. Next he turns to the congregation and invites people to come to...the front of the sanctuary to stand on the podium and share anything they believe God is speaking to them that might benefit the entire congregation. A few people from the congregation immediately come to the microphone. There are three different women who speak; one is Asian American, and two are white. One says, "God wants us to know that he is pleased with our worship." The guitar-playing gradually comes to a stop after the speakers are finished. Following some announcements, Pastor Simeon gives a sermon that lasts about an hour. As he speaks, the people in the church remain seated, but they occasionally let out a loud "Amen." As on other Sundays, the church service lasts about two hours.[4]

Similarities and Differences

These vignettes reveal striking similarities between Grace and Manna. Both congregations are located next to a fairly impoverished urban area, which I call Old Town. Mainly young professionals and students attend each church. The leadership and members of each are primarily Asian American. At Grace the leaders are Korean American, while at Manna they are both Chinese American and Korean American. Each church is evangelical and nondenominational—that is, they have no denominational affiliation—and both churches rent space from other congregations.

Yet spending time in each church also reveals significant differences. These differences are relevant to how the Korean Americans in each talk about civic life, the ways they participate in their local communities, and how they identify themselves as American citizens.

The Community

When I began searching for a Korean American and a multiethnic church to study, I wanted to select two churches that were in the same community. In 2001, I moved to a community about 30 miles away from Old Town.[5] Both Grace and Manna consider Old Town their nearest urban area. Manna is about a mile from the center of the city, and Grace is located about 10 miles outside.[6] Being in the vicinity of the same community means that Grace and Manna share similar resources related to civic life: they are close to the same group of social services, the same religious communities, and the same group of nonwhite and non-Asian residents—a group that they must come to understand if they are to serve it.

I chose Old Town for several reasons. First, for practical reasons: it is a community that has a second-generation Korean church and a multiethnic church in close proximity to one another. Second, because the community is not a Korean enclave, the Korean Americans in these congregations have access to non-Korean individuals to serve if they desire to do so. In addition, I wanted to study churches near a community whose members had fewer resources than the individuals in the congregations I was studying. I thought this would allow me to compare and contrast how each church, and the individuals within the two churches, reacted to or created opportunities to help those in their local community whom they perceived as needy.

With a population of only 48,573, Old Town is small to be called urban.[7] Yet walking around the center of the city, I quickly realized why my respondents think of it as such. I saw high-rise buildings, shopping centers, and residential homes packed tightly together. There were also homeless people who asked me for spare change. Although many of Old Town's residents are white, a substantial number are from nonwhite racial groups. At stores and gas stations, I would often hear Spanish or Mandarin spoken by the people around me. Twenty-four percent of the population identify as black.[8] The city and surrounding area also have several universities. One major university is in the middle of the city, and some of the Korean Americans who are members of Grace or Manna are graduates. Old Town is somewhat more impoverished than the United States population as a whole and has nearly double the amount of unemployment, as shown in table 3.1.

TABLE 3.1. Income Characteristics of Old Town Compared to U.S. Population

	Old Town	U.S. Population
Median household income (1999)	$36,080	$40,816
Mean earnings (1999)	$50,527	$56,604
Percent unemployed (2000)	7.1	3.7
Percent earning less than $10,000 (2000)	12.5	9.5
Percent earning $50,000 or more (2000)	35.2	42.0
Percent of families below poverty level (1999)	16.9	9.2
Percent of families below poverty level with children under five years of age (1999)	24.3	17.0

Source: 1999, 2000 U.S. Census Bureau, Current Population Reports, P60–209.

Grace: A *Distinctive* Second-Generation Congregation

After I had attended several second-generation Korean churches in Old Town, a colleague introduced me to a Korean American woman he had recently met. She told me about Grace, and invited me to attend. I visited Grace for several Sundays before approaching the head pastor, explaining my research, and asking for his permission to study the church. I presented myself as a Christian to the pastor and other members of the leadership team and told them the research was about how Korean Americans relate to their communities.[9] Since all church services and meetings are conducted in English and members of Grace are generally more fluent in English than Korean, there was no language barrier, and I was able to fully experience the services and talk easily with congregation members. Although I took two years of Korean language training in preparation for the study, all of the interviews were conducted in English.

The members of Grace did wonder why I was interested in studying Korean Americans. I generally told them that I was a researcher and interested in how a variety of different Christian churches relate to their communities. My similar socioeconomic class, education, and faith background were all assets to gaining entrée to Grace. These commonalities, coupled with regular attendance at services and church meetings, allowed me, over time, to develop relationships with the church members.

History and Organization

Grace started in 1997 as the English ministry of Bu-Hual, a first-generation Korean congregation.[10] At first, Bu-Hual had a youth group for second-generation Korean American English speakers. However, as the children of the first generation became older, the congregation realized the young people of the church needed their own pastor, someone who could be more than a youth group leader. They needed someone who could conduct services entirely in English for a second-generation Korean population, whose native language was English, not Korean. The pastor and other leaders at Bu-Hual approached Joseph, a second-generation Korean American and a recent college graduate who was attending a seminary in the area. Bu-Hual told him they would provide the financial resources if he was willing to start a distinct congregation for second-generation Koreans.

Joseph eventually agreed to the request, but felt strongly that in order to be distinct from the hierarchical structure of first-generation Korean American churches, the congregation should be led by a pastoral team rather than a single pastor. Consequently, he asked two of his seminary friends, Jacob and Joshua, to start the church with him. In addition to Jacob and Joshua, two other men later joined the leadership team, all of them second-generation

Koreans.[11] Although the five members of the group work largely as a team, those in leadership see Joseph as the central leader of Grace. According to Joshua, "[Jacob and the others] are the pastors of our church ... [but] Joseph is the *head* pastor [his emphasis]." Pastor Joseph gives most of the church sermons and is largely responsible for directing church leadership meetings and charting the mission and vision of the congregation. Pastor Joseph and two of the other leaders receive a small, part-time salary from the church, but they all have full-time jobs apart from their work at Grace.

Initially those who attended Grace were former members of Bu-Hual and mainly college students and young professionals. Yet, as Grace grew, the congregation attracted second-generation Korean Americans who had not been raised in the area. Some moved there to attend one of the nearby universities or had jobs in Old Town or one of the other surrounding urban areas. As they explained the history of the congregation, the leaders told me that Grace was similar to most other second-generation Korean American churches in that it continued to share a building with Bu-Hual. In a cryptically gendered way, the leaders explained that this meant Bu-Hual was their "mother" or founding church, even though Grace considers itself an independent congregation.[12] They use "mother church" to signify their relationship to Bu-Hual, because they think of the congregation as having given birth to their church. Other Korean Americans I interviewed who are involved in second-generation Korean congregations also use the term "mother church" to refer to the first-generation Korean congregation with which they are affiliated. Describing the founding of the church, Joshua, one of the church leaders, told me:

> I guess it [Grace] was first founded by Joseph and the elders of Bu-Hual, which is our mother church. Bu-Hual's parents thought they wanted an English ministry their kids could grow into. They had kids in high school at the time and some of them had kids in college and they realized that when their kids came back home they couldn't participate in the Korean service [because they didn't speak Korean]. And they approached Joseph and said, "Why don't you think about broadening your ministry to include college students?" And Joseph kind of went from there and said, "If I am going to form an English ministry then I want to do it all the way and form an English ministry [church]."

His words show the clear desire of the leadership team to have an autonomous congregation—something more than hinted at in the fact that the congregation has its own name and pastoral leadership team. Although Bu-Hual gives Grace financial and other resources, Grace is clearly a distinct congregation and not merely the English ministry of Bu-Hual. Jacob described Bu-Hual as somewhat atypical for a first-generation church because it does not exercise control over the leadership of the second-generation congregation.

Although Grace is not completely independent from Bu-Hual financially, Bu-Hual's method of monetary support underscores their desire to see Grace become financially independent. Bu-Hual simply provides a fixed amount of financial help, but the leadership of Grace determines how that money is spent. Grace's leadership team develops a ministry budget based on what Bu-Hual gives them combined with what comes directly from their own members. According to Pastor Joseph, "Our relationship with Bu-Hual is great. We have a great rapport. The first-generation congregation supports us financially. They also offer spiritual accountability.[13] I think they would rather see our congregation grow than their own congregation. They pray for us every day." It is significant that both Bu-Hual and the leaders of Grace want the congregation to work toward becoming completely financially and structurally independent.

The five members of the leadership team are primarily responsible for making decisions that influence the church. They, in turn, set up several committees and appoint heads of these committees. These include the welcome, social service, and outreach committees. The leadership team decides which committees will form the backbone of the church. The committee heads and members meet on a monthly basis after church services to discuss programming related to their specific areas. There are no formal voting procedures in the church. Instead, church members voice their views about programming by joining and participating in the committees.

Grace wants to be more progressive than first-generation Korean churches with respect to women, and allows women in all leadership roles except pastor and elder. While the five members of the leadership team are all men, committee heads are both men and women. In practice, however, women fill most of the care-taking and service roles at Grace. I never saw a man from Grace helping with the preparation or service of food for the post-Sunday-service meals, for example.

The People

About 80 to 90 people attend Grace each Sunday, almost all Korean Americans. The survey I conducted in the church reveals that only two members of the church are not Korean American, one a white American and one a Chinese American.[14] Aside from being nearly homogenous in ethnic background, the church is also fairly homogenous in a number of other ways. All of the members of Grace are young adults, ranging in age from late teens to early thirties. They are somewhat homogenous with respect to class status. Although their first-generation parents come from a variety of occupations, such as self-employed store owners, business people, and engineers, those who attend Grace are mainly from the upper middle class.[15] Younger members are generally enrolled in prestigious four-year universities.[16] Those older than college age are students in professional programs or medical schools. Both men and women work in professional occupations such as medicine, engineering, or banking.

One of the first things I noticed at Grace was the indicators of class and professional status. Women often wear trendy, expensive clothes. Designer names appear on many of their handbags. The men dress a little more casually than the women, but even during warmer months they wear crisp short-sleeved polo shirts and slacks, coordinated with matching belts and leather shoes. Those who speak in front of the congregation dress up more; the pastor always wears a suit and tie, as do most members of the leadership team.

Approach to Christianity

As I will explain further in chapter 4, Grace focuses on "just the basics" of Christianity and tries not to link Korean culture to faith—in part to be different from first-generation Korean churches.[17] When they classify the congregation as evangelical, the leaders and members of Grace mean that they adhere to certain core beliefs that describe American evangelicals more generally. These include, as mentioned in chapter 1, the Bible as trustworthy, human nature as sinful, hope for salvation in God's son, Jesus, absolute moral standards, and a personal knowledge of God.[18] Pastor Joseph describes his approach to evangelicalism and the theological and spiritual labels appropriate to his church this way:

> I would have to say "heady" and "evangelical and reformed." I guess I would make some sort of chart where I would have evangelical at the top and then underneath I would have "reformed." And then I would have "biblical theology." But, we would join with other churches, which are not part of our theological tradition, in doing things like helping with the yearly church retreat, for example.[19]

By "reformed," Pastor Joseph means an emphasis on the sovereignty of God and the "final authority of the Bible," in contrast to the authority of a religious hierarchy, as found in the Catholic Church. In practice, this approach stresses God's control over all, as opposed to a focus on the decision-making power of human will. The church joins with other congregations in the reformed arm of evangelicalism in deemphasizing the particular "gifts of the spirit" such as speaking in tongues—when it is thought that a believer is given by God the ability to speak a language other than his or her own for the purpose of benefiting the Christian mission.[20] During the time I attended Grace, they started the process of becoming affiliated with the Presbyterian Church in America, a largely evangelical denomination of Presbyterians.

During my discussions with the leaders at Grace, they also tried to link the congregation with other American evangelical churches and talked about the spiritual resources they have in common. Although the leaders did not mention them as such, the resources they mentioned were those used most generally by white, evangelical churches. For example, members of the leadership team told me they draw heavily on the writings of J. I. Packer, a professor of theology at Regent College, an evangelical seminary, and John Stott, a noted international evangelical leader.[21]

Ethnicity at Grace

Although as a church Grace is distinct from the first-generation congregation it is affiliated with, it is difficult to escape the presence of Bu-Hual and of Korean culture—it is in some ways overt, at times revealing an insistence by the first generation that the second generation maintain Korean culture. For example, as the members of Grace filed out of the sanctuary after a service one Sunday, members of Bu-Hual began to file in for their service. Bu-Hual's pastor was among the first to come in wearing a stole and a formal black robe that covered his clothes.[22] Grace members, who were walking out, bowed and greeted the pastor and other members of Bu-Hual with "Annyonghaseyo," a formal way in Korean of saying hello to an elder. Even those I knew who did not speak Korean well greeted the pastor and members of Bu-Hual in this way.[23] In longer conversations, the members of Bu-Hual insisted on speaking Korean to the members of Grace. This happened although most members of Bu-Hual also have good English skills, and many of those who attend Grace either lack Korean language skills entirely or are able to communicate more effectively in English.

The two congregations share responsibility for preparing the postservice luncheons, although they actually eat together only on a monthly basis. The choice of food illustrates one way the members of Grace negotiate between American and Korean culture. I noticed that Korean and American foods are served on alternate weeks: The Korean food is usually seaweed soups or rice and *prugolgi*, a beef dish. There is always *kimchee*, or spicy cabbage, a Korean staple. Korean food is served on the week that the women from Bu-Hual prepare and serve the meal. American food is served on the week that the women from Grace prepare and serve the meal, and usually consists of hot dogs or pasta.

There was also negotiation between first- and second-generation Koreans through specific religious rituals. Members from Bu-Hual generally did not attend the services at Grace. However, perhaps because at the time I was attending the pastors at Grace were not ordained, the Grace members were dependent on the head pastor of Bu-Hual to administer communion to them. The only time I saw the head pastor from Bu-Hual lead at Grace was during communion service.[24] Pastor Joseph and the other leaders would lead the rest of that monthly Sunday service.

During one communion Sunday, Pastor Joseph began the service by talking about the meaning of this ritual.[25] Then, without introduction and without preface to his remarks, Pastor Chung, the head pastor from Bu-Hual, walked directly to the front of the congregation and started to read a passage from the Bible where Jesus talks about being the "bread of life."[26] Pastor Chung continued: "We sanctify the bread and wine." Then he served the communion elements to the pastors of the church. The congregation members filed to the front of the congregation, and the pastors from Grace served the communion elements to them. While communion was being served, a member from Grace played "Amazing Grace" on an electric guitar softly in the background. After the communion portion of the Sunday service was over, Pastor Chung immediately stepped down from the front of the sanctuary and walked quickly and quietly down the center aisle, and out the door of the church.

I noticed that in several ways during that communion service Pastor Chung seemed like an outsider to the congregation. His flowing black robe stood in stark contrast to the plain suits the pastors of Grace wore. He spoke in clear and understandable English, but with a pronounced Korean accent, while Grace's pastors speak in unaccented native English. As I discuss later, these and other examples reveal an internal tension for Korean Americans at Grace. On one hand, they want to be *just* an evangelical Christian congregation and distance themselves from what they perceive as a cultural Korean Christianity that is somewhat vacuous. On the other hand, the members of Grace very much negotiate "doing church" in the presence of the first generation.

Manna: Creating a Truly Multiethnic Church

Although there are several multiethnic churches in cities that neighbor Old Town, Manna is the only church within Old Town that is specifically committed to being multiethnic. I found Manna through an acquaintance who is a member. Upon learning about my research, he suggested that I attend Manna with him. After a few visits, I decided to contact the church leadership about studying the congregation. Whereas Pastor Joseph from Grace unhesitatingly gave permission to study his congregation, the pastors from Manna wanted me to meet with all of the church staff before granting permission. When we met, we discussed my research for almost an hour, including what I would do with the data I collected, and whether the research could be used to further a specifically Christian mission. Once they were comfortable with the study, they gave me permission to study their congregation.

I presented my research and myself similarly at Grace and Manna. As I had at Grace, I talked at Manna about being a Christian to those who asked about my religious identity. Neither those at Grace nor Manna really asked much more about what I meant by "Christian," and everyone seemed satisfied after they heard that we shared a common religious label. I also told the leadership of Manna, and any members who asked, that I was conducting a study of how Christian Korean Americans relate to their local communities. Because there are white members of the church, at Manna I was often perceived as simply another church member, and was seldom asked about my research unless I specifically requested an interview with a church member.

History and Organization

Manna officially began in October 1999 through a merger of a Chinese immigrant congregation and a second-generation Korean congregation. The pastors of each of these congregations met at a conference and later realized they shared a similar vision about being pastors of multiethnic congregations. The pastors and leaders of each church eventually decided to merge their congregations. The written brochure that tells the story of Manna says the churches merged to "symbolize that there are no boundaries to the Gospel, whether within the church or globally."[27] A large portion of each congregation agreed to the merger.

The pastor of the Chinese congregation, Pastor Phil, a first-generation Chinese American, and Pastor Simeon, a second-generation Korean, were well-known pastors of immigrant churches. Pastor Phil formerly worked with a large Chinese congregation in Old Town.[28] Pastor Phil and Pastor Simeon told me independently that as they began to encourage their respective congregations to embrace/welcome those of other ethnic groups, some members were resistant.[29] In my conversations with him, Pastor Simeon mentioned that when he wanted to break away from being a Korean church pastor, he received a negative response from the Korean community; leaders of Korean congregations told him he was abandoning the Korean church. After the two churches merged, many from each of the original congregations also left the church. During a focus group attended by the pastors and other church leaders, both Pastor Phil and Pastor Simeon mentioned that ethnic-specific churches are often afraid of losing their ethnic culture if they become multiethnic.[30] Pastor Simeon added that Korean pastors, in particular, are afraid of people abandoning the Korean language and culture, which is related to their fear of losing control over the second generation.

Although it cost these two men congregation members, the pastors see their vision to form a multiethnic congregation as a spiritual ideal and relate being multiethnic to the fullest realization of the Christian mission. In embracing this vision, they think of themselves as doing something new, something distinctive from ethnic-specific churches and from evangelical congregations in general. During the focus group, Pastor Phil mentioned that he often feels like "Moses with Joshua ... standing at the banks of the Jericho. We need to be strong and courageous.... But let me tell you that when the Chinese church sees God, they will have a lot of points taken away."[31] This is a reference to a Bible story where, at God's command, Moses passed on leadership of the Israelites to Joshua before asking them to cross the Jordan River. In the biblical account, God dries up the Jordan so that the Israelites can successfully cross and defeat the city of Jericho. This relating of Manna's mission as a multiethnic church to the mission of the Israelites reveals just how important Pastor Phil thinks that mission is. He believes that Manna is embarking on an original form of Christian ministry, and that ethnic-specific congregations are not fully following the plan of God to minister to all people. He feels this has implications for the ability of these other churches to "take the city" for the Lord.

After deciding to merge their two congregations, the pastors rented a space from First Baptist Church, a predominantly African American congregation. Pastor Phil meets regularly with the pastor of First Baptist. As I will explain further in subsequent chapters, I noticed throughout my time attending Manna, and in my experiences with the other multiethnic churches, that they often saw themselves as borrowing ministry ideas and forms from black churches. The first time I visited the church building, I noticed that a separate Mandarin-speaking Chinese congregation also meets in the same building as First Baptist and Manna, but in a different space. Manna convenes in the main sanctuary and the Chinese congregation in the fellowship hall. About once a month the two congregations have a monthly joint service, which, because of language differences, requires special measures, such as having a translator present. For these reasons, I initially thought the congregations were distinct. Only after attending the services regularly and beginning to do interviews did I realize that the two congregations are part of the same church.

Pastor Simeon is the primary pastor for Manna. In addition to him and Pastor Phil, Manna has three other staff members, all Asian American. One is of Chinese ethnicity and two are second-generation Korean Americans. These staff people are men who are not seminary trained but still work in pastoral roles at Manna. The church is also actively seeking pastors and staff from non-Asian racial groups. Although all of the pastors and staff were men during the time I attended the church, the pastors told me emphatically that being a man is *not* a prerequisite for having a leadership position in the church. Although the church has never had a female pastor, women have served on the central staff team. Manna is primarily organized around "cell groups," small groups of individuals who meet weekly to study the Bible. The pastors, staff, and cell group leaders, who are both men and women, meet regularly to decide on the mission and vision of the church. They make up a larger leadership team that also determines the church programs. Members of the church suggest possible church programs, and the leadership team meets together to discuss it and, as several leaders told me, to "pray about it" before developing and implementing a program.

The People

The survey I conducted at Manna revealed that during the time I attended the church, three years after the merger, 73 percent of those in the congregation were of Asian ethnic background.[32] The sociologist Pyong Gap Min argues that mixed Asian congregations are rarely truly pan-Asian; they are usually made up entirely of individuals from either East or Southeast Asia.[33] Manna differs from the region-specific pattern Min describes—while the majority are East Asian, a noticeable portion are also Southeast Asian. Members hail from Chinese, Korean, Cambodian, Asian Indian, Vietnamese, and Filipino backgrounds, with Korean Americans making up 20 percent of all Asian Americans in the church. A full 27 percent of the congregation identifies as either white, black, Caribbean, or Latino.

With 27 percent of its membership from non-Asian ethnic groups, the congregation would not be considered demographically pan-Asian.[34] Using the definition of a multiracial congregation suggested by sociologists Michael Emerson and Karen Chai Kim, the church is technically multiracial, because less than 80 percent of its membership is in any single racial group.[35] However, because the church consists mainly of Asian Americans, Manna's pastors and leadership do not think of the congregation as multiracial but prefer to call it "multiethnic." On the basis of their self-classification, I also refer to Manna as multiethnic.

The pastors of Manna told me they decided to start a multiethnic congregation because of a "calling from God," not because of demographic changes in the neighborhood or a denominational mandate—common reasons other churches give for becoming more multiethnic. Manna drew its initial membership from a "preexisting organizational package"—in this case, a merger of a Korean and a Chinese congregation.[36] But in addition to welcoming various ethnic groups of Asians, the leaders also want Manna to incorporate more blacks, whites, and Latinos. To this end, it is a goal of the congregation to draw additional membership primarily from the racially diverse community of Old Town.[37] During the last two months of my time attending the church, Manna started an extension fellowship group in Old Town, called Manna City Fellowship, to attract individuals from diverse ethnic groups and to realize further the church's vision of caring for the city's residents.

Manna is demographically similar to Grace with respect to the age and class of its Korean American members. In fact, with a few notable exceptions, the class composition of the church as a whole is similar to that of the Korean Americans at Grace.[38] In other ways Manna is different from Grace. Besides its diverse ethnic composition, the congregation has a more relaxed approach. It is not uncommon to see members of Manna coming to church in shorts and flip-flops during the summer months, attire I did not see at Grace during a Sunday service. Like the rest of the congregation, Pastor Simeon and others who give sermons at Manna often dress casually.

Approach to Christianity at Manna

Like Grace, Manna also understands itself to be an evangelical congregation. During an interview with Pastor Phil and his wife, May Ann, at their house, Pastor Phil described the theological perspective of the church:

> Our theology is evangelical. Evangelical. But, we are open to the work of the Holy Spirit. Typical evangelicals, they believe in apostles, but they don't believe in Jesus resurrected. They say to me, "There are no more gifts [of the Holy Spirit], because of what the apostles said [in the Bible]." And I say to them, "Do you believe in Jesus or the apostles?" Jesus used to be doing good and if Jesus is alive, then he is still doing good. So that is a difference and I am very strong on that feeling... I am the minority. I have an evangelical background, but now I believe in the work of the Holy Spirit. We don't emphasize the charismatic gifts, but we emphasize the life.[39]

In discussion with Pastor Phil about Manna's approach to Christianity, he also identifies the congregation as evangelical. As a graduate of a well-known seminary in the evangelical tradition, he has access to the broader resources of institutional evangelicalism, such as knowledge of evangelical biblical interpretations and access to evangelical literature, worship songs, and a network of key evangelical leaders. Still, he tries to distance himself from some of the aspects of the broader evangelical movement; his distinctive approach emphasizes the "work of the Holy Spirit."

While other leaders at Manna also stress the church's distinctive "free" or "charismatic" approach to evangelicalism, Manna does not define itself as Pentecostal. During the time I attended the church, I saw no evidence of typical Pentecostal practices such as "speaking in tongues."[40] However, the leadership and members of the congregation talk about the importance of helping members to understand their connection with the Holy Spirit and to learn to "hear from God."

Because they recognize that most evangelical churches do not have a specific mission to be multiethnic, Manna's leaders try hard to distance the church from the largely white American evangelical models of ministry. During our interview, Pastor Phil mentioned the importance of small church groups. I followed this comment by asking him whether the congregation used the small group model of Willow Creek, an evangelical and predominantly white church, with a popular model of structuring small groups.[41] He emphatically insisted that their church did not use a "program" for ministry and told me Willow Creek was "just a program. Nobody has succeeded in copying that model... because *every church is a different culture*, you cannot copy the model but you have to extract the principles and apply it to your situation. It is proven that it [a fixed model] doesn't work" [my emphasis].

Pastor Phil's discussion of Willow Creek Ministries and his mention of other well-known evangelical leaders and ministries during other conversations revealed that he has access to larger evangelical resources, and discerns what his own church might glean from these resources, while consciously rejecting other facets of them.

Ethnicity at Manna

Being a multiethnic church is about more than demographic makeup at Manna. It is a central mission, as well as an interpretive framework through which to see American evangelicalism in the congregation. The sermons, congregational literature, and my conversations with leaders all reveal that ethnic diversity is a specific goal. According to the literature disseminated by the church, one of Manna's core values is to "see the church as a group of people with different cultures and backgrounds." Being a multiethnic congregation is defined as "valuing the ethnic diversities of God's Kingdom, establishing an atmosphere in which we enjoy the synergy of a diverse community," and "raising up a multiethnic leadership and staff." In the church brochure, Manna justifies this multiethnic vision by citing passages from the Bible that talk about "developing a church without walls in the area of cultures and backgrounds."

A comment in one of Pastor Phil's sermons points to how Manna's leaders see the connection between being a multiethnic church and their mission as Christians: "Let's share [with others] about being multiethnic.... [The early church] was a multilingual church.... God wanted everyone.... God put it on their heart to do missions.... This applies to... Manna Fellowship." To further justify Manna's focus on ethnic diversity, Pastor Phil illustrated his sermon with a pertinent Bible story. For Manna's leaders, multiethnicity is legitimized by linking it to Christian teachings and connecting diversity to more effective outreach.

Pastor Phil said that being with the young people at Manna forces him to look outside of his own Chinese ethnic history and see the needs of the city and of the broader world. May Ann, Pastor Phil's wife, described attending a racial reconciliation conference.[42] She said that at the conference, "it was clear, while we were singing 'Break Down the Wall,' that sense of community. Churches want to preserve the Korean culture or the Chinese culture... but a lot of culture needs to be redeemed... what we should be promoting is God's kingdom culture." May Ann's sentiment is that Christian churches should recognize various ethnic cultures, while realizing the common culture that Christians have from being part of the kingdom of God.

Why Attend a Korean American or Multiethnic Church?

My goal is not to make a strict causal argument between the models of civic responsibility in each of these congregations and the views of individual congregation members, controlling for other factors.[43] Instead, I am more concerned with determining how Korean Americans in second-generation and multiethnic churches, and in particular those who attend Grace and Manna, use the resources of their churches to create civic identities and develop civic practices. It is still important, however, to pay attention to the reasons Korean Americans at Grace and Manna give for attending their specific churches. While most of the members have one central reason for choosing their congregation, some give more than one explanation. The reasons expressed by the latter group overlap with several of the categories I discuss.

Korean Americans at Grace

The motives the Korean Americans at Grace gave for attending their church fall into three broad categories:

1. *Nonreflective*: Some are members of a Korean American congregation because they simply have attended Korean churches their entire lives out of tradition or habit; they have not reflected on why they are part of this particular type of congregation.
2. *Mainly spiritual*: Another group tried churches with a different ethnic composition, generally a pan-Asian or white church, and then decided to come back to a Korean congregation because they see second-generation Korean congregations as more spiritual and more evangelical than other types of congregations. Some expressed it as a specific spiritual mission to reach out to other second-generation Korean Americans, and feel as if they would not fit in with the ethnic culture of a non-Korean congregation.
3. *Exclusively ethnic*: A minority of Korean Americans come to Grace simply to be with other Korean Americans. This group consists largely of Korean Americans whose parents have not been members of a Korean American evangelical congregation. Some have parents who are Buddhists or Catholics, and in their young adulthood made the decision to attend a Korean church English ministry.

Candace is in her early twenties and works in a legal consulting firm.[44] She is among the first category of Korean Americans—someone who has not reflected on her reasons for attending a Korean American church. She comes to Grace mainly because she has always attended Korean churches. She describes her decision to be a member of a Korean American congregation in this way:

> I don't know. I don't think it has ever been a really conscious decision. I stayed at my home church until my sophomore year of college, and that was when I met one of the pastors [of Grace] at my university, at Korean Christian Fellowship, and I started talking to him about church and things of that nature, like Christian books. He was really easy to get to know and was really fun. He would just call us up and say, "Let's go out and have dinner." . . . I just ended up at Grace. Because of one of the pastors, I got to know Joseph, and then through another friend, Joshua.

Jeremiah is 29 and completing his last year of medical school.[45] He fits in the second category—he comes to Grace for reasons that he described as "primarily spiritual." Jeremiah was born in the United States, and his parents are practicing Buddhists. He grew up in a town he described as "white and middle class" and decided to try a Korean Christian church when he was in high school. Jeremiah and his wife attended a predominantly Caucasian congregation while he was in medical school, but, as Jeremiah explained, he "didn't really grow as a Christian" when he went to the white church. When they moved they made a decision to find a Korean American congregation:

> We made a deliberate effort to look for a Korean American church because of our two years [in medical school]. We weren't sure if our experience was due to the age difference, or if it was the ethnic difference. So we thought we would just play it safe and go back to a Korean American church and find a Korean American church that had an English ministry and had solid teaching and hopefully had a group of people our age.

Jeremiah tries to frame his decision to remain part of a Korean American congregation not as entirely based on the desire to be with those from a common ethnic culture but as emanating also from his spiritual needs.

Jessica is in her midtwenties and works for a nonprofit organization. She also fits in the second category of reasons for attending a Korean American congregation, but she found it unproblematic to describe her decision as having both spiritual and ethnic components.[46] Jessica said her decision to remain part of a Korean American church is deliberate. In terms of ethnic draw, she "just feels more comfortable around Koreans" because they are "more familiar. They have the same stories." One of the things she said Korean Americans have in common is that when they are around other Korean Americans they joke a lot about who acts "white" and who does not. She explained this as similar to "code-switching" with African Americans, where members of a group talk and behave differently in one context from the way they do in another, and described these context-specific ways of acting as a form of code-switching for Korean Americans.

Unlike those in the foregoing cases, some explained their reasons for choosing Grace *entirely* in terms of ethnic culture. For this group of Korean Americans, explanations for attending Grace are largely devoid of reference to the spiritual. However, when these individuals explain their choice as based on ethnic reasons, the *qualifying* they do indicates that they don't perceive it as entirely legitimate to have only ethnic reasons for attending church.

Joanne is in her late twenties and fits in the third category.[47] She started attending Grace primarily to be with Korean Americans her own age, mentioning, several times during our discussion,

> I really like spending time with the people there.... There is a certain bond I think, when you go to a Korean American congregation. Even things like language. You know, I speak Korean at home. You know, when I go to a Korean American church, a lot of people I meet there will speak some Korean too, so we will throw in some Korean phrases when we talk. And we will talk about Korean movies that we have seen. Things like that, it is like a common ground.

Joanne believes in God, but she isn't pursuing an active spiritual life. She adds that most of the people at Grace are really religious, and she is pretty sure they would not understand "where I am coming from." Joanne added, however, that she is probably standing on the same ground as some of the other people in the church.

Korean Americans at Manna

Interestingly, all of the Korean Americans I talked with at Manna had at some point attended a Korean-specific ethnic fellowship or church. There are Korean American churches in close proximity to Manna, which means that the Korean Americans there have the option of attending a second-generation Korean congregation if they choose. Most of those I interviewed at Manna talked about their decision to attend the church as a deliberate move away from the Korean church setting. They choose Manna primarily because they were looking for a *non-Korean* congregation rather than because they were specifically looking for a multiethnic church.

Several motives for joining emerged from these discussions about their choice:

1. *Spirituality*: Korean Americans at Manna want to attend a church where spirituality and Christianity are experienced without an overt connection to Korean culture.
2. *Ministry pressure*: They stopped attending a second-generation Korean congregation because of the "burnout" associated with too much involvement in church activities.
3. *Socioeconomic distance*: They indicated that in Korean churches, even ones with second-generation congregations, there is significant pressure to succeed economically and educationally, and they want to escape from this pressure. Although Korean Americans at Manna are generally as successful educationally and economically as those at Grace, they want to escape what many perceive as pressure from first-generation Koreans to succeed.

Winston is in his midtwenties and falls in the first category. He moved away from a second-generation Korean American congregation because he feels Korean congregations are centered too much on Korean culture instead of Christianity. Winston explained the contrast between his experiences in second-generation Korean churches with those at Manna. He also told me that he was cynical about first-generation Korean congregations, which often have church splits and are more concerned about Korean culture than being a "house of God."

> The whole community is really the church. If you look at the studies on this... they go to church because everyone is there. Monday through Friday you go to work and then when you come to church it is like, "Oh Mr. Kim, Mr. Lee," and that is where you get your fellowship and you survive in your Korean ethnocentric. [In contrast] there is such a trust among the staff and encouragement to try new things at Manna.

Winston's mocking tone expresses just how strongly he feels that Korean immigrants are more concerned about whom they see at church—"Oh Mr. Kim, Mr. Lee"—then about "trying new things" as a way of glorifying God.

Eleanor is in her late twenties and is a librarian. She also decided to stop attending a Korean church because she felt Christianity and Korean culture were too intertwined there.[48] When she was in college, she had a Christian roommate who was white, and she made a decision to not attend a university-based Korean Christian Fellowship. After a brief postcollege return to a Korean church, Eleanor decided to stop attending Korean churches altogether:

> I think the big thing [I like about Manna] is the absence of feeling [negative aspects of] Korean culture or Asian culture. It is the whole "losing face" thing, where you don't want to lose face in front of people so you don't care for your family problems. Korean church,

because the culture is so well ingrained in our Christianity, it's sort of like that.... So there's a lot of healing and sharing and things [at Manna] that are not shared [at a Korean church].

Eleanor finds at Manna a place where she is able to share, without judgment, the unique struggles that come from being Korean. At Manna she can freely express that she is Korean and Asian, but she feels she escapes the negative ethnic cultural expectations that she links to participating in a church community with only other Korean Americans.

Helen, 25, talked with me about the benefits of attending a multiethnic church as we sipped hot tea at a Chinese restaurant in Old Town. Helen works as an administrative assistant for a trading firm and initially came to Manna primarily because she knew of Pastor Simeon. Her response falls largely into the first category.[49] "When I was in college for a little while I went to a Korean American church, and Pastor Simeon was the college pastor at that time. And then when he started Manna, then I came to Manna." Later in the interview, she told me that as the church became more multiethnic, her perspective changed:

And I was really glad that I went to Manna, because it opened me up. I never had many friends outside the Korean church. It was great just to meet people from different backgrounds and to be able to worship the same God together, even though their ways might be different, our heart was the same.

Helen also explained that the second-generation Korean Christian Fellowship she attended in college was fairly exclusive—it didn't make reaching out to those who were not Korean a priority. Since attending Manna, Helen has come to believe second-generation Koreans should not attend ethnic-specific congregations:

I would never go back to a Korean church. I feel strongly [about] that. Like I love my Korean Christian Fellowship friends, but I strongly feel there is a bias and those ethnic-specific fellowships, they perpetuate an isolationist church. I understand the purpose of the Korean church maybe for people who are the first generation. A place where [first-generation people] can find community. But, I think for people of my generation it is our responsibility to look outward and bless people because we are all worshipping the same God.

Helen's perspective on ethnic congregations was changed through attending Manna. She now thinks that multiethnic churches are more "spiritual" or "Christian" than ethnic-specific churches.

Carl is 23 and was born in Korea, but he moved to the United States with his parents when he was one. Carl largely fits in the second category.[50] He left the Korean American congregation he attended because of the "burnout" he said is often coupled with being a leader in a second-generation Korean church. He felt the only way he could escape it was to leave the church: "Because if I stayed in the church that I was at, I would sort of be stuck in that teaching position [teaching Sunday School]. And that is not really something that I wanted to do. So I felt like the only way [out] was to stop attending the church altogether." Carl told me coming to Manna also meant escaping the hierarchy of the Korean church and the expectation that he would be in a leadership role:

> I think for most people who are college age or young adult, and in a Korean church, the older generation will ask the younger generation to be the Bible study leaders for the younger kids. At a church like Manna, there isn't that younger generation. It's people who are all the same age. There isn't really anyone who is expecting you to lead anything. You are on an equal level with everyone.

Although Carl was actively involved in ministry at Manna, there was a difference from his involvement in the Korean churches he had attended. At Manna, Carl felt he could choose whether to be involved in a ministry at all and the specific ministries he wanted to commit to.

Sue is 23 and works in the fashion industry.[51] She exemplifies the third category and feels that Korean Americans who remain part of the Korean church might feel more pressure to achieve economic or educational success: "I think it's very atypical that we [her brother and she] are in such nontraditional fields, or non-money-making fields. I think a lot of Korean families are really into stable, money-making fields like engineering and business." Sue told me that coming to Manna means she doesn't need to try and please anyone with her choice of job or economic attainment.

Conclusions

What is most pertinent to the themes of civic life I examine in further chapters is that Korean Americans give a *variety* of reasons for attending Grace and Manna. All of the Korean Americans I talked with speak English fluently. They also speak Korean to varying degrees, ranging from "not at all" to "fluent."[52] Their different stories reveal, however, that religious association does not proceed along a straight-line continuum from purely ethnic to more diverse congregations on the basis of human factors like language skills. Some Korean Americans may attend a Korean congregation, in part, because of parental wishes or because of existing social networks in the Korean community. However, there are also those at Grace and the other second-generation churches I studied who attend Korean congregations to learn more about

Korean culture. Korean Americans at Manna and the other multiethnic churches I examined often choose a multiethnic congregation initially because they want to distance themselves from the Korean church, and they give several different reasons within this broad category. In neither church type do Korean Americans explain their choice of church in terms of the congregation's specific approach to civic activities or relationship to the community.

The variety of reasons that Korean Americans at Grace and Manna give for attending a Korean American or multiethnic church lends credence to describing choice of church as "ethnic negotiation" rather than "ethnic assimilation." Korean Americans do not move away from a Korean-only context in a progressive fashion over their life course, based on the degree of knowledge they have of Korean ethnic culture. For a small group of respondents, Korean culture is an important reason to remain part of a second-generation congregation. For others, even though they attend a non-Korean church, they still speak Korean fluently and practice many Korean customs.

Although I set the Korean Americans at Grace and Manna within the broader context of interviews in other second-generation and multiethnic churches around the country, this work is primarily about the Korean Americans at these two churches. In this chapter I have examined several different descriptive themes surrounding Grace and Manna. These themes will be relevant to the rest of the book, where I discuss the relationship between civic identities and practices. In chapter 4, we turn again to an in-depth look at Grace and Manna, in particular the different interpretations or cultural schemas each of the churches offered Korean Americans for developing ideas about civic responsibility.

4

Models of Civic Responsibility

American citizens have some agency in defining what "citizenship" means to them personally and to what extent it entails responsibility to their local communities and various wider American publics. Determining the content of civic responsibility is a topic of particular relevance for the roughly 27.5 million or nearly 10 percent of Americans who are the children of immigrants.[1] Second-generation immigrants, unlike their parents—who either are not American citizens or became naturalized citizens later in life—are American citizens by birth, and they construct aspects of civic responsibility without historical precursors as role models.[2] In a context distinct from their parent's experiences as foreign immigrants, they grow up facing the question "What does it mean to be a *good* American?"

This chapter is concerned with how second-generation Korean and multiethnic churches develop models of civic responsibility with attendant schemas—interpretive frameworks—that Korean Americans use to create civic identities and civic practices. Here I begin a discussion that will continue throughout this work, both of how these models of civic responsibility relate to the broader institution of American evangelicalism and of how congregational models of civic responsibility are used by the Korean Americans in each of these two kinds of church contexts. Although data for this chapter come primarily from lengthy interviews with Korean Americans at Grace and Manna, I also draw on data from other ethnic Korean and multiethnic churches.

Congregational Models of Civic Responsibility

Cultural schemas for civic life matter because they are resources for guiding action. The aspects of congregational culture I am most concerned with are the ways in which Korean Americans in second-generation and multiethnic churches use congregational schemas to develop civic identities and the implications these identities have for civic practices. This analysis also reveals how Korean Americans in these settings are different from, or the same as, other groups of American evangelicals in how they view civic life.

In some ways, Grace and Manna have similar models of civic responsibility. The leaders and members of each church prioritize the expressions of evangelism. Each church places some priority on community service as a means of living and spreading Christianity to those in the local community. Yet each congregation also uses Christianity to interpret its ethnic demographic composition in different ways. For example, Grace places a priority on being different from first-generation Korean congregations by developing a distinctive evangelical and nonethnic identity. Manna calls itself a "multi-ethnic church," yet the church has a racial makeup of over 70 percent Asian Americans, most of whom are second generation and have had negative experiences with ethnic-specific churches. Although the congregation is not really that racially diverse, Manna places a priority on being distinctive from ethnic-specific churches, including white churches within American evangelicalism.

The structural location (their class, race, and ethnic composition) of these congregations and the cultural resources of their members also contribute to different models of civic responsibility in the two church types, models that have implications for public involvement. The approach to the interconnection between ethnicity and spirituality results in congregation-specific models of civic responsibility. Grace, and the other second-generation churches I studied, has a model of civic responsibility that draws from American evangelicalism, rhetorically deemphasizes self-focus, and emphasizes obligations to the congregation and wider American society. I label this a *communal* model of civic life. In contrast, Manna and the other multiethnic congregations learn diverse possibilities for civic life from their diverse membership; the leaders place a priority on member self-understanding and leave community involvement up to personal decision. I call this an *individually negotiated* model of civic responsibility.

Group memberships are an important part of shaping moral order for individuals and serve as central mediators between institutional frameworks and individual actions. Such mediations result in strategies of action for individuals.[3] Individuals in each of these churches bring consequent schemas from their structural locations; for example, Korean Americans in both types of congregations are demographically similar. They are second-generation Koreans, with immigrant parents. They are American minorities. Most attended first-generation Korean churches as children. They are, by and large, educationally successful American minorities, successful Asian Americans, and successful Korean Americans.

The form of evangelicalism in each of these church types confronts views based on the structural location of Korean Americans in second-generation and multiethnic churches, particularly those revolving around race, ethnicity, and class. Each of these churches uses evangelicalism to interpret ethnicity and class in different ways. As I will discuss in chapter 5, Korean Americans at Manna use the model of civic responsibility in their church to challenge images of Korean Americans as model minorities, while Korean Americans at Grace largely uphold the model-minority image. These different models for civic life have diverse yet patterned implications for local community service, as I discuss in chapter 6.

Although both groups of Korean Americans want to create distance from first-generation Koreans, each congregation has a different *Christian* approach to ethnicity.[4] Ironically, although they attend a second-generation Korean congregation, those at Grace talk very little about being Korean. They express tension over how their parents, first-generation Koreans, understand the connection between Christianity, economic mobility, and Korean ethnicity. In an effort to be different from first-generation Koreans, Korean Americans at Grace stress their responsibilities as a church community to help those outside their church and those outside the Korean community. The church also implicitly reinforces, however, that Korean Americans should be hardworking and not complain about adversity. Using Christianity to justify being hardworking and to deemphasize discrimination makes it difficult for Korean Americans to understand how they will relate to other ethnic minorities in Old Town. They perceive other minorities as less industrious and more apt to complain about what those at Grace see as a common history of struggle out of poverty.

Listening to Korean Americans at Manna reveals that they also want to be different from their immigrant parents. Being "multiethnic Christians" is part of the organizational schema for race and ethnicity at Manna. The leaders and members of Manna describe the church as multiethnic in interviews, and the pastors talk about becoming more multiethnic as part of their Christian mission. As a church, Manna encourages congregation members to see their ethnicity as a "gift from God" and to connect Christianity to valuing ethnic diversity and more general diversity. In practice, Korean Americans at Manna use the discourse of their congregation to embrace diversity, both in ethnicity and the politics of lifestyle within the limits of American evangelicalism. Korean Americans and the other members of Manna are also pushed by congregational leaders to develop an ethic of service to their community. As a church, Manna sponsors multiple local community service programs. Because of their ethic of individual negotiation, however, *how* to participate in community service is left almost entirely up to the individual. In Table 4.1, I contrast how faith perspective, class, and ethnicity relate to a prevailing model of civic responsibility within Grace and Manna.

Grace: A Nonethnic Christianity

Distinct schemas for ethnicity are part of the model of civic responsibility in second-generation Korean and multiethnic churches. Sociologist Pyong Gap Min, in his work on Korean immigrants, explains that immigrant churches often provide nonreligious resources, such as English language training classes and help with immigration documentation—practical resources that assist in adaptation.[5] Korean immigrant churches are also places where immigrants look for social networks and the reproduction of Korean culture in the United States, a place where their specific national and ethnic culture is outside the mainstream.

Korean Americans at Grace, consistent with findings from other studies of second-generation Korean congregations, construct ideas about their own organizational identities through doing what sociologist Michèle Lamont calls creating a "boundary ideology."[6] One way the boundary ideologies of specific groups are discovered is through documenting the criteria a group uses to evaluate or judge those outside its group. Especially since they are in close proximity to a first-generation church, sharing the same building, it is important

TABLE 4.1. Models of Civic Responsibility

	Grace	Manna
Approach to Christianity	Uniform doctrine Somewhat hierarchical approach to leadership	Diverse individual interpretations within evangelicalism Egalitarian approach to leadership
Relationship of ethnicity to Christianity	Distance from Korean immigrant churches Ethnicity deemphasized	Christianity leads to appreciation of diversity Distance from white evangelical Christianity Ethnicity emphasized
Relationship of class to Christianity	Hard work brings success Explicitly reject but implicitly accept the American Dream	Wealth and prosperity are unmerited blessings from God
Model of civic responsibility	Communal obligations to church, local community, and wider American society	*Ethic* of civic responsibility Individually negotiated civic practices in local community and wider American society

for members of Grace to have a cohesive group identity that clearly establishes the ways their church is different from that of the first generation. One way the members of Grace create a cohesive boundary is through describing second-generation Korean Christianity as a more authentic, pure form of Christianity than that held by their parents. Organizationally, as reflected in literature, sermons, and the opinions of leaders, Grace Church rhetorically emphasizes its desire to decouple Korean immigrant culture from Christianity in order to achieve a more "pure" form of faith. Although they are demographically a Korean ethnic church, their specific ethnicity is not examined overtly in the pastoral sermons and is discussed less often among individual members than it is at Manna. Even though this is not stated explicitly in their literature or sermons, Grace Church displays an unconscious schema that is reflective of the supposedly "nonethnic" Christianity of many white evangelicals. These ideas about ethnic identity of the organization have implications for how the church views civic life and specifically their ability to do community service in the surrounding community of Old Town, the largely low-income, ethnic minority community where the church is located.

A main priority of the congregation is to have a view of how ethnicity relates to Christianity that is distinct from that of their first-generation Korean parents. In an interview, Pastor Joseph, the main pastor at Grace, told me that second-generation Korean churches ought to be different from first-generation churches in developing a deeper and more sincere form of faith than that of their parents, one that separates Korean culture from Christianity.[7] He describes first-generation Korean Christianity in the United States as "ten thousand miles wide, but only an inch deep." In Pastor Joseph's view, immigrant Korean Christians concentrate on upholding the Korean culture to the extent that they stop focusing on the "real" tenets of Christian teaching.

Joshua, a Korean American in his early thirties, works in business and is a leader of the central planning committee for Grace.[8] Joshua told me that he and the other leaders on the planning committee wonder "how many people come to Korean American churches because of Christ, and not because of social reasons." Like Pastor Joseph, Joshua is a leader in the church who wants to help members move beyond coming to church for Korean cultural reasons.

It was initially surprising to me when I began to attend the church that although Grace is Korean, the topic of being Korean and the specific cultural issues that Korean Americans might face as nonwhite Americans are rarely discussed in congregational sermons or among the individuals in the church. Scholars may think that Koreans going to church only with other Koreans are actually trying to distance themselves from other Americans (by remaining in their own ethnic group), but I found among the members of Grace church that they are really trying to distance themselves from *first-generation* Koreans, not other Americans more broadly.

The sociologist Jean Bacon, in her work on Indian Americans, discusses the ways that these children of immigrants create ethnic identities by establishing boundaries between themselves and the first generation. I found that at Grace and the other second-generation churches I studied, second-generation Koreans also create religious identities with overlapping ethnic components through distancing themselves from the first generation. My conversations with the church leaders revealed that *because* of the church's structural location as a Korean American church affiliated with a first-generation Korean congregation, it becomes even more important, if the church is to be distinctively Christian, for it also to be distinct from first-generation Korean congregations. The boundaries that Korean Americans at Grace create between themselves and the generation of their parents are very much upheld by a spiritual logic. According to Lamont, boundaries between a group and those outside the group often have moral dimensions.[9] The American working-class men that Lamont studies create boundaries between themselves and others through labeling the individuals within their group as "the kind that work like you and me" and those outside their group as "lazy"—categories that draw a group boundary with moral dimensions.[10]

Although they are in a different social class, the second-generation Koreans in my study create boundaries that have moral dimensions, much like Lamont's working-class men. In particular, they create boundaries from the first generation through labeling them as "less Christian" or as having a "cultural Christianity," that is, a Christianity that results more from a commitment to an ethnic culture than what some of my second-generation respondents call "a desire to serve God." This is demonstrated in the way Korean Americans discuss conflict between their own and their parents' generation. Adam, a Korean American in his midtwenties who is pursuing a career in medicine, told me that even though his parents are Christians, his own desire to uphold the truths of the Bible often comes into conflict with his parents' Korean cultural expectations.[11] As he explains, this is a particular struggle, "when your parents are asking you or telling you to do things that are... against God." Adam later tells me that what he sees as a moral struggle often happens when his parents expect him to put school activities above church activities.

Other members of Grace indicate that while being part of a church for ethnic cultural reasons (such as a language barrier) might be acceptable for the first generation, it has no place among second-generation Koreans. The view of Samantha, a Korean American in her early twenties who is enrolled in a pharmacy program at a nearby university, reflects those of the leadership and echoes Adam's view that first-generation Koreans are less authentic or spiritual Christians because they connect Korean culture to Christianity.[12] She says it makes sense that for a short while Koreans who are part of her parents' generation will be members of a Korean church when they first immigrate. As

Samantha explains, Koreans initially need the safety of a first-generation church: "When you don't know anyone, one of the biggest places to meet people is church." However, Samantha contrasts this need with how she views being a more authentic Christian, thereby creating a boundary between her parents' generation and her own. She goes on to say that the second-generation Koreans who are the most "Korean," those Samantha describes as "Korean Korean Americans" are also "the least likely to be faithful Christians." Samantha's words may seem ironic, since she also attends church with other Korean Americans. Close observation, however, reveals that even though their church is made up of Korean Americans, those at Grace do not see themselves as "doing Korean church."

Explicit Rejection and Implicit Acceptance of Economic Mobility

The desire to create boundaries between "spiritual Christianity" and "ethnic Christianity" translates into second-generation Koreans trying to distance themselves from the first generation in additional ways. This further distancing from the first generation is reflected in how Korean Americans at Grace view class, and is linked with their "communal obligations" model of civic responsibility. This model of civic responsibility, reflected in obligations to uphold the social order in wider American society, is demonstrated by how those at Grace respond to the American Dream.

The American Dream is embodied in the struggling immigrants who come to the United States and seem, through hard work and sacrifice, to make a living for their families out of virtually nothing. Other Americans look to these immigrants who have "made it" and use them as symbols of inherent American equality.[13] In one sense, Korean Americans at Grace very much distinguish themselves from the first generation through their ideas about economic mobility. Many of my respondents describe this as "rejecting their parents' ideas about the American Dream" in pursuit of a more authentic Christianity. They tell me that those in their parents' generation think of the American Dream as the idea that if you "don't complain and work hard enough, eventually anyone can 'make it' in American society." During the time I regularly attended the church, I heard often in formal interviews, as well as casual conversation, that the first generation tries to pass the value of economic mobility on to the second generation through connecting economic success with being a good Christian. As we sat together in a coffee shop eating bagels, Jessica, a Korean American in her late twenties who works with a nonprofit, told me in an animated and cynical tone how common it is for the first generation to talk about the American Dream:

> Our parents all struggled at some point. All of our parents came to America with fifty dollars in their pocket.... Our parents all walked

five miles in the snow to go to school in Korea. That's why "education is so important and we should value it." They all... had to wash windows, or eat dog food because they couldn't read the label and it was cheap. They all got fired from their job because they didn't know English and so they had to start their own business.... So because they all had to struggle, status and wealth in the Korean culture are very important.

On one level, Jessica's description evokes haunting images of the immigrant struggle to overcome adversities of language and economic barriers. Later in my discussion with Jessica, however, I discover that her parents were professionals both in Korea and in the United States. That Jessica's description of the struggling immigrant making it in America is not actually true in her particular situation reveals just how important this story is as a cultural script. Cultural scripts are what sociologist Ann Swidler, in her work *Talk of Love*, describes as symbolically available stories that people use to make sense of their lives. Swidler analyzes the institution of marriage in her book, explaining that even though the "live happily ever after" ideal of romantic marriage does not fit with the actual experiences of individuals, the institution of marriage gives structure to this mythic view of love and becomes a way that people make sense of their lives when reality doesn't fit with expectations.[14] Even for those Korean immigrants who do not experience economic struggle, adopting the story of the American Dream allows them to fit in with other Americans. Whether or not "the American Dream" of upward economic mobility through personal achievement is an accurate description of Jessica's situation or that of other second-generation Koreans is not as important as what her statement reveals about the power of the American Dream as a cultural story. Being "good examples of the American Dream" is a script developed by first-generation Koreans for interpreting their own class position and passing it on to their children. Linking economic mobility to Christianity provides the kind of moral justification that some first-generation Koreans use to keep this message alive in their own churches and more successfully pass it on to their children.

Explicitly, Korean Americans at Grace and the other second-generation churches reject ideas inherent in the American Dream through redefining "good" Christianity and decoupling it from economic mobility. Consciously rejecting the connection between economic mobility and Christianity is a way that the congregations at Grace and the other second-generation churches I studied express a desire to be different from the first generation. Jacob, a Korean American in his early thirties, and another member of the central planning committee at Grace, told me that members of the congregation really struggle with how to hold being a good Christian in tension with the desire for economic success:

> I think we have a yuppie mentality and I think it's very dangerous.... We look at them [Korean Americans who are financially successful] and we say "Wow, they're really Godly people." But on face value what looks Godly is not Godly under God. Because whatever they do, they're giving out of their wealth, not out of their poverty.... I think this yuppie mentality is very dangerous in our church.[15]

To be truly "Godly," according to Jacob, the members of the church should separate professional success from true faithful Christianity. Jacob also told me that he thinks most members of Grace are probably economically and educationally successful. Yet Jacob does not want to make being professionally successful synonymous with being a good Christian.

The members at Grace also reject making a link between economic mobility and Christianity. After she told me how her parents use the American Dream in her own life, Jessica said many Korean Americans feel negatively toward that framework. According to her, "some of the Korean Americans don't want to struggle with that any more. They don't want people to look at how big their engagement ring is or how much their bag cost." From Jessica's perspective, churches should not be places where people come to compare measures of economic success.

Through comparing my time at Grace to that in other second-generation churches, I found that explicitly rejecting a Christianized version of economic mobility is a fairly consistent theme. Haijoon, a Korean American in her early thirties, is married to the pastor of a Korean American congregation in New York.[16] On the day I met with her, we sat in a dessert café next to the university where her husband is pastor for the English ministry of the Korean church. Haijoon explained that after college she made the decision not to be a lawyer, a career choice that she came to realize was more about the wishes of her parents than her own desires. In response to her decision, Haijoon is currently experiencing negative criticism from first-generation Koreans:

> There is this thing with Korean parents, where we are brought up to please them. But, I felt God was not leading me to become a lawyer. And in the Korean Church there is this thing where being successful educationally and financially is the same as being spiritual or being a good Christian.... And that's just not true, right? That's not a right interpretation of Christianity. Because, I mean there are lots of people who are not well educated, who are really good Christians.

Haijoon told me later that she wants her current church to be different from immigrant Korean churches. As a leader of the congregation, when she mentors people, Haijoon encourages the members of her church not to look for the right interpretation of "Korean" Christianity but to focus more on being the right kind of "Christian." She wants the young adults in her church to have the freedom to make their own career decisions rather than to follow the aspirations of their parents.

National Civic Responsibility as Upholding the Social Order

Being different from the ethnic Christianity of their Korean parents means those at Grace and other second-generation churches see themselves as upholding a pure and nonethnic Christianity. However, their discourse reflects what is in essence another form of "racialized" Christianity—a characteristic of some predominantly white, evangelical Christian churches. Like some white evangelicals, Korean Americans at Grace use Christianity to uphold the existing social order and commitment to a Christian *civil religion*. Sociologist Robert Bellah defines civil religion as the "transcendent universal religion of the nation," including such principle elements as belief in God, belief that the United States is subject to God's laws, and the assurance that God will protect and guide the nation. Implicit in this concept are ways of setting boundaries that distinguish the American nation from other nations in being "chosen," and a means of separating American citizens from non-American "others."[17]

As a congregation, Grace reinforces the ideal that America is a special nation founded on Christian principles and that Christian congregations in the United States have communal responsibilities to make the nation stronger. Being a good Christian means upholding the social order of American society. For example, one Sunday, Pastor Joseph told members of Grace during a sermon that the Christian church, "when it is faithful, has brought blessing to America."[18] He explained that "the roots of many hospitals in America are through the church," and then told members that they needed to work hard within existing structures in America, such as in education and their places of employment, to make America a better place.

Korean Americans at Grace and the other second-generation churches also link their church and Christian values more generally with the idea that America is historically a Christian nation and Christians should support American government policies. The church leaders at Grace often pray for President George W. Bush during Sunday worship services, and thank God that "he is a Christian man." Those at Grace think individual Americans and the American nation sometimes act immorally; yet, in their discussion about what it means to be a good American, the dominant discourse is the connection between America's founding and Christian values. For example, according to Samuel, a Korean American in his midtwenties and in medical school, America was "Christian from the beginning [and] has a Christian mentality. I think the church helps. I feel like, as I become a better Christian, I will become a better American... America itself was founded upon Biblical principles of right and wrong."[19] Samuel believes there is something particularly

Christian about America; in his words, America is based on "Christian ideals and principles." The commitment to upholding American civil religion has the potential to motivate civic participation. He later told me that Christians have a responsibility to "get out there" and make the nation a better place through "helping the poor and needy" and upholding biblical principles.

Those from second-generation Korean congregations outside Grace echo the same sentiments that Christian teaching and church participation should be intertwined with and motivate support of existing American ideals. Daniel, a Korean American in his late twenties who works as a pharmacist and attends a Korean American congregation in New Jersey, explains, "The core of it, to be a good American is to be a Christian.... The country was founded on religious freedom and worship. To be a good American is to be a Christian... it is to work hard and to raise children who go along with what it is that makes this country as great as it is."[20] Daniel clearly thinks evangelical Christians should generally support and uphold the given social order. Implicit in Daniel's statement and those of other Korean Americans who talk about public religion is the assumption that being a good Christian will not be in tension with being a good American. Grace places little stress on upholding Korean culture and, in so doing, is different from the way many first-generation Korean congregations connect being a Christian to community life.[21] In moving away from Korean culture, however, members of Grace are *not* adopting a Christianity that is free from ethnic culture. Rather, they are moving toward a Christianity that makes faith synonymous with American rather than Korean culture. In so doing, Grace church and other second-generation churches align themselves more with American evangelicalism—American "white" evangelicalism, whose ways of connecting spirituality to civic responsibility often serve to reinforce existing categories of Christianity as *the* civil religion.

Narratives of Local Civic Responsibility as Reaching Out

Individuals have both conscious, as well as what the sociologist Harold Garfinkel sees as unconscious, interpretations of or ways of understanding the world.[22] Although Korean Americans at Grace explicitly reject the way their parents connect Christianity with economic mobility, I noticed through attention to how those in the church informally talk about upward mobility and respond to discussion of discrimination among other nonwhite ethnic minorities that they *implicitly* also adopt a Christianized version of the American Dream. This means they sometimes connect Christianity to being industrious, or not complaining about discrimination, poverty, or other life problems. The implicit connection of Christian teachings and church life to facets of the American Dream is sometimes evident in church sermons at Grace. According to the church leaders and Pastor Joseph, "good" Christians are those who work hard in service to the community and to the church and do not spend a lot of time complaining about or focusing on life problems, particularly issues related to racial discrimination. In a Sunday sermon, Pastor Joseph tells the congregation: "We will not make excuses [about doing church service]. We won't say we have to study as if it is in competition with the things of God. You would study in advance, so you could serve the Lord." According to Pastor Joseph and the other church leaders and members, part of being faithful to church service is being what I call "communally focused"—an approach reflected in practices of spending more hours in service to the church, not talking about individual problems, and not complaining. Pastor Joseph calls this framework "working hard and getting rid of the 'victim mentality.'" In multiple sermons, he tells congregation members they should focus less on their own problems and concentrate instead on God and serving others. One Sunday I heard him say during a sermon: "There is the victim mentality. A lot of people feel they have a bad lot in life. They may think they are poorer than others.... If only we read the Bible, we will see Jesus set us free.... If a person would meditate on that truth, then they would never see themselves as a victim again." Here he emphasizes that those who read the Bible closely will realize it is not about understanding one's own problems, but about deemphasizing poverty and other troubles, and "not acting like a victim." It is important to note, as I will demonstrate further in subsequent chapters, that the church does stress community service. As those who do not focus on their ethnicity and do not want to act like victims, however, they find it difficult to relate to individuals in the local community whom they think "make too much of discrimination."

Decoupling Christianity from a focus on problems, as well as caring for the community over the individual, has implications for the discourse Grace and the other second-generation churches use to talk about interacting with the residents of Old Town, those who are poor, nonwhite, and seem—in the minds of Korean Americans at Grace—to "have a lot of problems." Explicitly, the communal obligations model of civic responsibility means that Grace places an emphasis on commitment to community service in Old Town. Since they perceive first-generation Korean churches as mainly focused on serving the needs of other Korean immigrants, particularly those in their own churches, these second-generation Koreans want to be outward focused largely in order to be different from first-generation Koreans. The church leaders told me that one of the central ways Grace will be distinct from first-generation churches and will be a more fully Christian congregation is through its community involvement. Pastor Joseph explained to me his goals of distinguishing his *second*-generation congregation from *first*-generation Korean churches through helping "our church members not to be too comfortable at our church, but to be a blessing to the world." Instead of being focused on retaining Korean culture or increasing economic mobility, in Pastor Joseph's view, churches should be places where people come to "learn more about God and to serve the local community."

Through church sermons, informal discussions with members, and their responses to interacting with the residents of Old Town, however, it is evident that Korean Americans at Grace believe that class differences between themselves and the residents of Old Town create a cultural chasm that makes community service difficult. As I will discuss further in chapters 5 and 6, those at Grace implicitly adopt the principle that America is a meritocracy. Although they do not believe pursuing wealth should be synonymous with being a good Christian, they do suspect that those who are not "making it" are simply not working hard enough. This cultural schema—this interpretation of what it means to be a good American and a good Christian—has direct implications for community service for the residents of Old Town.

Manna Fellowship: Learning to Appreciate Diversity

As a multiethnic church, Manna helps its members develop an understanding of how being a Christian is connected to appreciating ethnic diversity. Although Korean Americans at Manna are the same ethnic group and social class as those at Grace, the very core of Christianity at Manna includes the conscious embrace of ethnic diversity. These Korean Americans gain from their church a completely different model for the relationship of ethnicity to Christianity. Ironically, at Manna an outwardly focused appreciation for ethnicity in its myriad forms translates into what seems on the surface a very individualized focus on the specific needs of members in the church. The type of Christianity at Manna emphasizes that each individual should hear directions for action in the local community through a personal relationship with God rather than through church-based ideals. These factors coalesce to provide those at Manna with a more individually negotiated model of civic responsibility. This same model of civic responsibility is reflected in the other multiethnic congregations I examined.

The church upholds the model of multiethnic Christianity in a number of ways, including sanctions against other views. After attending Manna's services and congregation-sponsored functions for a number of months, it became clear to me that there are sanctions against those in the church who do *not* make a multiethnic focus part of what it means to be a Christian. For example: Manna's cell groups, the small fellowship groups that meet weekly outside of Sunday services, are a central way in which the church members learn about one another's needs and provide care.[23] The leaders of the church think the cell groups should be both reflective of the church's ethnic diversity and a place where appreciation of ethnic difference and racial diversity in wider American society is fostered. This is a difficult mission to accomplish structurally, since most of the church is Asian American, but I found that the leaders at Manna carry out subtle sanctions against forming ethnic subgroups in the congregation. In a focus group I conducted with the leaders of the church, the pastors talked about the problem of small groups that are still "too ethnic," composed mainly of those from one ethnicity.[24]

The church's focus on ethnic diversity is reflected among the individual members of the church. Korean American members often told me that, through attending Manna, they came to see the spiritual value of a congregation that is ethnically diverse. Sue is a Korean American member of Manna; she is in her midtwenties and works in merchandising. She told me that her original reasons for attending Manna had to do with the church being "so embracing" compared to Korean congregations.[25] Sue says the acceptance she learns from being part of Manna is best exemplified in her cell group, where she is learning to relate to an ethnically diverse group of individuals.

Korean Americans in the other multiethnic congregations echo this focus on connecting ethnic diversity with American Christianity. These Korean Americans say that their churches—through small groups, teaching on the importance of ethnicity, and the chance to focus on people outside their own ethnic group—help them to develop a spiritual appreciation for diversity in wider American society. Jack, a Korean American in his late twenties, attends a multiethnic congregation in California.[26] Jack explains that his congregation helps him to become a better American through the moral and ethical topics that are discussed. Among these is an emphasis on "appreciation for racial and ethnic diversity." In addition to the idea of individual freedom for all, Jack's words also reflect the rhetoric of universal brotherhood—a more communal attribute. However, diversity in multiethnic churches is connected to an overall vision of freedom and appreciation for individual differences rather than universal obligations to American society.

Valuing social diversity goes beyond appreciation for ethnicity at Manna—it extends to support of political diversity. By valuing difference, Manna creates space for Korean Americans to appreciate diverse political opinions and diverse approaches to community service. Sue told me that the Korean churches she has attended have been conservative politically, but coming to Manna encouraged her to admire those with political perspectives different from her own. She said that through Manna she is learning to have respect for a white woman in the church who has "very liberal" political views, "supports Ralph Nader," and is often engaged in political protests. Sue goes on to say that she would be unlikely to encounter this type of person in other types of evangelical Christian churches.

National Civic Responsibility as Religiously Motivated Social Critics

Multiethnic congregations are still not the social norm in American society. As part of a multiethnic organization, Korean Americans at Manna consider themselves distinct not only from a communally obligated Korean immigrant worship context but also, more broadly, from other American evangelical churches.[27] The religiously motivated commitment that Korean Americans at Manna have to ethnic diversity, as well as their individualist approach to Christianity, provides them with a group mentality as part of the social margins. Korean Americans at Manna gain exposure to diverse opinions and legitimate Christian discourse for upholding ethnic diversity and for thinking about American institutions and history more critically.

The schemas for civic responsibility are more diverse at Manna than at Grace. Some at Manna view the social order in ways that are similar to the ways Korean Americans at Grace do so. For example: Hope is a Korean American in her early thirties who attends Manna. She had previously worked for an investment firm, but when I talked with her, she was a stay-at-home mother for her young daughter.[28] She told me that being a good American "means to be loyal to your country. I think it means to have pride in the country where you live and not bash it, or then you shouldn't be living here." Hope's connection between being a good American and upholding the social order is an approach to civic responsibility similar to that found among Korean Americans at the all-second-generation Korean American Grace.

More often, however, an individually negotiated model of civic responsibility is reflected in the space Manna creates for some Korean Americans to act as social critics. A similar social space is not as available at Grace and other second-generation Korean churches. Being a social critic involves sometimes looking at American symbols, such as the American flag and the American Dream, in alternative ways and upholding other American symbols, such as appreciation for diversity and personal freedom. What is unique is that Manna as a congregation, and specifically the Korean Americans at Manna, sometimes talk about American society in very disapproving terms, criticizing what they see as unthinking patriotism. When I asked Sue, the Korean American from Manna mentioned earlier, what it means to be a good American, she answered by discussing her feelings about the American flag: "I'm not at all patriotic. My parents have an American flag and I hate it. . . . I'm not into the whole flag thing, or obvious patriotic things. I'm very pro-America in a lot of things, I support the government and I support democracy." Sue supports what she thinks are the foundations of American society: democracy and the government. However, she distinguishes support for American institutions from what she sees as possibly superficial and potentially unthinking "flag-waving" patriotism.

Korean Americans at Manna also have a different approach to civil religion from those at Grace; in particular, the connection they make between America's founding and Christianity. Like those at Grace, Korean Americans at Manna think that Christianity should influence government institutions. Yet, while some Korean Americans at Manna believe the history of American society fundamentally emanates from Christian principles and ideals, more often they punctuate this focus on the good with explanation of America's downsides. Jim, a Korean American in his midtwenties, works for Manna as a youth minister and is a seminary student.[29] When I asked Jim what it means to be a good American, part of his answer was a discussion of America's history:

> It's about knowing our history. It is about knowing the good and the bad of our history, knowing the truth and appreciating it but also not accepting everything.... It is interesting to study the roots of America and see how they branch in to things. Gold, wealth, power and the raping of the Indians and their downfall. That's all embedded in who we are. Sometimes we just think about ourselves.

As a congregational leader, Jim's expression of negative views about America's history reveals that there is space at Manna to voice disagreement with American government and societal institutions, valuing what is seen as a more holistic view of the American reality.

Local Civic Responsibility as Individually Negotiated Civic Practices

In some ways, the approach to civic responsibility at Manna has communal elements. Like those at Grace, Korean Americans at Manna connect Christianity to responsibilities for participation in a wider American community as well as their specific local community. Unlike the members of Grace, however, they make this focus legitimate through valuing individual opinions and diversity rather than through fostering a sense of communal obligation for local civic responsibility. Korean Americans at Manna think that a focus on a multiethnic Christianity means they have a responsibility to help those who are different from them. Young-Mi, a Korean American in her early twenties, works as a teacher and attends Manna.[30] Young-Mi gives her church and her school credit for providing her with a particular life ethic, which justifies valuing and caring for all Americans regardless of race or ethnicity:

> I can remember when I was young, how you talk about Martin Luther King...how he wanted equality for blacks and whites. That kind of leads to a discussion on how we need to accept all people...how God accepts us, no matter what we look like or where we're from.... To help people who aren't like you, reaching out like that kind of makes you a better American because that's what this country is: helping people out...regardless of what people look like or their backgrounds or what language they speak, you kind of help each other regardless of those things.

In her definition of being a good American, Young-Mi connects overlapping religious and racial identities to civic responsibility. She reasons that because God accepts her no matter "what she looks like," she has a responsibility to accept and help people who "aren't like her."

Those who write about the "politics of diversity" discuss the difficulties of fostering group responsibility to make changes in societal structures legitimate among those who are very strongly committed to appreciation of individual differences.[31] Although Robert Putnam, in his work *Bowling Alone*, blames the decline of civil society, in part, on increasing individualism among Americans, for Korean Americans at Manna an individually negotiated ethic actually seems to *motivate* social service.[32] When the leaders and individual members of Manna talk about service to their local community, the dominant discourse is "Being of service to others first requires helping oneself." Leaders reason that if church members are spiritually strong, they will have more to give others. The leaders and members at Manna encourage one another to come to their own ideas about their "gifts," and "callings," and their implications for practices, via a "personal relationship with God." According to Jake, an African American member of Manna and a teacher in his late twenties, Manna is a place one can personally grow spiritually. It is "a place where people have the ability to try new things and be fostered in their individual spiritual gifts."[33] Jake has an attitude similar to that of the Korean Americans at Manna about the efficacy of focusing on developing one's own individual gifts and talents as a way of strengthening the ability to do Christian service.

Another example also reveals how Manna emphasizes personal healing as a means of becoming more equipped to provide service in the community. At one point during the nine months I was part of the church, Manna sponsored training sessions entitled "Ministry to the Poor."[34] Hearing the conference title, I imagined training in practical service skills, such as connecting the homeless with shelters in the area or sermons and talks motivating members to become involved in volunteerism. But, surprisingly, the sessions were mainly about understanding one's own gifts and focusing on the personal healing of individual congregation members. At the end of one session, the leader, a white woman who is a missionary to Asia, asked individuals who wanted prayer for "freedom from things that are holding them back from helping others" to stand and step out into the aisles of the sanctuary.[35] Probably 75 percent of the 80 people who were present stood and asked for prayer. The leader explained, "Many of us feel we have to pay our families back and we are not free to serve the poor. I want you to be free to do what God tells you." The injunction is for members to focus on themselves, and overcome their own concerns and issues before reaching out to others, so as not to reach out from motives that are based in guilt. The final goal of the session, however, is that each individual figure out how to use his or her talents and resources in the local community to some extent.

Linking appreciation for diversity with being both a good Christian and a good American limits the extent to which Korean Americans at Manna, however, have the ability to develop a uniform and group-based discourse of civic involvement. Winston, a Korean American in his midtwenties who is a leader at Manna, told me he thinks second-generation Korean Americans at Manna and other churches have strong responsibilities to be involved in American society.[36] He says his idea of civic responsibility is to have an "impact on American citizens, if I can." When it comes to group responsibility, however, he talks about each person as "having a different role." Sue, whom I introduced earlier, also told me her church shapes her views of civic responsibility by "encouraging [her] to think about how we as Christians can influence society and government, *but never we as some kind of group* [my emphasis]." Carl, a Korean American in his early twenties and a university student, says Manna motivates him to be concerned about community service in some way, not necessarily to be involved only in what the church is doing.[37] Winston, Sue, and Carl all give their church credit for helping them develop ideas about community service, and each believes Christians should care for those in their community in ways beyond evangelism. Yet such a focus also makes it difficult for them to see how their church should or could motivate communal responsibility and why, in particular, they ought to be more committed to church-sponsored service programs than other kinds of community services. In chapter 5, I further explore how the individually negotiated cultural schema for civic responsibility has the surprising characteristic of sustaining long-term commitment to individual acts of civic involvement for Korean Americans in multiethnic churches.

Origins of Organizational Schemas for Civic Responsibility

After describing the differences in models of civic responsibility for second-generation and multiethnic churches, it is important to reflect on their origins. Many of the civic life resources these churches have in common come from their structural location as evangelical congregations and the resources this religious tradition provides. These resources include sets of doctrines, spiritual literature, and patterned sets of practices.

What is different about the cultural schemas for civic life in each of these churches comes from differences in their interpretation of ethnicity, race, and the relationship these categories have to civic life. Each church is filled primarily with ethnic minorities: Grace with second-generation Korean Americans and Manna with its largest group being made up of Asian Americans. They use the resources of evangelicalism to spiritualize these differences and to legitimize group boundaries between themselves and other evangelical churches of certain types.[38] Grace wants to be a distinctively Christian congregation. To do this, the leaders and members distance themselves from first-generation Korean churches, which they perceive as practicing an ethnic rather than a truly spiritual Christianity. Because Manna has mainly second-generation people from various ethnic backgrounds, and the leaders and members of the church have had difficult experiences with ethnic-specific churches, they want to be a distinctive kind of evangelical church by being different from all ethnic-specific churches.

In their desire to be distinctively evangelical, each congregation borrows cultural schemas for church life from other evangelical churches. In order to draw on denominational resources, Grace is pursuing affiliation with the Presbyterian Church in America, a largely white, conservative evangelical denomination. The first-generation Korean church with which they are affiliated, however, is not part of this denomination. Grace borrows other practices from white evangelical churches, such as worship songs and ministry resources. The pastors and church leadership talk more about literature from noted white evangelical leaders, such as John Stott and J. I. Packer, than they do about works of Korean evangelical leaders, even though evangelical Christianity in Korea has significant resources from which to draw.[39] As the leadership explained to me, using these broader American evangelical resources is part of becoming a purely Christian rather than a Korean congregation. Trying to be uniquely evangelical and nonethnic has implications for their model of civic responsibility—a model that does not take into account their structural location as a demographically Korean congregation. By focusing on developing a nonethnic Christianity, the members of Grace do not draw on the ethnic resources of being nonwhite in the United States, which could serve as an asset in community service through helping them link with other nonwhite Americans.

In a desire to be a distinctively multiethnic church that is committed to appreciating diversity in its myriad forms, Manna also sees itself as a minority church within American evangelicalism. As Pastor Phil tells me, they do not have much help in a mission of diversity from the resources of American evangelicalism, even though both of Manna's central pastors are graduates from well-known evangelical seminaries. Consequently, Manna borrows from the other "major minority" church in American Christianity—the black church. Their congregation meets in a building owned by a black church. The pastors of Manna meet regularly with the pastor of this congregation. They also use programs and resources on Christian social justice and service in public teaching that are published by a major black church ministry in another city.

Conclusions

I started this research with the assumption that citizenship is something to be held as a constant or control. I found, however, that even for a group of Korean Americans who are all citizens, the *meaning* of civic responsibility is socially constructed and varied. Other institutional arenas, such as families and work environments, also shape ideas about civic responsibility for these Korean Americans. In their discourse, however, evangelical Korean Americans prioritize congregational participation in providing interpretations of what it means to be a "good" American.

Their churches provide specific understandings of the relationship between evangelicalism, ethnicity, and class, which result in implicit models of American civic responsibility. Both of these congregations are evangelical. In some ways, both are also religious individualists, that is, the leaders and members of Grace and Manna stress a focus on the relationship between God and the individual person rather than a commitment to a hierarchical religious structure. Yet members of Grace, the second-generation Korean congregation, rhetorically reject personal negotiations in favor of collective obligations and responsibilities. They explicitly reject the ideas first-generation Koreans have about the American Dream yet sometimes implicitly make adherence to an American work ethic synonymous with Christian spirituality.

In contrast, the personal understandings of Korean Americans who attend Manna, the multiethnic congregation, have considerable complexity, combining elements of intense self-reflection and self-focus with elements of appreciation and communal concern for others. This individually negotiated model stresses developing an ethic of civic responsibility. Korean Americans who attend Manna, as well as those who attend the other multiethnic congregations, also develop group identities as social critics and a less prescribed view of how to practice civic responsibility.[40]

The rest of this work is devoted to understanding how congregational models of civic responsibility relate to civic identities and civic practices for these churches and the individual Korean Americans in them. I show that the congregational model of civic responsibility is one kind of organizationally based schema that individuals use to create identities and strategies of action surrounding civic responsibility. Congregational models do not completely determine civic life for the Korean Americans in second-generation and multiethnic churches; rather, as one resource, they mesh with other resources individuals use to create civic identities and shape practices.

Analyzing the differences in *how* various potential cultural schemas generated by evangelicalism and other structural locations are adopted and implemented in local organizations adds both empirical and theoretical insight to a cultural sociology. Empirically, this way of looking at the interactions between these two groups of Korean Americans and their congregations provides broader insight into how people in basically the same structural location develop different approaches to civic life. In addition, by way of implication, this work has relevance to issues of institutional change. I show here that connecting individual identities to institutions through organizational and individual-level schemas provides understanding of the mechanisms by which Korean Americans and other Christian new Americans, as a growing percentage of the evangelical population, might bring change to American evangelicalism. This work broadens insight about how levels of culture interact with and shape one another—in ways that are not necessarily top-down from institutions to individuals—and reveals the multiple sources that individuals use to create civic identities, and how social civic identities relate to practices.

As I will now show in chapter 5, these congregational schemas provide Korean Americans with legitimate ways to view and construct social civic identities, as well as ways to create identity hierarchies. It simply is not legitimate at Grace, for example, to say that one is *more* Korean than Christian, because the cultural schema indicates that the congregation is fundamentally evangelical. Korean Americans, therefore, prioritize Christianity as a lens through which to interpret experiences of being Korean when negotiating their civic identities. These congregational schemas also provide individuals in the churches with a means of doing boundary work, legitimating certain practices as more "right" or "holy" than other practices.[41] This happens in ways one might not expect without an understanding of the particular cultural schemas of the respective church types.

5

Civic Identities

Michael Schudson wonders aloud, in his book *The Good Citizen: A History of American Civic Life,* whether the process of citizenship reaffirms the social hierarchy of the American community.[1] In some sense, the Korean Americans in my study must respond to existing conceptions of American citizenship as racialized, where they are viewed as "other" in American society. Yet, as Schudson explains, we live in a modern age where the web of citizenship is widening. With the advent of what Schudson calls the rights-regarding citizen, I would argue that there is more possibility for individual agency. Under certain conditions, individuals have the possibility of challenging prevailing notions of what it means to be a good citizen and how an identity as an American overlaps, conflicts with, or is even shaped by one's religious identities. For my respondents, racial categorizations and religious interpretations of race are a central way citizenship is defined.

Sandra is a second-generation Korean American in her mid-twenties and attends Grace. I asked her if she thinks non-Koreans view her as an American, and she responded:

> I don't think that I ever felt very different from them, but I remember once my brother came home—this was when he was very young and he must have been in kindergarten or first grade. When he came home he was making fun of Chinese people, how their eyes are small. I just looked at him and I was like: "How do you think you look?" And he said: "What do you mean? I am white." Yeah, I think that

is kind of funny. Though he was different, he didn't see himself as being different.[2]

In the story Sandra told me, she and her brother are responding to existing American racial categories, which, in part, determine facets of their civic identities; real Americans are white, and nonwhite Americans are different, or "other." Yet Sandra and her brother are not completely without agency in this situation, using imposed racial categorizations as cultural resources to construct their own identities.

In some ways, civic categories are imparted by outside structures, such as national governments. According to Schudson, the state has decided who is a citizen and who is excluded from citizenship through narrow definitions of race, class, and gender, particularly during certain times in history.[3] Categories of citizenship have the ability to reaffirm the social hierarchy of the community, with nations ranking and giving some citizens fewer social rights than others. Scholars pay less attention, however, to how individual citizens construct civic identities, and in this context, to how individuals decide what it means to be a United States citizen. In particular, how do American citizens decide which groups they have allegiance to and whom they have a responsibility to help? How do ethnic and religious categories overlap for new Americans in the construction of identities? How, specifically, do local organizations mediate civic identities?

I started this work by asking how Korean Americans understand what it means to be an American and how religion plays a part in this process. I explored how the churches they attend provide Korean Americans with models of American civic responsibility. This chapter explores how they use these models of civic responsibility to socially construct civic identities. I address these broader questions and issues by asking how Korean Americans construct social aspects of identities as American citizens and specifically how they use religion to understand their place in society relative to other racial and ethnic groups. A salient theme throughout my discussions with Korean Americans is the role played by their churches—how attending either Korean American or multiethnic churches is giving them cultural resources to construct civic identities.

Identities and Identity Formation

Racial and Civic Identities

The ideal of American citizenship is that "ethnicity is separate from belonging; America is a nation of immigrants, and legal citizens should not be ranked to determine who is more or less American."[4] Yet, contrary to this ethos, the historical and current place of race and ethnicity is contested in American society. Even a cursory look at American history would lead most to agree that, at least in the past, racial categories have structured American citizenship.[5]

Determining to which racial and ethnic groups one belongs is a key facet of civic identity and, rather than just a predefined census category, also has some of the moral dimensions Lamont discusses in her work on boundaries. One aspect of persistent racial inequality in the United States is what race theorists James Kluegel and Lawrence Bobo call "symbolic racism," moral feelings on the part of some white Americans that black Americans violate traditional American principles of hard work and self-reliance.[6] The concept of symbolic racism is a facet of the prominent view that race continues to be a category of exclusion that is imposed, and that shapes who is viewed as an authentic citizen—in part because America continues both structurally and institutionally to perpetuate a view of America as white and black, with black Americans viewed as less deserving of full citizenship. Aspects of this view are also formulated in "racial formation theory," put forth by race theorists Michael Omi and Howard Winant, who argue that race is a politically contested and important concept in American society that structures both state and civil relationships—primarily around the categories of "white" and "other."[7] Omi and Winant define "racial formation" as the "sociohistorical process by which racial categories are created, inhabited, transformed, and destroyed." They argue that "racial formation is a process of historically situated projects in which human bodies and social structures are represented and organized," and further explain: "we link racial formation to the evolution of hegemony, the way in which society is organized and ruled." Although Omi and Winant do not draw on insights from the sociology of culture, their work supports the view that the United States has almost completely predetermined schemas for racial categories and their meanings. For example, they argue that the racial structure of the United States is predetermined and that individuals have little agency in deciding where they fit in its landscape. Indeed, there is some evidence of this lack of agency among the Korean Americans I interviewed. They said they have a hard time figuring out where they belong within the evangelical as well as the broader American landscape—a landscape they perceive as too often broken up only into the categories of black and white, with little room for Asian Americans.

Existing racial categories are factors that have structured the civic belonging of new Americans—something that is historically evident through a study of U.S. immigration.[8] As part of the increasing body of literature on the social construction of "whiteness," the historian Noel Ignatiev discusses Irish migration during the eighteenth and nineteenth centuries. Although the Irish were fleeing from oppressive conditions, they quickly adapted to the American social system in which race is an important means of distinguishing and ranking groups.⁹ The Irish deemphasized ethnic identities and rejected their common characteristics with black Americans as minorities in order to become "white."

Sociologist James W. Loewen explains that Chinese Americans who settled along the Mississippi Delta in the late nineteenth century initially tried to carve out a niche as distinctively Chinese. Other Americans, however, labeled them as either black or white, and they responded to such categorizations by trying to fit in more with white than black Americans.¹⁰ They sought to construct outward symbols that would convince white Americans of their own "whiteness." We have modern examples of racialization of new immigrant groups as well. For example, because of existing negative stereotypes of black Americans as dangerous and less successful than other groups, sociologist Mary Waters argues that some Caribbean Americans try to retain their ethnic culture in order to resist being labeled "black."¹¹

Yet there is also emerging, in our current climate, a new perspective on race—one that infers that legal and cultural changes brought on by the Civil Rights Movement and changes in 1960s immigration law (while certainly not completely eradicating racism) have led to a broader range of accepted racial and ethnic categories.¹² Diverse political coalitions have pressured the government and other public institutions to more fully recognize America's demographic diversity. Census categories evolved dramatically as a result of this political pressure and, in the 2000 census, individuals had the option of identifying with more than one race.¹³ Whereas others labeled Loewen's Mississippi Chinese black, coalitions of nonwhite Americans themselves consciously adopt the collective identities of black, Hispanic, and Asian, for the purpose of political and social mobilization and solidarity.¹⁴

This view of racial categories as emergent and changing, while not the entire story, does form an important backdrop for my research. Still, neither of these views of racial categories, as structured a priori or as emergent, fully addresses intragroup differences in the moral construction of identities. I argue in this chapter that organizational memberships mediate racial and ethnic identities, and I discuss how these categories overlap with and are structured by other identities to shape the construction of "good" citizenship in potentially *different* ways, even among those within the same ethic and racial group.

I came to this study with the presupposition that the content of racial, ethnic, and religious identities for Korean Americans in ethnic-specific and multiethnic churches was still open to discovery. Because of the openness of American evangelicalism to multiple interpretations, Korean Americans in ethnic and multiethnic churches have the possibility of using evangelicalism to (1) legitimate a more individualistic understanding of racial relations, like many white Christians; (2) identify with a more structural understanding of race relations, like many black Christians; (3) embrace aspects of both of these; or (4) develop altogether different constructs for racial, ethnic, and religious identities, and their relationship to civic identities and practices.

Scholars who study Asian America increasingly argue that this group has the ability to transform existing racial paradigms in the United States.[15] I am in agreement with this view. One area of scholarly discussion about the meaning of the category "Asian American" centers on the public construction, in media and educational institutions in particular, of Asian Americans as model minorities, those who are inherently predisposed to success. In some instances, this stereotype is used to legitimate continual racism against black America through the logic of "if Asian Americans can succeed, then why can't black Americans?" I found that ethnic-specific and multiethnic congregations provide Korean Americans with the resource of different yet patterned *new* cultural schemas to negotiate the public image of Asian Americans as model minorities. Korean Americans' churches help them manage their immigrant parents' expectations of success, and their own ethnic and spiritual understandings. Korean Americans use the in-group and out-group boundaries in these different church contexts, which they perceive as having moral components, to determine social aspects of their civic identities. Such identity constructions have very real consequences for how Korean Americans relate to other racial and ethnic groups, and in particular black Americans.

The ethnic-specific churches I studied are more likely to create boundaries between Korean and black Americans by changing racial boundaries into class distinctions. In contrast, churches that are self-consciously multiethnic provide their members with a theological language to discuss race and diversity. Consequently, and in contrast to the ethnic-specific churches, many of the Korean Americans in the multiethnic churches stress their commonality with black Americans. Those in the multiethnic churches more often discuss the tension between being Korean and being American. Their interpretations of Christianity help them to negotiate this tension; Korean Americans in multiethnic churches use Christianity consciously to construct protean or fluid social identities.[16]

Such constructs specifically use Christianity to interpret race, ethnicity, and class. Korean Americans in ethnic-specific churches hold views of the relationship of religion to civic life that differ from those of Korean Americans in multiethnic churches. If there is this kind of diversity in interpretations of religion's relationship to civic life among members of one ethnic group, there may be a lot more diversity among nonwhite evangelicals than is currently being realized—not to mention the diversity that new Americans might be bringing to forms of Christianity other than evangelicalism, as well as to non-Christian religions.

The Model-Minority Stereotype

Public societal conceptions of one's group are a kind of institutional cultural resource that individuals use to create facets of civic belonging or civic identity. The image of Asian Americans as "model minorities" is one such image that my respondents use in creating civic identities. Often perpetuated by media, government, and schools, the model-minority stereotype has as its center the thesis that inherent ethnic cultural traits make Asian Americans more financially and educationally successful than other groups of nonwhite Americans.[17] Scholars have challenged this view by revealing the socioeconomic diversity in the Asian American community and the differing resources with which Asian immigrants come to the United States.[18] Scholars pay little attention to how Asian Americans utilize facets of the model-minority stereotype in forming their own personal identities, or how they internalize the stereotype to create boundaries, with civic consequences, between themselves and other Americans.[19]

Korean Americans at both Grace and Manna, and those in other Korean and multiethnic congregations, discuss the role of the model minority stereotype in their lives. My respondents often mentioned how they respond to the model-minority stereotype in understanding aspects of their own identities. Helen, a Korean American in her midtwenties, is a member of Manna and works as an administrative assistant in a financial trading firm.[20] When I asked her if she is discriminated against in American society, she told me that it often happens in what others think of as "positive" ways or when teachers and authority figures see her as a "good" minority. Helen explains:

> You know the role of the good minority, of Asians as overachievers. I would get teased a lot. And the teachers would really love you. And I would draw something really simple, and the teachers would say, "Asians are good artists." And I started to not care if I got a B. And I started to not care about college.

For Helen, the model minority is a culturally available concept. It is also one that might be imposed by others at any time and has the effect of attacking her individuality. However, in this story, Helen also socially deconstructs the stereotype through her actions. She does not think of herself as a model minority and begins to demonstrate this to others by "not caring about college."

Korean Americans' congregations provide them with different cultural schemas for interpreting the image of "Asians as successful." Some aspects of their interpretive frameworks help them to interpret the model minority image positively, even reinforcing images of themselves as model minorities. Other research, too, finds that Korean American congregations and university Christian fellowship groups often reproduce intertwined images of prestige, cultural hierarchy, and Korean Americans as model minorities.[21] Ethnic and religious studies scholar Rudiger V. Busto argues that American evangelical Christianity often reinforces a spiritual version of the model minority by seeing Asian Americans as super-spiritual "zealots."[22]

Grace: Implicit Affirmation of the Model-Minority Image

At its core, the model-minority image makes a statement about the origins of wealth. It is clear that Korean Americans in both churches are financially and educationally successful relative to most other groups of Americans. However, at Grace, there is tension in how the church leaders socially interpret the connection between spirituality and wealth. On one hand, they think being a Christian makes *seeking* financial wealth contradictory to the spiritual life. On the other hand, the congregation implicitly affirms that, for Korean Americans, financial success is an inherent ethnic cultural trait. During our interview, I asked Pastor Joseph what kind of needs people in the congregation face. He responded:

> I think, for instance, the second-generation Korean American mentality, they need success. Partially because they are kind of spoiled, myself included, because the first generation immigrated to the states and they worked really hard. They worked so their children could have a better life, and the children do have better lives, but at the same time everything was just handed to them. So it's very common to see a child driving a superior car to their parents'. To me that is a little odd, but it is something frequent, and the second generation oftentimes think that they're entitled to it. So it kind of comes up in their attitude. They think they need success, need good jobs, and need to make a lot of money.[23]

Clearly Pastor Joseph wants to be different from the "Korean mentality to need success." He also told me that his congregation should focus on things he considers most important to Christianity, such as commitment to understanding the Bible.

Conversations with other leaders and individual members at Grace, however, reveal a tension in this area. Joshua, in his early thirties and a church leader, told me one of the biggest struggles faced by Koreans at Grace is the resistance to making financial attainment the ultimate marker of meaning. Joshua thinks this kind of struggle is simply an ethnic cultural trait for Koreans.

> Because of our *ethnic identity and our culture*, we are very ambitious as a people. *Korean Americans are very ambitious.* Our parents tell us we have to go to school and we have to get an A and we have to

become lawyers and doctors. And if we don't achieve some sort of social status, then we feel kind of belittled and inferior. If you look at our church, we have twenty people who are out of college. Out of that, maybe only one or two people are not in graduate school, or are not doctors or lawyers. So we are very ambitious [his emphasis].[24]

Because these churches are evangelical Christian congregations, the churches and individuals in them have, as part of their institutional culture, multiple ways (or, as Ann Swidler writes, "cultural tools") to interpret wealth.[25] For example, Joshua could view congregation members' resources as an "undeserved blessing" from God. Yet he uses the image of a large number of Korean professionals in the church as further evidence that "being ambitious" is something inherent to Korean American ethnic culture.

The sermons and public teachings at Grace help the Korean Americans there develop civic identities by giving them spiritual categories for distinguishing between individuals who are spiritually strong and those who are weak or act like "victims." In his sermons, Pastor Joseph often tells the church that to acknowledge discrimination or poverty is to "act like a victim" and remove one's focus from God. He cautions the church members against devoting too much attention to their problems, poverty, or discrimination. In a sermon one Sunday he said:

> Grace Church needs to get their eyes off themselves and their own problems. We cannot have that mentality and be a blessing. . . . We need to focus on the needs of other people. . . . How many people in this church see themselves as a victim? Jesus did not come so you would be a victim, but that you would overcome. Let's share that blessing. Get your eyes off yourself.[26]

As I will discuss in chapter 6, "getting one's eyes off oneself" helps Korean Americans at Grace to be more involved than those at Manna in *church-sponsored* community service.[27] However, the very fact that the leadership connects discussing one's poverty or other difficult social conditions to being less spiritual has the unintended consequence of creating distance between Korean Americans and those they perceive as members of a class or ethnic group that talk about experiencing discrimination or being victimized.

Manna: Rejecting the Model-Minority Image

Korean Americans at Manna are just as educated and financially successful as those at Grace. Because the congregation is predominantly Asian American, rather than creating social networks with non-Asian ethnic minorities within the church, Manna provides its members with a framework for interpreting social interactions with nonwhite Americans outside the church. Korean Americans at Manna have access to cultural resources through sermons and church teachings that help them to focus on the solidarity and commonality, rather than the differences and boundaries, they have with other ethnic minority groups in American society.

Manna connects being a multiethnic congregation to being a more spiritual congregation. This framework is a cultural resource that the Korean Americans there use to construct civic identities. One of Manna's core values is to "see the church as a group of people with different cultures and backgrounds." Being a multiethnic congregation is defined as "valuing the ethnic diversities of God's Kingdom, establishing an atmosphere in which we enjoy the synergy of a diverse community," and "raising up a multiethnic leadership and staff." In the church brochure, Manna justifies this multiethnic vision by citing passages from the Bible that discuss "developing a church without walls in the area of cultures and backgrounds." The leaders discuss multiethnicity during teachings and sermons, and link being a multiethnic church with a more effective evangelical mission. In one sermon, Pastor Phil, a Chinese immigrant, told the church:

> Let's share [with others] about being multiethnic.... Pentecost was a multilingual church. The Greeks and Jews didn't distribute things well enough. But, God wanted everyone.... God put it on their heart to do missions. They had different quarters. But, when they shared the gospel, the walls broke down. They had become a big group, so they called themselves Christians, little Christs. This applies to... Manna Fellowship.[28]

Here, Pastor Phil used a story from the Bible to justify the congregation's current vision for being a multiethnic church. This consequently facilitates discussion within the congregation about the differences between individuals. Church leaders and members make a point of emphasizing that race should be openly discussed and should not form barriers between people in the church. Manna and the other multiethnic churches I studied help Korean Americans see the importance of ethnic diversity by providing a Christian theology or spiritual lens through which to more broadly view diversity in American society.

Jack is a Korean American in his late twenties who attends a multiethnic congregation in California.[29] At the time of our interview, he had recently resigned from a position in business to work full-time for his congregation. Jack had previously attended a second-generation Korean church, but left because he thought the first-generation church affiliated with his former congregation exercised too much power over the second-generation church. He told me that being a member of a multiethnic church really "opens his eyes" to thinking about race:

> A topic that we recently covered was racial reconciliation. That's a huge belief I think the church really opened my eyes to. I don't know if I've reconciled. But I know there needs to be some kind of change in my belief system or my attitude toward the whole idea of racial reconciliation.

As Jack understands it, he was not thinking about racial reconciliation before attending his church. Through attending the church, he has come to see the importance of racial reconciliation because, in his words, his congregation provides a sort of religious lens through which to view race relations.

Stressing unity and equality carries over to how leaders and members of Manna think about class and wealth accumulation. The church teaches that pursuing spirituality is more important than gaining wealth. When members accumulate wealth, it is a result of God's blessings rather than their own hard work. This lays the foundation for Korean Americans to deemphasize wealth or to admit to poverty in their own backgrounds. Jim, a Korean American in his midtwenties and the youth pastor at Manna, explained:

> I hope to be used some way to channel the resources God has blessed us with to the poor, to those that don't have as much.... Because my dad didn't have much when he came here. He started as a busboy. And now he put us all through college and bought us all cars when we graduated, and it is extravagant. Yeah I never had to worry about money or anything like that. I didn't have everything. But, I feel like God has blessed us [Korean Americans] with that kind of work ethic and it is something we can give back.[30]

Jim's discussion of a "special work ethic" among Korean Americans echoes some of the ideas about the model-minority image held by the members at Grace. However, instead of seeing material wealth and the work ethic as something he and his parents have acquired mainly through a special cultural or ethnic predisposition, he views the resources of his family and even their work ethic as "gifts from God." That a church leader sees wealth accumulation as part of God's blessings rather than as an inherent part of being Korean reveals that discourse is available in the congregation to challenge the model-minority image for Asian Americans.

Defining the Self through Defining the Other

Part of civic identity construction is determining where one fits among various racial and ethnic groups in American society. For Korean Americans, it is particularly important to negotiate their place vis-à-vis black Americans. The ways that Korean Americans' congregations connect Christianity to race, ethnic, and class relationships are resources they draw on to negotiate boundaries with other groups of Americans.

Korean Americans in Second-Generation Churches

Media images, as well as some scholarly work, focus on the interracial conflicts between first-generation Korean business owners and black American customers in urban areas.[31] It is important to note, however, that none of those I talked with, at Grace or other second-generation Korean congregations, overtly discuss not liking black Americans or even experiencing interracial conflict with black Americans; it's a theme that is more common among members of the first generation.[32] The second-generation Korean Americans in my study specifically try to distance themselves from what they see as the overt discrimination Korean immigrants sometimes have toward black Americans. The same Korean Americans, however, do display unconscious schemas that uphold a boundary between themselves and black Americans. In less overt ways than their parents, they, too, emphasize their distance from and difficulty in relating to black Americans, based on the perception that black Americans don't try hard enough and sometimes act like victims.

Bill, a Korean American in his midtwenties, works as an engineer and attends Grace. When I interviewed him, he talked about the desire he has to sustain a good job to support his parents.[33] As Bill puts it, his parents succeeded "against the odds" and are worthy of help. In contrast, even though he mentions positive friendships with African American coworkers, Bill sees black Americans in general as a group he finds it challenging to identify with. He also finds it difficult to help them in a community service setting, explaining: "Maybe because of slavery, they always seem like they have a chip on their shoulder. Some are very proud and they don't want help. They can do it on their own." Bill finds it hard to support African Americans who think of themselves as current victims of racism. As evidenced by Pastor Joseph's sermons, "acting like a victim" is also an attitude that Grace views negatively. Neither Bill's friendship with black Americans at work nor his motivation as a Christian to help those who have less is able to overcome his opinion that many African Americans have "a chip on their shoulder" and are difficult to help in the social service arena.

Occasionally, the defining of Korean Americans as different and better than black Americans is demonstrated in a more overt way among the second-generation churches I studied. Daniel is a Korean American in his late twenties who works as a pharmacist and attends a second-generation Korean congregation in New Jersey.[34] He told me that he thinks African Americans are often jealous of Korean American prosperity and that, from the Korean perspective, black Americans have been in this country for generations and generations and are still looked down on and not accepted. When I asked

Daniel why, in his opinion, African Americans "don't get ahead," he explained that it is largely because they do not value education or work hard enough:

> They need to go to school and to work hard and not complain and spend so much time rioting like the Malcolm X people. Martin Luther King I respect immensely, but not Malcolm X.... African Americans sometimes don't want to get ahead it seems, and just don't work.

Daniel tries to make it very clear during our discussion that he does not discriminate against African Americans. This statement is most salient because of what it indicates about the way Daniel creates group boundaries. He thinks of himself as a typical Korean American: a Christian and hard-working young professional. Daniel also tells me the best American citizens are often Christians and work diligently in their chosen profession. Those whom he perceives as "working hard" are more worthy and deserving of help. Those who spend time "rioting" or "complaining" are less deserving. For Daniel, many black Americans fit in the latter group.

To the extent that Korean Americans champion "hard work" as their sole means to economic advancement, they are establishing their own respectability and using a schema that equates being Korean with being hard-working to create a boundary between themselves and black Americans. So, while some aspects of the model minority stereotype are a source of irritation to Korean Americans, an overt commitment to viewing hard work and merit as the sole means of advancement can be interpreted as an effort to establish moral superiority to black Americans.

Korean Americans in Multiethnic Churches

Korean Americans at Manna also draw on religious resources to interpret their relationship to black Americans; however, they use these resources to see the place of Korean Americans as part of ethnic minority America. Categorizing themselves as *minority* Americans shapes the way they disestablish group boundaries with black Americans. They discuss what blacks and Koreans have in common, emphasizing that both groups experience poverty and have family-oriented cultures. When there is conflict, Koreans at Manna attribute it to spiritual rather than personal causes. They have respect and admiration for what they perceive as the collective approaches black Americans have to political life and are more likely to feel favorable about helping black Americans in social service settings, or, as I will discuss further in chapter 6, even learning more effective social service techniques from black congregations.

Individuals at Manna tend to emphasize similarities between Korean Americans and African Americans. When there is evidence of conflict between the two groups, it is more often attributed to external forces that are beyond the control of either group. Jeremy, a college student in his early twenties who attends Manna, implicitly rejects the idea that Korean Americans are model minorities by saying that they, like African Americans, have not always had economic success. He told me:

> At my church now, I feel like I fit in the most with a guy [who is] an African American from Florida.... My view is that African Americans and Koreans would get along really well, but that Satan, the enemy, has tried to make it so that we would hate one another.... I think we would get along so well because we both go through similar issues. Like debt and poverty and... just the whole thing with family and I just think that both are very warm. Like we have warm sides to the parents and a very disciplinary side to the parents as well.[35]

His congregation provides Jeremy with a frame for the conflict that sometimes occurs between the two ethnic groups: the two groups are meant to be together. Conflicts are not due to the unwillingness of black Americans to follow the work ethic of Koreans; rather, the root of conflict is spiritual; it is simply the work of spiritually evil forces, the "work of Satan."

The civic identity at Manna as being part of "ethnic minority America" is reflected in how Korean Americans understand the political actions of African Americans to fight against discrimination. Eve, in her early twenties, works in business and attends Manna.[36] In contrast to those at Grace, she speaks favorably about the political achievements of African Americans, mentioning the cases of conflict between the two groups as isolated incidents that should not influence their overall relationship: "Despite their [African Americans'] history and discrimination and what they went through, they're still able to voice it and they stand up for their rights and even their mistreatments in the past." Both Bill and Eve have exposure to middle-class and poor black Americans. Compared with Bill, however, Eve treats the racism experienced by black Americans as genuine. Exposure to non-Korean racial and ethnic groups is not enough to dispel images of Korean Americans as model minorities; instead, religion as it is understood at Manna helps Korean members to renegotiate, to some extent, the boundaries with other racial groups. In so doing, Manna provides Korean Americans with a cultural schema to implicitly challenge the reproduction of the stereotype of Asian Americans as model minorities.

Race and Civic Identity

Korean Americans at Grace and other second-generation churches often talk about civic identity—their sense of who they are in America—as characterized by distinct categories: an individual is either black or white; she is an immigrant or not an immigrant. To become an American is to decide precisely where one fits within these categories. Some Korean Americans rhetorically deemphasize their ethnic ties as a way of being "just American," even stressing they are really racially more white than Korean. When I asked Bill, mentioned earlier, what role his ethnicity plays in his life, he explains that it makes no real difference:

> The only time I really think about it is with those forms, Asia-Pacific, white... but honestly I never thought about it. I kind of view myself as Caucasian or American. I know some Koreans that are really into their heritage, but for me, I don't even think of myself as a Korean American. I'm just an American. I don't really view race very much. I try really hard not to categorize people. The easiest thing to do is to describe somebody, you know, white girl with gray hair, or Asian girl. It's the easier way to describe somebody, but I try not to.

Bill recognizes that there are racial categories in the United States, but he is trying not to become part of these categories. In his mind, real Americans are those who choose to ignore race. His words, however, also reflect Bill's unconscious schema for understanding race. In trying to distance himself from racial categories, Bill makes himself part of a very real racial category—to be an American is really to be racially *white*.

Both because of their race and their immigrant heritage, others at Grace have ambivalence about where Asian Americans are situated along the black/white continuum. I asked Joshua, a Korean American in his early thirties, and one of the leaders at Grace, where he fits in American society:

> For Korean Americans I think it is very complex. Or for any immigrant church, I think it is complex. If you ask a Korean person who is very confident to define himself, he will never say or acknowledge that he is Korean. That person will always try to pitch himself as an American. In true analysis he will acknowledge, however, that no matter how much they see themselves as an American person, that person is not white or even black. He is yellow. So how does that person fit into the entire American context?[37]

Joshua thinks that, because Korean Americans are neither black nor white, others do not perceive them as true Americans.

Jacob, a Korean American in his late twenties and a leader at Grace, also tells me white and black Americans do not see Asian Americans as real Americans or real minorities:

> We are accepted because supposedly we're colored a little bit better, so we're a little bit better than blacks, but then I think blacks don't

look at us as minorities. [*How do they see you?*].... I don't think African Americans they consider us minorities, but then Asians don't want to think of themselves as *poor* minorities [his emphasis].[38]

Jacob clearly sees black Americans as "real" minorities. On the one hand, he laments that others do not classify Asians as minorities. On the other hand, there is also ambivalence in his words about whether Asians even want to be categorized this way. Jacob perceives a social and class association that is attached to being a minority, and particularly, in his mind, to being associated with black Americans. In this view, black Americans are perceived as "poor" minorities.

Korean Americans at second-generation churches most commonly think others view them as foreigners. Jennifer, a Korean American in her midtwenties, works as a social worker and attends Grace.[39] As we talked over lunch I asked Jennifer if she thinks other Americans see her as an American:

> Probably not. [*Why wouldn't they think you were an American?*] Because I am obviously Asian. I am obviously Asian. I don't even have the highlighted [blonde] hair. Mine is straight and dark brown. [*So, these would be white people who would not perceive you as an American?*] Yeah. They would not think of us as American. We are Korean. That is the first thing that comes to mind: "Oh what are you? Chinese? Japanese?" You don't get offended by that. But, you notice it. The texture of my skin, my flat face, by everything, I am Korean. But, when you get to know me, I am more than that.

Jennifer tries not to get offended by racial categorizations. As she walks through her physical description, her view almost falls in line with the kind of racialized view that Omi and Winant discuss in their work. She uses a very real physical description of herself to document that she doesn't really fit in in the United States. In Jennifer's opinion, others, and especially white Americans, do not think of her as a real American. And it was clear from our discussion that in some ways Jennifer is not sure whether she views herself as a "real" American either.

Joshua, Jacob, and Jennifer all talk about how other Americans view them. As Joshua explained, in some sense, to try and be fully American is to separate oneself from Korean immigrant culture. For Joshua, becoming American involves the rejection of being Korean in some way. An individual should try to "pitch himself as an American." Yet, as one moves further from being Korean, where does one fit in the American landscape? It is so much a part of Jennifer's framework that other Americans will think of her as a "foreigner" that she responded to my question "Why wouldn't they think you are an American?" with a sense of exasperation, as if the question itself betrayed how clueless I, the interviewer, was about the racial classification of citizenship in the United States. She responded, "Because I am obviously Asian." Being "yellow," as Joshua also says, is to be outside the American racial classification. Yet, although other Americans might view them as immigrants, Korean Americans at Grace find little solace in embracing the immigrant ethnic culture of their parents. They are left with the "either-or" categorizations. They feel they must decide to be the ways they perceive white Americans are, even coloring their hair blond or noting "Caucasian" on the U.S. census, or they will not be enough like other Americans racially to "count" as real American citizens.

Creating "Multiple" Identities

While those at Grace accept either-or categories for their identities as Americans, I found that many of the Korean Americans at Manna and other multiethnic churches constructed identities in more fluid and individual ways. Sociologist Fenggang Yang describes multiple immigrant identities as "adhesive," in that immigrants often grow more American in some parts of their lives while reinforcing ethnic lifestyles in others.[40] They attach some part of American culture to their existing ethnic identity. In contrast, civic identity for Korean Americans at Manna and other multiethnic churches is better described as what the psychiatrist Robert Jay Lifton calls "protean"—fluid and overlapping.[41] Having fluid identities does not mean that all identities are weighted equally for Korean Americans. Rather, those in the multiethnic churches use aspects of Christian identities to hierarchically order their other identities, interpreting and organizing race, ethnic, and class identities, while not replacing them.

Like those at Grace, Korean Americans at Manna also create identities through generating a boundary between themselves and first-generation Koreans. Sasha, a Korean American in her early twenties, attends Manna and works at a Korean school.[42] She originally left the Korean congregation she was attending because she thought the environment was too constraining. After beginning to attend Manna, Sasha told me her view of the connection between spirituality and success began to change:

> I was made to be a certain way, and in the Korean church I wasn't able to be who I was made to be. I was kind of shut out. And then when I found Manna I felt like "Wow," this is it. God created me to be a certain way, and I felt like I finally found help, the help I needed to discover all the great things that God wanted me to pursue.... I think that even though our parents go to church, and are very committed, they don't really practice it, putting God first.... A lot of second-generation Koreans see that in their parents....When it

comes down to it, in the house, when they talk to you about your career decisions or when they talk to you about what they think you should do, it's not about God first, it's about succeed, success first.

For Sasha, creating her own identity is a spiritual pursuit and an individual negotiation related to finding out who God made her to be. Sasha also told me that Manna gives her freedom to think about what "God wants her to do" with her career beyond what her parents want or what would be most impressive in the Korean church. Manna gives Sasha a way to talk about reorienting her view of success. She begins to see pursuing her own career decisions not merely as gaining distance from her parents or becoming more assimilated in mainstream American culture but also as developing an individual sense of self in a specifically Christian way, one that is connected to understanding what she sees as God's plans.

Korean Americans at Manna and other multiethnic churches also use spiritual categories to interpret and hold in tension their "in-between" civic identities as both Americans and Koreans. Manna gives Korean Americans spiritual categories for understanding how they can be Americans, even though they experience discrimination as a result of being Koreans living in America. A good example of this comes from a discussion with Collin, a Korean American in his late twenties, and a member of Manna. As Collin and I sat in his small apartment, eating the watermelon his wife brought us, he told me about his struggle to reconcile being Korean and American, and how his Christian faith helps him come to terms with the conflict endemic in holding the categories of "Korean" and "American" in tension. He told me:

> It's interesting, because I grew up in America my whole life, I was born here, but then I am also Korean. So I kind of have this dual understanding of myself. . . . I believe that when you become born again [or become a Christian], you are a citizen of the Kingdom of Heaven, so ultimately your allegiance is to that Kingdom. But we are not living there. We are living here. And I happen to be living in America. And I think that is one area where second-generation immigrants have an advantage, because they can understand that dual residence kind of thing. Because we understand that we are in America, but we are not fully American. We are different because we are Korean.[43]

Collin's understanding of what it means for him to be a Christian gives him an advantage in understanding the tension between being an American and having a Korean immigrant heritage. His Christian framework also provides him with categories for constructing a new approach to American civic life. Collin does not need to be fully accepted by others to think of himself as an American citizen. Being a Christian provides him with ways of understanding that multiple identities can coexist. He is living in "this world" as a Christian, yet knows his allegiance is to a different "kingdom." Collin finds a way to live and serve in the context of American society, even though he is also Korean and might not be fully accepted as an American.

For other Korean Americans, too, being a Christian helps them to develop a deeper appreciation for their ethnic identity in the face of discrimination. Jeremy, mentioned earlier, also told me that Christianity helps him to accept being Korean, even though he might be denied opportunities because of his race.

> I am always going to feel that it [being Korean] is going to be my exterior, it is the shell that I am in, the Korean framework.... I am Korean, rather than any other race or shape or whatever. God decided to make me Korean. And I don't know what I am going to be when I go up to heaven. And hey, it's pretty cool, this Korean thing. Korean people are in tune with you. I don't know what role it plays in my life, honestly, because I don't speak Korean.... Being Korean I feel like I won't be able to get to places as easy as it would be for someone else to get to that place.[44]

For Jeremy, his spiritual framework provides a way to interpret his ethnic identity. He acknowledges that being Korean means he "will not be able to get places" as easily as other Americans or that he might experience discrimination, yet he is able to accept and even embrace being Korean, because his faith gives him a way to talk about his ethnicity as something positive that God provides. His spiritualized sense of identity—"God decided to make me Korean"—provides him with the strength to continue to fully embrace his Korean identity in the midst of struggles he might face.

Conclusions

Through their church communities, Korean Americans have access to cultural schemas or interpretive frameworks that enable them to use spirituality to order race and socioeconomic positions that they then can use to construct civic identities. Korean Americans at both Grace and Manna churches create boundaries with first-generation Koreans. Yet their churches also give them different resources for understanding where Asian Americans fit in American society. Those at Grace and other second-generation churches seem more likely to develop distinct, more compartmentalized identities as "Americans" and as "Christians." Korean Americans at Manna seem more likely to develop multiple and overlapping categories for civic identities that hold in tension the categories of Korean, American, and Christian.

Their churches also give Korean Americans different resources for understanding societal images of Asian Americans as inherently successful or "model minorities." While members of Grace use interpretations of Christianity to put constraints on financial success, the teaching of the church still largely defines Korean Americans as inherently successful and thus different from other ethnic and minority Americans. They construct boundaries between themselves and those they think of as less hard-working and express difficulty in helping these "other" Americans.

Even though they have largely the same socioeconomic and professional status positions as respondents at Grace, Korean Americans at Manna and other multiethnic churches say that church teachings have changed their approach to interracial relationships. They come to view themselves more as ethnic minority Americans than as middle-class Americans. They interpret financial success in ways that stress their commonality with other groups, seeing wealth accumulation as a result of "God's provision." This perspective allows Korean Americans to challenge aspects of the stereotyping of Asians as model minorities, the idea of their inherent superiority to other racial and ethnic groups. Such interpretations have very real consequences for civic relationships, particularly those with black Americans.

I show here the importance of group memberships in providing new ways for Korean Americans to understand civic identities that structure civic life. The Korean Americans I quote in this chapter are all American citizens. In some ways, living in America means that aspects of their civic identities are structured for them. These Korean Americans are ethnic minorities, and they are financially and educationally successful.[45] Yet the material I have presented here shows that Korean Americans also possess individual agency. They are able to use the cultural resources of their churches to interpret the particular *meanings* that class and race locations have for civic identities. Even though they are part of the same ethnic group and largely of the same financial and socioeconomic class, my respondents socially construct civic identities in different ways.

Theoretically, this research reveals that civic identities are not merely personal, internal constructs but also are reflected in day-to-day practices. Since most congregations are monoracial, remaining part of an English-speaking Korean congregation or Asian American congregation would be a more natural step toward identity assimilation for Korean Americans. In contrast, Korean Americans in multiethnic and multiracial churches may actually gain resources for collective identities that have the potential of reclassifying group boundaries and the symbols surrounding such boundaries. If, for example, out of their identities as minority and Christian Americans, second-generation Koreans act as if discord between black and Korean Americans is not the result of inherent ethnic and class differences but simply "the work of Satan," such reorientations may change the actual relationships between these two groups into one of cooperation and support.

These findings have relevance beyond the lives of religiously involved second-generation Koreans. More broadly, they address how the civic identities of new Americans are reflected in the groups they belong to and how they create defining lines around their groups and others.[46] These findings also have implications for how multiethnic and multiracial group memberships might structure identities. Merely being a member of a diverse organization may not be enough to change individuals' perspectives toward racial and ethnic diversity in American society. Despite the frequency of demographic diversity in organizations, particularly as regards the presence of women and racial minorities, these groups still experience discriminatory practices.[47] Being a member of a multiethnic organization will change the attitudes and identities of individuals most when racial diversity is crucial to accomplishing the core purpose and mission of the organization.[48] Manna and other multiethnic churches studied here make being a multiethnic church central to their core mission of evangelism. They find ways to break barriers between Asian ethnic groups and develop relationships between those groups and non-Asians so that they might "share the gospel" more effectively. This has an impact on the way individual Korean Americans understand their identities relative to other groups.

Local organizational memberships, particularly religious memberships, play an important role in providing moral categories that both shape and are used by individuals in the construction of civic identities. These findings expand how we think about identities. Identities are often multiple and overlapping. Rather than different institutional contexts providing clear ideas for which identities are uniformly preferred by individuals, it may be more accurate to think of contexts as providing different schemas that individuals use in diverse yet patterned ways in constructing their identities. Although the data I gathered do not make assertions about direction of causality, they do show that exactly how identities are hierarchically structured may depend on the nature of the cultural resources provided by the organizations of which individuals are members.

This work joins with that of other researchers who show that race and ethnicity are not only imposed on individuals but also used by them in the construction of identities.[49] For some individuals, religious identities overlap with and even order racial, ethnic, and class identities in the social construction of civic identities. This is what Lifton calls the "protean self"—identity that is many-sided and fluid.[50] The schema for Christianity in multiethnic churches gives Korean Americans resources to reconcile the seemingly different identities of being both American and Korean. They do not see themselves as fully belonging to America or Korea. Yet they are able to construct cohesive identities while living in the midst of this interstitial space. Future research should examine not only how nonwhite immigrants adapt to existing civic identity categories but also how new Americans might challenge and even reconfigure such categories. All of these issues involve understanding what it means to be an American in one's own terms. Identities are not only mental maps or constructs but also lived out in practices. In the next chapter, I turn to a discussion of connecting the models of civic responsibility and the identities that Korean Americans in multiethnic and Korean American churches develop to actual acts of community service.

6

Civic Models and Community Service

Each of the following vignettes from my field notes provides a typical example of how Grace and Manna, and the Korean Americans in each church, view community service. In particular, the vignettes show how each church views the relationship of evangelism—telling others about one's faith with the hope of conversion—to service to the local community of Old Town.

Vignettes from Two Churches

Each of the vignettes describes an experience I had while participating in community service with the members of Grace and Manna. First, an experience with Grace, the second-generation Korean congregation:

> I count 15 teen-age residents housed in the youth shelter this afternoon as I enter the building with members from Grace.[1] We are here to spend time as volunteers with the mainly white, African American, and Latino youth. Karen, a Korean American woman from Grace, is leading the volunteer project for the day. She asks the youth center director, a tired-looking African American man, if we might take the kids outside to play a game of kickball. After the game is over, Karen goes to the middle of the recreation room and opens the snacks brought by the church volunteers.

Then she gathers everyone from Grace together and gives the church members a survey to pass out to those in the youth shelter. I take a quick glance at the piece of paper in my hand. It includes the questions "Do you believe in God? If you were to die today, what do you think would happen to your soul? Would you like to know how you could have love, joy, peace, contentment, and eternal life?" and "Do you have any prayer requests?" Karen nudges me toward Jasper, an African American teenager who is wearing an American flag bandanna on his head. I ask him if he believes in God. Jasper tells me he does and then adds: "I go to church with my grandma." Without any prompting from me, Jasper asks me if I can pray for his family. We pray together, and I decide not to ask him any more questions from the survey.

After this, Karen, Wayne (also a member of Grace), and I sit together on the old couch in the center of the room. Wayne asks Karen how things went. She replies: "He [the young boy she was talking to] is a Catholic, but I am not sure if he knows what it means to be a Christian." As if a little disappointed, Wayne replies, "My girl is already a Christian, too." Later, we spend about an hour and a half in the gym playing volleyball with the kids. Although they were listless when we first arrived, by the end of our time there, every teenager at the shelter is in the gym playing volleyball.

The next vignette describes an experience I had with members of Manna, the multiethnic congregation, during a service at their small satellite branch, Manna City Church. The goal of this new fellowship is to provide practical help and bring an evangelical message to the impoverished residents of Old Town:

Thirty or so people are gathered at Manna City Church this Sunday.[2] They are mainly of different Asian ethnic backgrounds, with a few African Americans and Caucasians.[3] Most are young adults I recognize, still in college or recent graduates working at jobs in one of the metropolitan areas near the church. A couple of people appear out of place. There is a middle-aged white woman wearing an old, somewhat dirty, long coat. She moves around in her seat quite a bit during the service, shifting nervously from one side to the other. There is also a middle-aged African American man who wears a leather jacket and a worn hat. He sits by himself at the end of a pew. A young Asian American woman, whom I recognize as a regular member of Manna, comes and sits next to the woman in the worn coat. She sits fairly close to the woman, clearly trying to demonstrate her friendliness to this stranger.

After the service is over, refreshments are served in a room behind the sanctuary. Before I walk back to the refreshment area, I notice Jim, a Korean American who led the time of singing for the service, standing at the back of the sanctuary talking quietly with the African American man who sat alone during the service. They stand close to one another, and Jim listens intently as the man explains the requirements of his parole. Jim both offers to help the man complete his parole-required community service and to give him a ride home from church.

Similarities and Differences in Volunteerism

These accounts uncover several similarities in how Grace and Manna as organizations see volunteering in Old Town. Both Grace and Manna are interested in providing tangible help to those in their community, such as through volunteering at a youth shelter, helping an individual meet a parole requirement, or offering transportation. Korean Americans in both congregations also view their respective religious centers as important places to find frameworks for community service. For Korean Americans in both churches, providing service to residents in the local community of Old Town involves relating to people who are largely different from themselves in terms of race, ethnicity, and social class.

One of the main goals of this chapter, however, is to examine the differences between the two groups of Korean Americans at Grace and Manna. I discuss how the models of civic responsibility presented in chapter 4 relate to specific ideas and practices of volunteerism for Korean Americans in these religious centers. I also examine the ways Korean Americans use the organizational schemas that contribute to the distinct models of civic responsibility in these two congregations as cultural resources for understanding specific acts of community service.

In addition to the survey I conducted at Grace and Manna, in this chapter I draw on data from the long interviews I did with Korean Americans in each church and participant-observation notes from the time I spent attending the two churches. Focusing on Korean Americans in the two churches where I spent the most time allows the clearest picture of how organizationally based models of civic responsibility relate to ideas and practices of local community service for Korean Americans. This combination of data also provides possibilities for assessing how two groups of Korean Americans, who come largely from the same structural location (in terms of class, education, race, and ethnicity) and who attend churches in the same community could come to different understandings of how to participate in that local community.

Korean Americans in these churches draw on other resources besides congregational models of civic responsibility to construct community service practices. Those at both Grace and Manna often say that they first had exposure to community service through their schools. Family attitudes toward community involvement are another important part of developing ideas about community service.[4] Some Korean Americans mention responding to a particular Korean immigrant church model of caring only for other Koreans as being significant in helping them to decide how to participate in a local community and serve those who are not Korean.[5] However, it is significant that Korean Americans in each church prioritize their respective congregations as the primary place where they negotiate ideas about community participation and decide specifically how to participate in Old Town. Korean Americans in each of these churches also participate in distinct ways that are patterned according to a church model of civic responsibility.

Grace has a *communal obligations* model of civic responsibility. This means that, in the context of volunteering, Korean Americans at Grace express both strong obligations to their congregation and strong communal obligations, as a church, to help the needy in their local community. Practically, the church serves the role of sponsoring volunteer activities. Because of congregational sanctions, the congregation is able to encourage members to have a high level of commitment to church-sponsored community volunteer activities. The congregation's approach to spirituality also structures volunteer activities. At Grace, being an evangelical congregation means that the most legitimate volunteer activities are those with specifically evangelistic purposes. As my conversations with Wayne and Karen demonstrate, Korean Americans at Grace are disappointed when evangelism is not a component of volunteering or if the person served is already a Christian. Communal obligations to the congregation have implications for the role of organizational identities in shaping volunteer activities. Because of obligations to the church, volunteers are more likely to go together as a group, rather than individually, to participate in community service.

Korean Americans at Manna also think that they have communal responsibilities to help the needy in Old Town. However, they have what I call a more *individually negotiated* approach to civic responsibility. Congregation members are encouraged by their leaders, through the specific types of activities the congregation sponsors, to personally discern their own individual gifts and their approach to spirituality. This means that church leaders do not heavily encourage members to participate in a specific set of programs, but rather try to help them to develop an ethic of volunteering. Church leaders help members to advance in what they call "learning to be like Jesus" in his compassion and concern for the needy. Being like Jesus takes many forms, including inviting others to church, helping those in the community one-on-one through small groups of volunteers that are sent from the church, or simply deciding that one's motivations are currently not "right" to be a volunteer.

Korean Americans at Manna find this approach appealing as a way to gain distance from what they view as the "Korean church model" of group-based, obligatory duties and service. The Korean Americans at Manna, compared to those at Grace, spend more time talking about their own motivations for volunteering and see volunteering as an individual enterprise. Because the vision of the church is also less uniform than that at Grace, Korean Americans at Manna have more room to develop a unique "moral self" for volunteering.[6] Practically, church leaders find it difficult to get members to commit to a high level of participation in church-sponsored community service activities. Surprisingly, however, this individually negotiated ethic of service has the consequence of fostering more participation in nonchurch community service activities for Korean Americans at Manna than at Grace.

From Forms of Capital to Moral Meanings

Korean Americans in ethnic-specific and multiethnic churches, in part, use the identities they develop in their congregations to legitimate certain kinds of civic practices over others. Asking what kinds of interpretive frameworks congregations provide their members with to help them develop religious, ethnic, and civic identities challenges the way theorists often view the role of congregations in civic life and, in particular, in new immigrant communities. Both researchers who study immigration and those who study civic participation often regard congregations primarily as purveyors of capital. For scholars of immigration, the social capital of congregations is the network of relationships that helps immigrants find jobs, gain additional education, or secure noneconomic rewards like social approval and status.[7] Congregations generate social capital by providing immigrants with personal relationships that may link them to business associations or, for the second generation, networks with the first generation that facilitate the retention of ethnic culture.[8]

Most literature on the relationship between religious participation and civic participation also sees religion through a "forms of capital" lens.[9] Examining the forms of capital a congregation provides to its members is helpful in explaining, for example, the positive or negative relationship between certain kinds of religious participation and rates of volunteerism. Religious communities often provide individuals with social networks and skills that aid societal participation, for example, by connecting them to civic activities that are not specifically religious.

A forms-of-capital approach, however, does not provide insight into how organizational differences might structure diverse forms of volunteerism for individuals even within the same religious tradition. It does not provide knowledge of the meanings individuals attach to community service. And in particular, it does not explain why individuals preference some types of volunteerism over others. Insight about these topics is best found through talking to people about how they view the relationship of religion to volunteerism and observing them as they work out this relationship in the context of a congregation and a local community.

While churches certainly provide their members with useful forms of capital, seeing churches only as purveyors of capital neglects what is most distinctively religious about congregations—their role in generating cultural schemas with attendant moral frameworks for deciding how to act in the world. As social scientists have long explained, religion is inherently set up around moral meanings, oppositions of good and bad, this world and the other world, right actions and wrong actions.[10] What sociologists of culture have come to describe as "moral meanings," the kinds of frameworks individuals use to determine good actions, are a central aspect of congregational schemas.[11]

This is especially so when examining the link between church membership and community service. Congregations vary markedly in how they influence larger moral understandings of social and political issues.[12] Work on discourse and organizational cultures shows the importance of paying attention to these cultural schemas as a way of gaining insight into actual practices, and into how moral understandings shape and legitimate certain practices over others.[13]

Differences in Volunteerism between Grace and Manna

The survey I conducted among the members of Grace and Manna provides an initial mapping of volunteer practices for the members of each church. During the fall of 2002, I passed out a survey on civic practices at Grace and Manna during a Sunday service, and left extra surveys with the leaders of each church for members who were not present. Through this combination of activities, the survey achieved a response rate of 83 percent. Seventy-three members of Grace and 118 members of Manna filled out the survey. The survey questions were taken mainly from the Social Capital Benchmark Survey (2000).[14] Because these results are only from Korean Americans who attend two churches, they should not be generalized to the entire population of second-generation Korean Americans in the United States. From the survey I learned that Korean American members at Grace participated, on average, in fewer volunteer activities than Manna as a congregation and, on average, in fewer such activities than the Korean American members at Manna. Table 6.1 summarizes the results from the question "How many times have you volunteered in the past 12 months?"

TABLE 6.1. Volunteer Activity in Past 12 Months

How many times in the past 12 months have you volunteered?	Mean	Total (N)
Grace	8.36	73
Manna (all)	11.04	118
Manna (Korean American members)	13.59	29
Benchmark Survey respondents	9.50	3003

That overall the members of Manna and, in particular, the Korean Americans at Manna participate in more community service activities than do those at Grace is also confirmed by my participant-observation in both churches, on the basis both of how much Korean Americans talked about volunteering in the longer interviews and how much they discussed volunteering more informally.

These findings about practices, however, tell us little about the meanings Korean Americans attach to community service or the ways they use their church's models of civic responsibility to negotiate the kinds of volunteer activities they participate in. To this topic I now turn. Table 6.2 describes the volunteer activities sponsored by each church and provides an overview of how each church's model of civic responsibility relates to community service.

Grace: A Communal Obligations Model of Volunteerism

As a congregation, Grace has a strong desire to look beyond the needs of its own members to those of the wider American community. Consequently, Grace's leadership views volunteering in Old Town as one of its central goals. I asked Pastor Joseph what role congregation members should have in interacting with those in the community.[15] He explained that he wants church members to "have a powerful testimony of charity and mercy," stressing that members of Grace should want to benefit society spiritually as well as materially. Pastor Joseph further explained that his goal for the congregation is for it to relate more to Old Town in the future, and gave examples of setting up a medical clinic or providing an after-school program for children in the community. Another church leader, Joshua, a Korean American in his early thirties, said: "I would like to see the church do or become more engaged in mercy ministry [community service]. Actually helping people around the community where our church is [located]."[16] The desire to serve is clearly present at Grace.

TABLE 6.2. Volunteer Activities Sponsored by Each Church

	Grace	Manna
Model of civic responsibility	Communal obligations	Individually negotiated
Approach to community volunteerism	Different from first generation in strong responsibility to volunteer in non-Korean community. Obligation to participate in community service activities sponsored by church	Different from first generation in de coupling service, in any form, from being motivated purely by obligations. Church leaders encourage members to consider participation; developing an ethic of service is more important than participating in any specific activities
Gender and community service	Women feel more obligation than men to do community service activities	Women have freedom to engage in a variety of activities challenging the Korean church role of women as care-takers
Community service sponsored by church	Group-based activities: youth shelter, nursing home volunteers	Individually based activities: sock drive, handing out coffee to homeless, training for single parents

The Immigrant Generation and Volunteering

The impetus Grace has to reach out to the local community is shaped by the congregation's perceived relationship to first-generation Korean churches. As a second-generation Korean congregation, Grace wants to make itself distinct from first-generation Korean churches. Pastor Joseph told me how second-generation Korean congregations should grow beyond first-generation churches, especially in how they approach hierarchy, gender relations, and class:

> There are certain sins that have been institutionalized. There are "corporate sins." Sin is equal to injustice. I am optimistic in the sense that I can make changes. Judging in the Korean first-generation church: Social class is important. The church needs to work on this. Confucian hierarchy is important. Men are above women. The older are superior to the younger.

Later in our conversation, he also explained he wants Grace to be different from the first generation through having a more outward focus. That Grace sees itself as having a specific mission to help non-Koreans in their local community means that it is making a significant departure from the mission of first-generation Korean Christians.[17]

Coupling Evangelism and Volunteering

That Grace is part of the broader institution of American evangelicalism also shapes its approach to volunteerism. In the public discourse of the congregation, evangelism is strongly connected with obligations to volunteer. Because evangelism is central to the mission of the church, coupling evangelism with volunteering means members have a nonnegotiable responsibility to participate in church-sponsored community service activities. Such a connection also structures the types of volunteer activities the church sponsors; activities where evangelism might occur are more legitimate than other activities. Congregation members are more likely to participate in church-sponsored activities because they are sure such activities will have a narrowly defined evangelistic focus. They do not have this kind of assurance when participating in service activities sponsored by nonreligious community organizations.

The leadership of the church strongly encourages members to participate in as many church-sponsored volunteer activities as possible. For example, before each service project church leaders send e-mails to the church-wide list; often these e-mail messages demonstrate the connection between evangelism and volunteerism and encourage participation. In one such e-mail, a coordinator for the youth shelter outreach—a Korean American woman—wrote:

> I know that we get so accustomed to the idea we will all be going to heaven that we forget to spread the [news]...so come on brothers and sisters, let's spread the news to those who don't know.... I know that youth shelter only meets once a month....

This e-mail demonstrates that, in part, church members are expected to participate in the youth shelter outreach both because of a desire to show mercy to others and because of the potential such outreaches provide to do evangelism.

Another e-mail was sent by a Korean American woman who is the coordinator of a different church-sponsored volunteer effort at Grace, this one at a nursing home:

> I just want to encourage you all to take the time this week to lift up a prayer for the upcoming [visit] to the nursing home this coming Sunday.... We don't know yet what condition they are in, be it their physical condition, or even their spiritual condition, but we can still pray, not only that they will be blessed, but be open to receive the gospel message via our deeds and actions.[18]

Community service is linked to reaching a more diverse population to evangelize. Participating in church-sponsored volunteer activities is almost nonnegotiable because of its link with evangelism.

Communal Obligations to Participate in Church-Sponsored Community Service

At Grace, the church leadership stresses that members have collective obligations to be involved in community service efforts sponsored by the congregation. The church sermons encourage members to be specifically dedicated to church-based activities, rather than individual volunteer pursuits, further reinforcing the collective nature of the congregation. The leaders occasionally motivate members through public commendations of those who are heavily involved in volunteer activities or by comparing the leadership or members of the church to one another during sermons. In one sermon, Pastor Joseph remarked: "In the last six months, I have seen some stellar examples of people who are serving God.... Joshua encourages us, as a businessman by going out to the youth shelter."[19] Through singling out by name those in the congregation who are serving the church by doing community service, Pastor Joseph structures for congregation members an attitude and value of serving others and a specific way they might do so, as well as creating strong pressure to be involved in the organizational activities of the church.

As an organization, Grace has high boundaries, a strong distinction between those outside the church and inside the church. Interviews with church members demonstrate that they spend most of their time outside of work involved in church activities.[20] This means that the central friendship circles for congregation members are with other members. Such organizational boundaries give Korean Americans at Grace the ability to reinforce norms of church participation with one another. For example, numerous e-mails are sent over the congregation-wide list serve before the day of a church-sponsored volunteer outreach. The content of such e-mail communications and their frequency display the spirit of obligation to church activities.

In one instance, a Korean American woman who coordinates outreach to the youth shelter sent out an e-mail the week before the activity. She began her e-mail by quoting a song: "Whom shall I send? Who will go for me? To the ends of the earth? Who will rise up for the King? Here I am, send me. Whether foreign land or neighbors, everyone's the same, searching for the answers that lie within your [referring to God] name."[21] The coordinator goes on to use the words of this song as a way to link social outreach with evangelism and further motivate congregational participation.

> I know the youth shelter only meets once a month and we're only there for three hours tops, but you know what, I am sure God is using us. You know how a split second can totally change someone's life? For example, [what about] a car accident? Imagine what three

hours can do with God's mighty hands. Man we can do so much.... Thanks for reading this real long e-mail. "Here I am send me."

This e-mail underscores the high level of social pressure that is put on members to participate in church-sponsored community service, as well as the evangelistic focus of such activities.

Volunteerism as Obligatory and Group-Based

Grace's members talk about volunteering in ways similar to their leaders'. This was communicated to me in my discussions with Jeremiah and Candace, both members of the church. Jeremiah, a Korean American in his late twenties, was finishing a degree in medicine when I interviewed him.[22] We talked about the reasons he believes being a Christian is connected to helping the poor and the needy: "I think it is important the church demonstrates mercy to the world, partly in obedience to Christ, because he calls us to reach out to the poor. But also to really demonstrate Christ's love to the world. We should definitely be doing that." Candace, a Korean American in her late twenties, told me that her church provides her with the motivation to focus less on her own needs and desires and to become more concerned with obligations toward others.[23] To provide an example of this commitment to service, Candace explained that even after working 12 hours a day as a legal consultant, she often stops by a local hospital to volunteer at the children's ward. Although she is an exception to the general church-based volunteering of other members at Grace, Candace invoked a model of collective obligations similar to the other members when I asked why she helps children at the hospital instead of, for example, "going home and watching TV, like many people would after working such long days." She explains:

> I feel like I don't like to waste my time. I feel like there [are] twenty-four hours and how much sleep do I really need? There is so much of a bigger world out there then my own little circle and me ... there are times when I feel like I am just bogged down with a lot of things to do at church. But then I realize I am just being selfish, like I am totally thinking about myself and I am just giving myself a "pity party." When I think about how the other people [in church] help me, and how we serve each other, then I can't say that I am the only one serving.

Whereas Jeremiah uses the words "responsibility" and "obedience" to describe the connection of being a Christian to reaching out to the poor and the needy, Candace talks about volunteering as being part of what I would call her own unselfing and compares herself to other members of the church, using their apparent commitment as a reason that she also should be committed to selfless service.

Gendered Volunteerism

Both the institutions of American evangelicalism and American volunteerism reflect views about the differences between men and women, particularly the perspective that women are more inherently caring and nurturing, and belong in caring and service rather than leadership roles.[24] Some scholars, trying to broaden Christian Smith's ideas about the evangelical "subcultural identity concept" to the realm of gender, argue that evangelical Christians try to be distinctive by forming a subcultural identity that is different from others in the broader U.S. population in its specific approach to gender—an approach that appears to essentialize differences between men and women into particular roles. For example, sociologist Sally Gallagher, in her work *Evangelical Identity and Gendered Family Life*, argues that individuals in evangelical families use aspects of a subcultural identity when championing rhetoric of different roles and consequent responsibilities for men and women. For example, borrowing from Smith's work, Gallagher argues that evangelicals often see themselves as embattled with the mainstream culture when it comes to issues related to gender roles and child rearing, and effectively create an "out-group."

Sociologists of culture, however, stress that ideologies are often different from practices. And this is true in the case of gender within much of American evangelicalism. When Gallagher examines the men and women who sit in the pews, rather than paying attention only to the voices of church leaders, she finds that there is considerable disjuncture between the official discourse of evangelical views on family life and what individual evangelical families are actually doing. Gallagher finds that to practically work out division of household labor and care for children, evangelical families also draw on broader American cultural approaches to the family. These approaches gleaned from American culture include egalitarian approaches to child rearing, household tasks, and contributions to family income. According to Gallagher,

> while written materials, pastors, and theologians may consistently teach either developing complementarities and hierarchy or mutuality and egalitarianism, most ordinary evangelicals find themselves much more ambivalent; women's physiology seems so obviously to point to a deeper reality of women's maturity, yet most women spend the majority of their adult life in the labor force rather than at home.[25]

Looking at the cases of second-generation Korean American religious participation and gender that I examine here reveals that Korean Americans at Grace want to be distinctive in their approach to gender from the first generation, and give women more opportunities to lead in churches. While those at Grace, unlike those at Manna, believe that only men should serve in the roles of pastor or elder, Pastor Joseph continually renews a commitment to breaking down the hierarchies "between men and women."

Practices at Grace are sometimes different from ideologies, just as with the evangelicals Gallagher studied. Women at Grace do more of the organizational, administrative activities involved with coordinating volunteering, and they participate more in these efforts as volunteers. As the aforementioned e-mails reflect, the youth shelter and the nursing home outreaches are generally organized and initiated by women. And most of those who attend the outreaches are also women. While Korean Americans at Grace talk about volunteerism in ways that reflect the congregation's outward approach to gender, the church leadership and individual Korean Americans at Grace often look at volunteerism in particularly gendered ways.

Even though many of the women at Grace are professionals, in demanding occupations such as medicine or business, they often express misgivings that they were not involved in *more* care work. I heard these sentiments less often among the men in the church. For example, Pastor Joseph's wife, Miriam, also works full-time as a physician. Miriam told me after church one Sunday that she had been up all night "on call." Yet, later in our conversation, Miriam explained that she feels a lot of guilt about not participating in the youth shelter outreach, particularly because she is the "pastor's wife." In other conversations, she said she wants to spend more time attending Bible studies and doing church-based volunteer activities, in order to be an example "to the younger women in the congregation." In evangelical circles, physician is an uncommon occupation for the wife of a pastor. In spite of her busy schedule, however, Miriam is very involved in the activities of the church. I saw her there most Sundays, and she often stays after the Sunday services, sometimes for a couple of hours, to connect with the other church members during the weekly after-church luncheon. Still, a particular gendered view of evangelicalism that provides a view of what responsibilities a "pastor's wife" should have leaves Miriam believing she should be doing more in service to the church and the community.

Consequences of the Model at Grace

Korean Americans at both Grace and Manna said that their church is the primary place for them to locate volunteer activities. Sixty-five percent of Korean Americans at Grace said they would find volunteer opportunities through their church. Only 11 percent said they would locate volunteer activities through their own personal investigation. In addition, only 16 percent are involved in an organization outside their church that provides health or social service to the needy.[26] Table 6.3 summarizes these results.

The longer interviews, however, reveal more specifically how members of Grace view the relationship of their church to community service. Members

TABLE 6.3. Where Respondent Locates Volunteer Activities: Grace

	Frequency	Percent
A community volunteer organization	8	10.1
Through my college or university	8	10.1
Through my church	51	64.6
Some other place (please specify)	3	3.8
My own personal investigation	9	11.4
Total	79	100.00

told me being a member of Grace almost determines specific acts of volunteerism. Dan, a Korean American in his midtwenties, attends Grace and is a student in medical school.[27] He told me that Grace is crucial in helping him locate community service activities: "Through Grace, I went to help in the youth shelter... Like that is something that I definitely would not have done by myself, because it would have been awkward for me to just show up. Just by myself. But, wherever Grace went, I went." For Dan, his church plays a strong role in providing him with opportunities to volunteer and in structuring the community service activities in which he takes part: "Wherever Grace went, I went."

There are certain benefits and challenges to volunteering primarily through the church. Because Grace is a second-generation Korean church, having a common ethnic background makes it easier to motivate members to work together. When I asked Pastor Joseph how the ethnicity of the congregation influences volunteer efforts, he told me: "These are people who have a common background. They can have passion that will galvanize people to do things. It is easier to get people to move towards a desired goal." As I mentioned earlier, being an entirely second-generation Korean congregation also makes it easier for members to sanction one another to participate in congregation-wide activities.

However, the fact that Grace is a second-generation Korean congregation also structures volunteerism in ways leaders and members think are limiting. Groups that an organization links with see individual volunteers as acting on behalf of their organization, and therefore as embodying that organization's characteristics. For this reason, organizational-level volunteering might have stratifying effects.[28] When bringing those they help to church, or in relating to other community organizations that are not ethnic-specific, being an ethnic-specific congregation makes the chasm between non-Koreans and others more difficult to cross. Members in some ways feel forced to go outside the congregation to volunteer rather than bringing people to the church and helping them there. Joshua explains, "[That the congregation is Korean] is limiting, most notably to draw in people other than Koreans."

My time volunteering with members of Grace also brought some insight into how non-Korean organizations view the church. Joshua says the ethnic-specific makeup of Grace was a hindrance when they first approached the youth shelter. He told me the directors of the shelter probably "considered it twice" before allowing the church to come, because everyone at Grace is Korean. When I asked Joshua how he thinks things might have been negotiated if the church were white, he replies, "I could imagine that it would not be an issue." In an informal discussion with one of the leaders of the youth shelter, an African American man in his midfifties, I was also told that the shelter initially had some reservations about whether an all-Asian church would be able to connect with the youth in the center. These examples demonstrate that nonethnic volunteer organizations might see ethnic churches *only* as "other," not realizing the potential such congregations have to provide services in their local neighborhood.

Manna: Individually Negotiated Community Volunteerism

Like those at Grace, the leaders at Manna also think it is important to provide services to Old Town. The congregation makes it a goal to provide specific volunteer programs and actually sponsors more of them than Grace does. During the time I attended, Manna initiated an after-school tutoring program for the community, participated in the March of Dimes, started a drive to provide socks for men in a homeless shelter, and had a program to help parents in Old Town develop better parenting skills. They also talked about expanding their ministry to start a nonprofit, "nonreligious" ministry arm to make applying for government grants to do community service easier.

Spending time at Manna quickly reveals that the role of the church in the lives of its members differs from that at Grace. While Grace emphasizes communal obligations to participate in church-sponsored volunteer activities, Manna's leaders make a point of *not* exercising communal control over members. Instead, the leaders of the church see their primary role as helping members develop individual motivations or an "ethic of service" to the needy in Old Town.

As at Grace, part of the approach to volunteering at Manna comes from its organizational identity as an evangelical congregation. Different from Grace, however, the approach to spirituality at Manna is that members should focus on their own spiritual development rather than be overly concerned with following "legalistic" rules connected with Christianity, for example, governing whether one smokes, drinks, or watches certain movies.

Sociologist Robert Wuthnow explains that religious conservatives often have an individualistic approach to religion, speaking about faith in "a very personal way." He argues that such religious individualism may decrease the positive influence religion has on motivating people to provide for others.[29] As Wuthnow's thesis might suggest, Manna exemplifies a more individualistic approach to Christianity than Grace, and holds this approach as one of its core values. Before members are equipped to reach out to others, the church leaders believe, they should become "personally healthy." According to a church brochure, one of Manna's central goals is to "minister healing and freedom to the spirit, soul, and body of a person so that he or she could become a strong disciple of Jesus Christ." This approach to Christianity means the church views volunteering in more personal and less uniform ways than does Grace. During my discussion with one of the staff members of Manna, Winston, a Korean American in his midtwenties, he explained his desire to see members of the church grow in their "heart for the poor," or their concern for the welfare of those who have fewer economic resources than they do.[30]

Manna's framework for connecting Christianity to appreciation for ethnic diversity shapes the church's approach to local community service. Sue, a Korean American in her midtwenties and a small group leader, sees her experiences at Manna and at an inner-city government-sponsored social service as two important life experiences, both of which give her a desire to help the "poor ethnic community."[31] Although she believes Manna is limited in its ability to do community service because the church is not yet *truly* multiethnic, Sue told me that the goal of "having a multicultural church is such an asset." She explains that as the church becomes more multiethnic in the future, it will be easier for it to serve the community, because it will help individuals in the community take Christianity more seriously. Being multiethnic, in Sue's mind, will also help the church reach out to a broader diversity of individuals. It is noteworthy that having an interpretive framework that stresses a multiethnic Christianity is connected in Sue's mind to doing more effective social services in the local community.

Korean Americans at Manna

Like those at Grace, individual Korean Americans at Manna say that they are most likely to locate volunteer activities through their church. Table 6.4 shows the responses to the church survey question I asked of the membership as a whole: "Where would you be most likely to locate volunteer activities?" Table 6.5 shows the responses to this question of only the Korean American members of Manna. Sixty-nine percent of Korean American members at Manna and 59 percent of the entire congregation said that they would be most likely to find volunteer opportunities through their church. The survey indicates that

TABLE 6.4. Where Respondent Locates Volunteer Activities (All Manna)

	Frequency	Percent
Through a community volunteer organization	8	6.1
Through my college or university	14	10.6
Through my church	78	59.1
Some other place (please specify)	9	6.8
My own personal investigation	23	17.4
Total	132	100.00

Korean Americans in both churches think their congregations are important sites for locating volunteer activities.

Individually Negotiating Motivations

Although members of Manna said they would be most likely to locate volunteer activities through their church, I realized from attending the church that Korean Americans there actually participate much more in individual than church-based volunteer activities. Korean Americans at Manna most often view their congregation as helping them to develop their "thinking" about volunteering, rather than motivating them to participate in the specific volunteer practices connected with the church. In particular, they say that Manna helps them develop the right motivation for volunteering. Jeremy, a Korean American in his midtwenties who is finishing his undergraduate degree, told

TABLE 6.5. Where Respondent Locates Volunteer Activities (Korean American Members of Manna)

	Frequency	Percent
Through a community volunteer organization	2	6.9
Through my college or university	4	13.8
Through my church	20	69.0
Some other place (please specify)	0	0
My own personal investigation	29	10.3
Total	132	100.00

me that attending Manna encourages him to think about community service "in my own backyard."[32] According to Jeremy,

> right now it is starting to happen. Before, the church didn't even have that in our vision, reaching out to the community.... All of the sudden, we found ourselves being led right to our backyard. And now that is what is happening, we are praying and focusing on reaching out to our community.... It wasn't so much "We should do this because that is what Christians do." That would be horrible. It was something that we were going to do because we saw the Lord calling us and leading us so much, so convicted out of love.

To Jeremy it is more important to examine one's motivations, which he describes as being "convicted out of love," rather than to encourage participation in specific types of community service. Jeremy's ideas about embodying good or bad motivations for reaching out to the poor in a community are clear: giving the poor help is something for which a church or an individual should have a "particular vision" rather than something that is a universal obligation for all Christians. He describes the perspective of reaching out "because that is what Christians do," or simply having an obligation, as a "horrible" sort of motivation.

The most common discourse for community service is one in which Korean Americans at Manna connect caring for the poor and needy to "being like Jesus." Being like Jesus could take multiple forms; what it actually means, particularly what kind of specific volunteer activities it generates, is negotiated individual by individual. Such negotiations make it difficult to decide whom one has a responsibility to help and what form such help should take. "Being like Jesus" could mean helping those who lack financial resources, but it could also mean helping those who are "poor in heart," that is, those whom Korean Americans at Manna generally view as spiritually or emotionally troubled rather than those who have economic or material needs.

Like others I talked with at Manna, Carl, a Korean American in his early twenties and a college student at a nearby university, told me volunteering and helping the poor are simply an extension of "being like Jesus." The following is an excerpt from our discussion:

> *[And what kind of things does being a Christian imply in the rest of your life? For example, does it mean helping the needy and the poor?]* Personally, for me, it means becoming like Jesus. *[And what would that mean? How would you know that you were more like Jesus?]* To be more compassionate. *[To certain groups of people?]* To everyone. But, to certain groups in particular, to the poor and the homeless. *[Why them?]* Because that is what Jesus did.[33]

While Manna helps Carl think it is important to reach out to the poor and needy, the congregation does not provide him with a specific structure for the types of volunteer activities he should engage in.

Later, when I asked Jeremy if he thinks being a Christian and helping the poor and needy are necessarily related, he told me:

> I think if someone is truly following Christ, then they will be led to the lost and they will be led to the poor naturally. They will be led to wherever the Lord leads them to: spiritually poor, physically poor, and financially poor. It's just a natural thing. Just from following Christ and not our own comfort and ambitions and selves.... Not only so much from pressure, like if you are a Christian then you will have to do these things. I don't really think that. If you are just following the Lord and are led by faith then you will be led there.

Jeremy's description of the process by which he should help the poor and needy emphasizes "leading." Who the poor and needy are, however, is relative. The poor and needy might merely be those who are "spiritually poor" in addition to those who lack financial resources, depending on the context.

Conversations with individuals reveal that an individually negotiated approach to volunteering makes it difficult for congregation members to collectively decide whom they have a responsibility to help.[34] At times, helping the poor and the needy involves a negotiation process of deciding *who* the poor actually are. Emma, a Korean American in her early twenties, is finishing an advanced degree in nursing.[35] During my interview with her, she also connects helping the poor to being motivated by attention to Jesus' example:

> I just think all people in general find it easy to neglect them. And that all people should not forget the poor. And that doesn't mean everyone has to go to the inner city, because I think God calls people in different areas. But in your heart [do] not forget them. Just take a moment to smile at them.

Emma has a strong motivation to help the poor. But her comments also illustrate a relative approach to what this might mean for each individual person. This ethic entails no particular responsibility other than to examine one's own motivations. Caring for the poor could mean something as simple as "smiling" at a homeless person on the street.

Immigrant Generation, Gender, and Volunteerism at Manna

That most Korean Americans come to Manna to reject what they view as the obligations and "legalistic" spirituality of first-generation Korean churches means that they find in Manna a place where they have freedom to resist obligations to do service work. In particular, this is relevant to the Korean American women I talked with, who mention differences in the meaning of volunteer work between Korean churches and Manna.

Korean Americans see Manna as providing them with a new sort of spirituality, one that is more their own, and based on their individual understandings. This perspective on Christianity structures how Korean Americans at Manna understand community service. When they talk about volunteerism, Korean Americans hold their experiences with Manna in contrast to the Korean churches of which most have been a part. Korean Americans at Manna told me that, in Korean churches, being a Christian is more a matter of obligation, and that the routines and rules of the congregation determine activities. Leaving the Korean Church entails reacting against ways of doing community service as practiced there. According to Helen, a Korean American in her midtwenties who works as an administrative assistant for a trading firm, Manna stresses individual approaches to serving that are very different from those of the Korean congregation she previously attended:

> At the Korean churches, everyone is cookie-cutter. Everyone talks the same way. At Manna, I just feel everyone is different, and you can be that way and you can contribute to the church in your own way. There is just so much freedom. If someone has a heart to serve the poor, like my friend Korine, she does, and then it turned in to another core value the church wanted to incorporate. And they encourage that. And it is a combination of the structure being flexible and just being who you are.[36]

Gender is also an important lens through which Korean Americans at Manna view civic life. They hold their experiences of gender in Korean churches in contrast with those at Manna. Women at Manna feel freedom to negotiate gender roles in different ways; in particular, they do not feel locked in to doing service work. Eleanor, a Korean American in her midtwenties, works as a librarian. She describes herself as "really outspoken, independent, and strong for an Asian girl."[37] Eleanor told me she appreciates that Manna is breaking down gender roles and allowing her to do more leading in the church, particularly in the role of small group leader.

In contrast to the pastor's wife at Grace, Pastor Simeon's wife, Hope, a Korean American in her early thirties, said she has freedom at Manna to reject the image of the "Korean pastor's wife."[38] When I asked Hope what "rejecting this image would mean," she responded: "They [Korean pastor's wives] are quiet [and] submissive, always backing up the pastor. A pastor's wife doesn't speak out; they don't have a voice." Even though both she and her husband are Korean Americans, she ended her answer by saying, "But that's a *Korean* pastor's wife [her emphasis]," as if to make a distinction between being a Christian who is ethnically Korean and adopting a "Korean Christianity."

Later in our discussion, Hope further explained that at Manna she is not pressured to do many of the service roles that are expected of women, and particularly of pastors' wives at many Korean churches. The ability of Korean American women at Manna to engage in more individual ideas about gifts and callings is part of the contrast between Grace and Manna regarding commitment to church-based volunteer activities. Having the ability to negotiate individual church activities means it is more likely that Korean American women have the opportunity to personally discern whether they are more equipped for leadership than service roles.

Consequences of Individual Negotiations

The struggle to decide who the poor are, or whether Korean Americans have the "right" motivations for volunteering, keeps some at Manna from actually volunteering at all. According to Sue, the Korean American in her midtwenties who works in merchandising,

> I want to be involved in a community but I don't really have a community here. And I don't want to do it haphazardly; I want to be involved with a church. I don't want to go to the community doing just one thing, like going to a soup kitchen.[39]

Sue clearly has a desire to eventually be involved in community service. However, the ethic of service at Manna makes it acceptable for Sue to examine her motivations for service to be sure she doesn't serve "haphazardly," instead of committing to a specific church-sponsored community service.

Peter, a Korean American in his early twenties who is finishing an undergraduate degree, also makes relative what it means to be poor and needy.[40] He told me he "doesn't like to categorize people as 'poor and needy' or whatever. They are just people, and all people have to be loved." Just as Sue currently does not volunteer because at this time she is not part of the "right community," Peter, too, is waiting until the "right time" to volunteer. If he were to volunteer, he would not tell anyone at his church, but would probably do it on his own in order to preserve good motivations.

Korean American members at Manna told me they resist any reasons for reaching out to the poor that are based in a sense of obligation or imposition. In comparison to the approach at Grace, an individually negotiated approach to volunteering makes it difficult for members to challenge one another to become more involved in their community *and* for the congregational leaders to motivate participation in church-based community-service activities. For example, during the announcement time at a service at Manna City Church, a young Asian American man came to the front and gave an announcement about a church-sponsored community service activity to provide tutoring every evening for an hour after school to three children from the community.[41]

When I talked to one of the coordinators after the service, she explained that the congregation is having a difficult time getting people to commit to the activity on a regular basis, leaving mainly the church leaders to provide the tutoring.

Although community service is more personally negotiated at Manna than at Grace, it is also important to remember that, *surprisingly*, Korean Americans at Manna also participate in more volunteer activities than do those at Grace. Although Manna leaves to individual members how they should participate in the community, instilling an ethic of volunteerism in the members at Manna means that the church encourages everyone to be involved in local community service in some way. Although people's specific practices might be quite diverse, the church provides a legitimating framework for everyone to be involved. Korean Americans at Manna are more involved in volunteerism overall, although they feel less obligated than those at Grace to be involved specifically in church-based volunteer activities.

Conclusions

The children of recent nonwhite immigrants often have high socioeconomic and educational status, structural locations that foster community participation among the population at large. This demographic reality makes it vital to understand the differences in motivations and practices of volunteerism between diverse groups of second-generation immigrants and between subgroups of individuals even within the same ethnic group. The findings in this chapter demonstrate the importance of different models of civic responsibility in structuring ideas and practices of volunteerism for Korean Americans.

Beyond provision of human and social capital, congregations provide moral narratives based on Christianity that legitimate volunteering and particular forms of volunteering over others. The approaches to volunteering in a congregation are important in structuring how individual Korean Americans see their role as volunteers. The *communal obligation* framework of civic responsibility at Grace makes church-sponsored volunteer activities seem obligatory for congregation members. They participate in activities as a group. Volunteer efforts involve the congregation going outside its walls and linking with existing community services, and providing group support for these services through volunteer hours. The ethnic-specific character of the church makes it easier to facilitate members working together and motivating one another toward volunteerism, but it sometimes limits access when relating to non-Korean community organizations.

In contrast, the model of civic life at Manna encourages members' *individual negotiation* of civic activities. The Korean Americans there draw on a Korean ethnic history and, particularly, a history with ethnic Korean churches as a place from which to understand the relationship between religious faith and volunteerism. They try to distance themselves from a particular ethnic value system or brand of spirituality that places unexamined obligations above a personal, reflective, or more "genuine" spirituality. The approach to spirituality reinforces this outlook, and emphasizes hearing individually from God and discerning a "special mission" rather than motivating everyone to have the same volunteer goals. This could mean adopting an evangelistic purpose for volunteering, or it could mean providing only for the physical needs of others.

Examining the differences in motivations to do community service between Korean Americans in these two churches expands research on the interaction between religious participation and ethnic adaptation in a civic context. When attention is given to the relationship between congregational ideologies and volunteering among individual members, considerable complexity arises even among evangelicals within the same ethnic group. As the vignettes at the beginning of this chapter demonstrate, Korean Americans in both congregations are motivated to help those who are less fortunate. Both groups see their congregation as a base for volunteer activities. Yet Korean Americans at Grace and Manna have different views of how this should take place.

Based on evangelical motivations, members of Grace value providing help for non-Korean Americans in their community. Of the congregations social work scholar Ram Cnaan studies in his research on congregation-sponsored community services, those made up of immigrants are the ones he finds *least* likely to provide social services.[42] Yet, even though it is an entirely second-generation Korean church, Grace views linking with other community organizations as part of its role. The desire to provide help to those outside the Korean community may indicate a more general shift from the insular focus of first-generation churches to the outward focus of second-generation Korean congregations.

The narratives of Korean American members at Manna reflect the congregation's focus on an individually negotiated approach to spirituality and volunteerism. Consequently, although the congregation of Manna stresses community service, its leaders are less able to galvanize the entire congregation, or Korean American members in the congregation, toward specific volunteer activities in the same way the leaders at Grace do. Because personal discernment is valued, it is difficult to keep members accountable to doing specific activities. The perspective on evangelicalism of these Korean Americans is somewhat reminiscent of Sheilaism, the individualized faith of Sheila Larson, who said—according to sociologist Robert Bellah and his coauthors—"My faith has carried me a long way. It's Sheilaism. Just my own little voice."[43]

In another sense, however, it is important to note that, unlike Sheilaism, the form of religious individualism at Manna sustains broader communal commitments to actually remaining involved in local community service. The individual and informal volunteering of the type done among Korean Americans at Manna, such as providing a ride to and from church or helping out a neighbor, is important.[44] Korean Americans use Manna's congregational appreciation for diversity and a relational, personal approach to spirituality, to legitimize very real acts of service in their own lives.[45] Practically, this means that volunteer efforts are not limited only to participation in programs sponsored by the church. "Being like Jesus" implies thinking about caring for the poor and needy in all areas of life. These sorts of obligations do not stop within the walls of the church. Rather, a clear understanding of one's personal mission is something that travels with members to all situations, and is not limited to those situations where a set moral code has already been discussed in congregational teachings. As such, this type of volunteering has the potential to be more pervasive and long-lasting among individual Korean Americans.

That a more individually negotiated approach to spirituality has the potential to sustain *more* acts of community service than a communally based approach may also change how we view religious individualism. It is possible that, in a more individualist society, a spirituality that one owns and carries to all areas of life may have increased potential to sustain civic involvement. This finding also changes how we view a religious institution such as American evangelicalism. Evangelicalism thus emerges as an institutional field within American religion that uses both a religiously based communal rhetoric and an individual rhetoric to foster commitment. Which type of discourse is dominantly connected to community service may depend on local congregational contexts. In the next chapter, I continue to look at the relationship of ethnicity and spirituality to civic life, this time through the consideration of political narratives and practices.

7

Evangelicalism and Politics for Korean Americans

Michelle is in her early twenties and an active member of Grace. A recent Ivy League graduate, she was searching for a full-time teaching position when we met.[1] As we sat for three hours sipping coffee in a bookstore near Old Town, I asked her about her role in American politics. She answered my question with tension in her voice, drawing inferences about her political position in American society as both an ethnic minority and as a Christian:

> I feel like more Asians should be involved in politics and more Christians as well... in general I would like to see more minorities just step up in politics.... And I think that's why there needs to be Christians and integrity in the government... in general my mom is not really involved in politics.... I mean she keeps up with the news. I think she, like a lot of other people, just feels it is a hopeless cause.... Just being aware of your values and giving you a set of values and refining what you believe in... I kind of never associate it with the church. We have an America where church is church and state is state.

Several themes in Michelle's conversation overlap with those I heard in my conversations with the other Korean Americans I interviewed. They do not see their local congregations as political entities, reflecting the view that "church is church and state is state." Their congregations do not impart models of political life in the same way that they impart models of community service.

Korean Americans do not have unpatterned individual opinions about the relationship between evangelical Christianity and American politics, either. Rather, immigrant histories, their place as ethnic minorities in American society, and frames of American evangelicalism result in several dominant narratives of American political life. Among the respondents, some Korean Americans used rhetoric that mirrors that of politically active conservative Christians. Others, like Michelle, think that as Christians they ought to be involved in politics. Yet, lacking models of political involvement from their parents, Korean Americans do not have a sense of how they might be active in meaningful ways. For those studying the influence new citizens may have on American civic life, this group of Korean Americans is particularly interesting, in that they want a renewed model of American political participation that accounts for immigrant and minority histories of discrimination and their values as evangelical Christians.

The word "politics" may bring to mind obvious behaviors such as voting and lobbying legislators. Yet the children of immigrants do not have a family history of political participation in the United States. For this reason, studying what their narratives reveal about underlying political motivations and potential may tell us more about the future impact these children of new immigrants will have on the American landscape than will surveys of their existing political participation. In examining politics, here I am interested primarily in understanding how Korean Americans relate to power structures in the United States—both in their local communities and nationally—and how they develop rhetoric for change. Political action could take the form of influence on national government or legislative life, but it could also express itself simply in efforts to rectify inequalities in a local community.

The discourse Korean Americans have about politics and political participation illuminates the values and ideas that are central to their thinking or their political consciousness. William Gamson describes three aspects of political consciousness that are the underpinnings of social movements: (1) individuals must develop a frame that allows them to see "injustice" in the world and a shared sense that there is suffering that ought to be alleviated; (2) individuals require what Gamson calls "agency," or a belief that one's group can bring real change; and (3) individuals must have a sense of "identity" as a group to form a social movement that can make a difference.[2] Injustice, agency, and identity do not *necessarily* lead to involvement in social movements, but they do form the basis of developing the potential to align with groups that seek to challenge and change power structures.

Religious organizations and individuals are an important part of shaping public policy, legislation, and social movements. Congregations provide people with resources for political involvement in tangible forms. These include leaders, social networks, and places to meet.[3] These forms of capital result in a payoff greater than their specified religious utility, in that they can nurture efficacy for political action.[4] Those who see the connection between religion and politics primarily in this way might say Dr. Martin Luther King Jr. was a successful leader of the Civil Rights Movement largely because of the human capital he gained through his church work as a pastor, skills that included the ability to speak well in front of a crowd.

Religion also provides intangibles such as motivations and meaningful rhetoric for political actions.[5] These are the moral meanings that support political action. For example, the emphasis some religious teachings place on caring for the poor brings an awareness of injustice.[6] Moral frameworks are best understood through observing what people do, listening to how they talk, and then discerning what such discourse and actions reveal about the underlying meanings they attach to political life.[7] Thus, when pastors implicitly endorse candidates through whom they pray "for" and even whom they pray "against" from the pulpits of their sanctuaries, they impart partisan views to their churches. Churches and pastors model for their participants whether it is more in keeping with being a good Christian to be a pro-life Republican, a social justice Democrat, or neither of these or to remain largely uninvolved in political life.[8] Such categorizations are important to American politics: when individuals don't vote in community elections because pastors categorize voting as unimportant, then people in churches lose their voice in local and national politics. Likewise, when religious individuals form movements around fighting racial injustice, on the basis of the belief that "God created all people equal," then religion serves as a source of mobilization.

Evangelical Models of Political Action

The Korean Americans I talked with draw from several different and institutionally evangelical models for political action or inaction. The most public model of engaged evangelicalism is that of the Christian Right, as shown by recent media images of the resurgence of conservative Christianity in American politics.[9] The political scientist Clyde Wilcox describes the Christian Right as "a social movement that attempts to mobilize evangelical Protestants and other Orthodox Christians to conservative political action." Their focus is on a variety of social issues, ranging from lobbying on behalf of those who homeschool their children to supporting antiabortion legislation.[10] The Christian Right is largely a demographically white movement, with 10 to 15 percent of white Americans supporting it.[11]

While politically conservative evangelicals receive the most media attention, more evangelicals are either politically moderate or uninvolved. According to sociologist Christian Smith (1998), in his comprehensive work on American evangelicalism, many of evangelicals' cultural antagonists worry that the so-called Religious Right contains an authoritarianism, which is prepared to run roughshod over the public system of liberal democracy. While those elements certainly may exist in evangelicalism, almost all of the ordinary evangelicals we interviewed were studiously committed to and confident about expressing their views through voting and polite lobbying. Relatively few expressed interest in protests and demonstrations; others expressed deep reservations about the confrontative actions of Operation Rescue and similar groups.[12]

Rather than centrist in their political actions, some evangelicals believe that Christianity is primarily about forming individual relationships that lead to "saving souls" rather than structural change in this world. This view gives evangelicals little motivation to be involved in politics.[13]

Interestingly, those of my respondents who are most concerned about politics look not to white but to black Christians for a model of connection between social justice and Christianity in America. Among white evangelicals, there are fewer approaches that link commitment to social justice with traditional religious beliefs. Among black congregations, however, there are plenty of examples of a conservative Protestantism joined with socially liberal political action.[14] Although they align with white Christians on issues of doctrine and some social platforms, such as opposition to abortion, black Christians are markedly more liberal than whites on issues of economic policy and civil liberties.[15]

This chapter primarily examines the discourse Korean Americans develop for the relationship between faith and political action. During my discussions with those at Manna and Grace, as well as with Korean Americans in other congregations, I asked Korean Americans how they understand their individual roles as well as the role of their church in American politics. Even when the discussion was not about actions they viewed as overtly political, their mentions of injustice and their ability or inability to bring changes were as illuminating as the thoughts they shared when directly asked about politics. Korean Americans rely on evangelical identities—yet my respondents do not fit neatly into groups such as the Christian Right on one hand or noninvolvement on the other. Instead, they draw on evangelicalism selectively, in ways that take into consideration identities as Christians, as immigrants, and as nonwhite Americans.

How Korean Americans talk about politics centers on several core themes. They have very local understandings of civic life when it comes to volunteerism, understandings that are largely similar to the approaches of their respective congregations. They view their local churches as bases for community involvement. However, they routinely explain that their congregations are not political organizations, and rarely is there overt mention of politics in sermons and public teachings at Grace, Manna, or the other second-generation or multiethnic churches. Korean Americans primarily think of their congregations as locally involved entities, while they view politics as a national and more abstract pursuit. My respondents told me that their first-generation parents provided them with few models for political action. This led many of my respondents to look toward broader Christian ways of understanding American politics. In order to structure their political understanding, respondents also connected evangelicalism with what it means to be ethnically Asian American and, more broadly, with what it means to be an "American minority." Some legitimate political noninvolvement through an evangelical theology. Yet those who are most politically involved take aspects of social justice rhetoric from black churches and individuals. Like black congregations, these Korean Americans develop a minority consciousness and a model for political action that links social justice inextricably to Christianity.

Political Practices

Korean Americans in Grace and Manna are similar in their level of political participation. While a greater percentage of Korean Americans at Manna than at Grace say they are "very interested" in politics and national affairs, the majority in both congregations are only "somewhat interested" in political life. For example, only half of the Korean Americans in each church are registered to vote. Tables 7.1 and 7.2 summarize the results from the survey of each church where I asked questions about voting and interest in political and national affairs.

Korean Americans at Grace and Manna are only minimally involved in politics and appear to be less active overall than the American population. According to the 2000 census, 70 percent of American citizens are registered to vote.[16] In comparison, even though all of those I interviewed are eligible to vote, only 47 percent of those at Grace and 52 percent of Korean Americans at Manna are registered to vote. These results could be explained, in part, by the young age of my respondents. Yet, to gain the fullest picture of their civic lives, we need to listen to *how* Korean Americans connect political and religious participation.

TABLE 7.1. How Interested Are You in Politics or National Affairs?

	Very	Somewhat	Not Interested	(N)
Grace Church (%) N	(18) 15	(59) 49	(23) 19	(100) 83
Manna Fellowship (All) (%) N	(22) 32	(59) 85	(18) 26	(100) 143
Manna Fellowship (Korean American) (%) N	(23) 7	(48) 15	(29) 9	(100) 31

TABLE 7.2. Are You Currently Registered to Vote?

	Yes	No	Not Eligible	(N)
Grace Church (%) N	(47) 39	(39) 32	(15) 12	(100) 83
Manna Fellowship (All) (%) N	(61) 88	(24) 35	(15) 21	(100) 144
Manna Fellowship (Korean American)	(52) 16	(26) 8	(23) 7	(100) 31

Frames for Noninvolvement

The Local Work of Saving Souls

To understand the future of political participation in American society, it is as important to study motivations for *lack* of involvement as for involvement. Some Korean Americans have a well-thought-out narrative for justifying their lack of political involvement. These individuals told me they are more concerned about the local, individual work of saving souls than about being involved in changing political structures. Jessica, in her late twenties, attends Grace and works with a local nonprofit devoted to improvement of public education.[17] This work causes her to reevaluate how she thinks about the relationship of politics to Christianity:

> I found myself getting sucked in to that attitude, that you need to make sure people's human rights are recognized. . . . And there was a part of me that knew something was wrong with that as a Christian. And I wasn't able to put my finger on it for a long time until I went home and talked to my uncle who is a Christian. And he was in social work. . . . And he told me there is nothing wrong with trying to improve people's lives. But, ultimately, if charity doesn't lead people to accepting Christ, then ultimately it doesn't mean anything.

Jessica actually cares deeply about human rights. During the time I attended Grace, I had numerous conversations with her about alleviating the conditions of those who are poor. Yet her statement here eloquently captures the tension some Korean American evangelicals feel who struggle to make sense of why they should be involved with changing society if such changes do not lead to "sharing the gospel." These examples reveal the priority that these Korean Americans place on making evangelism the centrally important aspect of their faith. As Jessica explained, such acts of charity do not mean much if ultimately they do not lead to individuals accepting Christ.

While they rarely appeal to their congregations for models of political involvement, the views Korean American evangelicals have about noninvolvement often reflect those of Korean American pastors. None of the nine pastors I interviewed think evangelical theology necessitates separation from world affairs. However, both those who minister in multiethnic and in second-generation churches emphasize that their central mission should be local in nature. When I asked Pastor Simeon, from Manna, how he sees his congregation connecting with national or local politics, he told me that local churches are primarily "in the business of changing lives."[18] This kind of perspective aligns with the evangelical view that it is more important for Christians to be concerned about the individual and local aspects of ministry than larger structural changes, such as those that involve government policies.

Korean Americans told me that in sermons or public teachings their pastors rarely encourage political action, whether through partisan or more neutral encouragement toward involvement. Joanne, a Korean American in her late twenties, works as a resident in a local hospital and attends a second-generation Korean church in New Jersey.[19] Joanne said politics is not something her church discusses. She told me that her church's role in helping her become a more civic-minded American is through helping to change her character:

> Our church, in particular, we pray for our country. Our church doesn't get involved. We don't really talk about political issues among the church at large. Like in sermons, our pastor doesn't talk about world affairs. You know, he doesn't talk about terrorism or anything. [Our church helps us to be better Americans] mostly through our character.

Prayer for government leaders is seen as a spiritual pursuit; yet signing petitions or asking members to engage in voter registration drives is viewed as involving churches too much in the affairs of the state.

In contrast, there is a distinct group among these pastors who want very much for their congregation members to be involved more structurally in lobbying government officials for changes to public policies that affect the poor. The pastors told me it is difficult to get their congregation members to be more involved politically because some Korean Americans view political actions as being too removed from their concerns. Jeff is in his early thirties and the pastor of a second-generation Korean congregation in New York.[20] He explained why it seems so much more difficult to get Korean Americans involved in politics than it is to get them involved in local acts of community service:

> The political is abstract, huge. One has to decide whether to be a Democrat or a Republican. It is a bigger leap for Korean Americans than community service. Community service is something that can be seen. One can see the results, the interactions happen on an individual level, not changing systems. Second-generation Koreans have largely had "the ghetto mentality" passed on to them by the first generation, and political involvement seems too daunting.

In part, Jeff explains what he sees as a lack of political involvement on the part of Korean Americans as resulting from an attitude that politics is daunting, an attitude that is passed on from the first generation. Yet Jeff's words show that this group of noninvolved Korean Americans also fits into a noninvolvement model of broader American evangelicalism. Local community involvement is tangible, whereas it is difficult to decide how changing public policies or government structures are relevant to being a Christian. Also embedded in his sentiments is the idea that second-generation Koreans have a difficult time caring about others because, like their parents, they are too concerned about their own ethnic communities.

Agency

Pastor Jeff's sentiment that Korean Americans are more concerned about ministry to individuals than about changing societal conditions is a reality for some of my respondents. However, other Korean Americans actually think they *should* be politically involved but have trouble seeing how their involvement makes a difference. A prevailing theme that resulted from my analyses of these interviews is that Korean Americans who do not participate or who participate minimally in politics sometimes lack "agency," the sense that they can make a difference in changing society.[21] When asked why they do not vote, most of these Korean Americans told me that one's vote does not matter. Sonyoung, a Korean American in her early twenties, attends Manna and is pursuing an advanced degree in education.[22] Sonyoung does not believe she has the ability to make changes, and explained, "I don't really feel like I have very much influence." She told me that the single time she voted she thought her vote probably "didn't make a difference."

Even those who are minimally involved in politics, for example, those who occasionally vote in national elections, also think one's vote does not matter. Miriam, in her late twenties and a resident at an urban hospital, commented, "As important as it [voting] is, I don't think it is that crucial. I mean I am going to vote, but it's just one vote, I guess."[23] It became clear that those who lack agency could become politically involved if they were given a frame for political action that emphasizes the impact of state and national government on their lives and the lives of the poor and needy.

Lack of Models

What we learn about political life from our parents is centrally connected to how we view politics in our adult lives.[24] It is significant that second-generation Korean Americans often describe the political life of first-generation Korean immigrants in cynical terms. The Korean immigrant community is seen as being "insular," concerned only about their own well-being. As I explained in chapter 6, this perceived insularity on the part of the first generation is a central reason that Korean Americans give for becoming involved in community service.

For second-generation Koreans, the approach their parents had to American politics is also given as a reason for their own relationship to it. Being the children of immigrants is part of their unique experience as immigrants and a way they are different from other American evangelicals, to whom they may be similar in other ways or whom they may surpass in education and wealth. Few of those I interviewed have parents who speak English fluently. Many have parents who are not American citizens. My respondents' stories reveal that their parents either see themselves as able to do little to change the American political system or are concerned more with Korean than American politics. Michelle, after she told of her mother's noninvolvement in politics (in the quotation at the beginning of the chapter), went on to say of politics: "I don't talk about it with other Koreans, with Korean parents or with my Korean relatives as much. I mean, they will talk about Asian politics." Other Korean Americans mentioned their parents are more connected to the Korean than the American political system. They also told me their parents travel often to Korea and are interested in American politics only when the United States government is involved in foreign policy that has an impact on Korea. This provides evidence for what sociologist Peggy Levitt calls "local-level political linkages within the transnational village." I did not find similar connections to Korea or Korean politics among my second-generation respondents, however.[25]

My respondents who want to be involved have a hard time knowing *how* to be involved when they receive few models from their parents. Some told me that their parents are simply uninvolved or that they disagree with their parents' tacit involvement. Sasha attends Manna, is in her early twenties, and a recent college graduate.[26] She had recently started a job as a teacher when I talked with her. I asked her, "What do you think of as your role in American politics?" She answered:

> Maybe if I were a fifth-generation Korean American, then maybe it would be a lot easier to answer the question.... Like my town, of all Korean people, they would never vote for the school budget. So the school budget would never pass. I think what happens is that the first generation is ignorant. Not in a negative way, but we are ignorant of the politics of the new country, and so it inhibits a lot of what we can do and how we can help. Because we don't know about it, it severely limits what we can do, and I think that is how I am.

Sasha blames her own noninvolvement on her parents and community, who did not teach her how to be involved in American politics.

Eve, a Korean American in her early twenties, works in business and also attends Manna. She expressed a sense of apathy when I asked about her role in American politics:

> I don't vote. I just don't do it because I don't know their platforms well enough. I don't read about it.... [*Why do you think you're not as involved?*] When I grew up my parents or nobody around me was into that. I thought my parents, the one time they did vote was for George Bush because he was a Christian and he wanted to bring prayer to schools. That was all they knew about him, and I was like, "That's all you know about?" And they said, "Yeah, we're Republicans, we don't like Democrats because they're prochoice" or whatever. And I said, "If that's the only reason, I'm not going to vote"; even if they say they do other things like raise taxes or do things that will just get money out of us.... I just don't vote. [*So it's because your family is not so involved?*] Nobody around me was very political.[27]

Eve is cynical about the approach her parents had to politics, an approach she thinks is based on a facile Christian agenda. She believes political actions should be more complex than merely voting for "prayer in the schools" because other Christians do, and her cynicism reveals that Eve wants a different model from the one her parents have for connecting Christianity and politics.

In two instances, my respondents' stories reveal the importance of family ties in motivating them to become involved in political life. Sooyoung is in her late twenties and lives in New York. She attends a multiethnic church and works as an attorney.[28] Sooyoung was somewhat different from the other Korean Americans I interviewed in the way she talked about her family's political involvement. I asked her, "Do you think of yourself as having a role in American politics?" She answered:

> Voting, oh yeah. My grandfather, when he came to the United States, settled in New Hampshire at sixty-seven; for the last twenty years of his life he was really involved in the Democratic party.... So he was very involved, and I think he's a good American... he's a better American than anyone I know because he got involved in the community.... I think that's how I should be. The least I can do is to vote.

Where other Korean Americans are not political because their parents are not political, Sooyoung is unique in that she does have a family role model for political involvement. She uses her grandfather's involvement in the Democratic Party as a model to guide her own political involvement.

Korean Americans also told me that, because so few Asians vote or are in legislative or government roles, they do not have the examples of political participation and representation among their ethnic group that they perceive other Americans as having. Jeremy, a Korean American college student in his early twenties and a member of Manna, told me that being politically *uninvolved* is a particularly Asian trait:

> I have no idea about politics and I always try to avoid it. And I think it is a very Asian thing to do. Asian people complain about bills and all those things.... And if they don't vote then that is going to happen. There is only, like, 4 percent of Asian Americans represented [or who vote]. And then they don't take it that seriously and are like: "Lets just focus on this [local] community."... I [feel] challenged that I should get into it and see what is going on and vote.[29]

On the one hand, Jeremy thinks lacking political models from other Asian Americans keeps him from being fully involved; on the other hand, his awareness of being underrepresented in government elections actually motivates his own involvement.

Jolie is a Korean American in her late twenties who lives in New York. She works as a reporter and attends a multiethnic congregation. Like Jeremy, Jolie echoes the view that American legislative life has few Asian representatives: "I also worked a little on Capitol Hill, as a Capitol Hill reporter as part of my program. I mean I walked around a lot and I was very aware there are not many Asian Americans in politics."[30] Jolie's perception reveals that lack of representation may make it difficult for Korean Americans to know how to be involved politically.

Sumi is a Korean American in her late twenties who lives in Missouri. She works in health administration and attends a Korean congregation.[31] The lack of nonwhite Americans in politics also influences how Sumi views her own involvement. I asked her, "What do you think of as your role in American politics?" She answered:

> Well, besides voting right now, it's hard to say. Of course, right now, you don't see as much minority representation in politics. And that could also be part of the reason why I don't feel that I have a strong influence in politics, because I don't see it modeled out right now.

In a very real way, Sumi, like Jolie and Jeremy, feels that she does not have a community of Asian Americans to show her how to become politically involved.

These Korean Americans think of Asian Americans in general as politically apathetic. Although they look outside of churches for models of political action, they find few representatives in government positions. My respondents invoke identities as "minority Christians" and "Asian American Christians" when discussing political participation, categories that are often used as the basis of coalition building.[32] Yet, although there are certainly coalitions of politically involved Asian Americans, aligning solely with other Asian Americans is not enough to foster involvement, because those alliances do not take into account the importance of maintaining a distinctive sense of what it means to be a Christian.[33] Korean Americans are left to locate unique Christian models of political action.

The Korean Religious Right?

It makes sense that those who do not receive categories of political action from their parents, and for whom a Christian identity is important, might rely on another model of political engagement. They might draw, for example, on the Religious Right model mentioned at the beginning of this chapter. Indeed, Korean Americans at Grace and Manna are more likely to define themselves as "moderately politically and socially conservative" than as liberal.

Forty-two percent of Korean Americans at Grace and 32 percent of Korean Americans at Manna are moderately conservative. When Korean Americans explain their perspective on American politics, many assume it is "most Christian" to be a political conservative, particularly in relationship to issues like abortion and homosexuality. Darrel, in his late thirties and the pastor of a second-generation Korean American congregation in New Jersey, told me that Korean American evangelicals tend to be conservative about social issues—what he describes as "right-wing" in terms of abortion and homosexuality.[34] Table 7.3 summarizes the results of a survey where I asked respondents to describe their political and social outlook.

Clearly, many of the Korean Americans at Grace and Manna think of themselves as at least "moderately conservative" when compared to other political labels. The longer conversations, however, reveal *how* the Religious Right model is realized in the lives of these individual Korean Americans. Those I interviewed often related Christian teaching to upholding American

TABLE 7.3. Thinking Politically and Socially, How Would You Describe Yourself?

	Grace	Manna (all)	Manna (Korean)
Very conservative (% n)	5.2 (4)	10.8 (15)	12.9 (4)
Moderately conservative	41.6 (32)	30.2 (42)	32.3 (10)
Middle-of-the-road	28.6 (22)	31.7 (44)	29.0 (9)
Moderately liberal	18.2 (14)	19.4 (27)	19.4 (6)
Very liberal	2.6 (2)	2.9 (4)	0
Something else	3.9 (3)	5.0 (7)	6.5 (2)
	100 (77)	100 (139)	100 (31)

civil order. Peter, a Korean American in his early twenties, is in his last year of an undergraduate program and attends Manna.[35] He told me about the connection between being a Christian and the way he thinks about American politics:

> Upholding the word of God. You have heard this. Americans are so relative.... America's foundations were in the Bible and we are deviating from that. And did you hear that thing in California where a judge ruled the pledge of allegiance was unconstitutional because it said, "under God."? I mean, that is crazy! But, I think upholding the word of God like "Thou shall not kill" and [opposing] abortion where everyone is like "freedom to choose" and that sort of thing.... And then there is that whole argument about whether the fetus is really life. But then in the Bible it does treat life as beginning at conception. It's just the standard of God's word.

Peter assumes that the most Christian position is political conservatism. He thinks a Christian morality should be implemented in the United States; he is prolife.

As if to underscore that being politically conservative is normative among Korean Americans, those who are more liberal politically see themselves as being on the margins when compared to other Korean Christians. Mary, a Korean American in her midtwenties, who is working toward a master's degree in business administration and attends a Korean congregation in New Jersey, said:

> I have to confess that when I voted this past November, I just voted Democrat the entire ticket.... [*So then, would most people at your church consider themselves liberal politically?*] Definitely not! I am *definitely* in the minority as far as the Korean church goes. I think most Koreans are Republican. I would also consider myself prochoice, which I think is really not a popular stand within the church. I think of sin as a personal choice. And I don't see anything clearly in the Bible to say that abortion is a sin [her emphasis].[36]

That Mary thought voting as a Democrat was something she needed to "confess" to me is very telling. From her perspective, being a Democrat put her among the minority when compared to other Korean American Christians.

Yet being a conservative is not the basis of coalition building for Peter or other Korean Americans. For example, I discovered during my conversation with Peter that he did not know that there are two major political parties in the United States—a fact that shows a disconnect with the American political system. Likewise, others who link political conservatism to Christianity rarely mention being part of the so-called Religious Right that has captured the allegiance of many white evangelicals.[37] Only 15 percent of those at Grace and

10 percent of Korean Americans at Manna had attended a political meeting or rally during the preceding 12 months.

New Models

The Korean Americans who talked most about politics and being politically involved are the ones who least easily fit the Religious Right model of evangelical politics. These Korean Americans try to gain distance from what they call a more "fundamentalist" approach in favor of a new approach to American politics. This group finds themselves dissatisfied with secular liberal approaches to politics because they perceive that political liberals do not share their religious convictions. Yet they have misgivings about individuals who bundle Christianity with political conservatism and what they see as implicit discrimination against nonwhite Americans.

Some Korean Americans feel dissatisfied both with evangelical conservatives and what they understand as secular political liberal approaches to politics. Sooyoung, mentioned earlier, explained:

> I think the very liberal people, the trouble with them is the educated liberals tend to be socially minded—they care about injustice—but the fault is that they've moved away from God and they have no basis for their moral outrage. They don't believe in a force that determines whether something is good or bad, so what right do they have to be angry at injustice? That's why I don't see validity to their point. The moral Republicans, I don't see them as being very active because I think they're very self-righteous, to the point where they don't like to help.

Sooyoung clearly thinks it would be difficult, as a Christian, to find an approach to politics that works for her.

Sangjoon is a Korean American in his midtwenties who, at the time I spoke with him, was attending a prestigious evangelical seminary while working part-time as a youth minister at Grace.[38] He, too, wants to be more involved in politics, but is uncomfortable with some aspects of political conservatism that he has seen among other evangelical Christians. When I asked Sangjoon about his place in American politics, he lamented, "We have not seen nonfundamentalists get really engaged in politics." Sangjoon views politics as something in which mainly "fundamentalist" Christians are involved, a category Sangjoon clearly did not want to identify with. Although he thinks Christians should care more about changing society, he doesn't know how to become political in ways that satisfy his approach to Christianity.

Korean Americans express particular misgivings about evangelicals over the issue of race, drawing on identities as Asian Americans and, often, with the category of nonwhite Americans broadly. Jolie clearly identified herself as an evangelical during the course of our discussion; she told me that being a Christian means there is "only one way to salvation" and that is "through Jesus Christ." But when she goes to the polls, an identity as an American minority is also a central part of her framework for political action: "I think those kinds of issues that are very minority-specific, like affirmative action, or things like that, those are the issues that I tend to be interested in right away as opposed to larger, broader, social issues.... Being a minority definitely encourages me to vote more often." An identity as a racial minority in America clearly defines for Jolie how she thinks about public policy and how she votes.

Michael is in his early thirties, attends Manna, and is pursuing a doctoral degree in the social sciences.[39] As a Korean American, he experiences tension over how he should align himself politically regarding the issue of race:

> I see some of the movements among the Republicans regarding Christianity or at least some of the values espoused by biblical principles, things like abortion—I guess a lot of traditional values that are consistent with Christianity. But, at the same time, I look at them and a lot of Republicans, a lot of real fundamental Christians; I just find them to be narrow-minded and racist. And I remember Chuck Swindoll once said, "It's good to be a conservative Christian, just don't act like one." And, I think that's true...when I look at the Democratic Party and what they believe in, there's a lot to be said about that. Jesus said, "I came to save the oppressed." And I really believe that the Democrats have a lot of emphasis on...the poor, and advocate for things like affirmative action and welfare, changing the school systems and really fulfilling the needs of the poor and equal rights and advocating for minorities in general. And so I think that's something I really believe in.

In this statement, Michael expressed misgivings about completely aligning with a conservative model of politics, which he perceives as not caring enough about the rights of minorities and the poor, and he connects these beliefs to the Christian mission and the idea that Jesus came to "save the oppressed." Identifying as both an evangelical and an ethnic minority shapes how Michael thinks about politics *but also* gives him conflict about how he should align politically.

Most relevant to the impact of Korean Americans on evangelical civic life are the stories of those who are involved in American politics in meaningful ways. None of my respondents talked specifically about creating political social movements. Yet, in their narratives, I find awareness of the kind of agency, injustice, and identity that are the basis of coalition building.

In particular, Korean Americans told me that they benefit from Korean and Asian American *evangelical* leaders and peers who help them see the specific connection between spirituality and political action. When my respondents find such public models, these people help motivate them to become more involved. Mi-Young, a Korean American in her early thirties, was finishing her Ph.D. in theology.[40] She was also preparing to begin a teaching position at a seminary that she described as "mainly white." Mi-Young also attended a majority white congregation in New Jersey.[41] When we talked, she had recently attended a conference for Korean Americans. The gathering was sponsored by the Presbyterian Church (USA), a liberal Presbyterian denomination that nonetheless has an evangelical Christian presence, and featured lectures by several prominent Korean American Christian leaders.[42] One particular talk by Paull Shin, a Korean American senator, captured her attention.[43] Shin made the argument that Asian Americans have a responsibility to be more political. While politics had been something she had previously left to others, Shin's injunction caused Mi-Young to reconsider her view. Mi-Young decided to start voting regularly and to talk with other Korean American evangelicals at her graduate school about becoming more involved in local politics.

I met Pascal, a Korean American in his late thirties, at a national conference for Korean American college students.[44] Although, unlike my other respondents, he had not come to the United States until he was in his early teens, Pascal still considers himself very much an American. He teaches at a well-known evangelical seminary in the Northeast and attends a mostly white evangelical congregation that he describes as being very American in the "flag-waving, right-wing Republican kind of way," adding quickly, "I think this is pretty true of evangelicals more generally."

At the conference, Pascal gave a lecture for both religious and nonreligious students about the role second-generation Korean American Christians should have in their communities. He mentioned, in particular, the responsibility second-generation Koreans have to help other minority groups. In a later interview, Pascal explained that as an ethnic minority, he finds himself "leftist leaning" on some issues, which distinguishes him from white evangelicals. "I identify with the call to justice along with the conversion of the gospel." Yet the tension with what he perceives as white American evangelicalism is the motivation for action. Pascal went on to say, "I think I fit into America by shaping the minds of the future leaders, of the ecclesiastical leadership of American society." Through shaping the minds of both Korean *and* non-Korean evangelical pastors, Pascal hopes to broaden the evangelical view so that it encompasses more concern about social justice.

Peers who have a framework for integrating a Christian identity with a minority consciousness and political involvement are also important in helping my respondents begin to value political social action. Samantha is a Korean American in her midtwenties who attends Grace and is in her last year in a doctoral program in pharmacy.[45] Samantha told me that she doesn't think of herself as being very political, but a friend helped her to see the place of Asian Americans in politics:

> The stereotypical thing I've heard, that the reason why Koreans in the beginning are not looked on favorably, is because we kept to ourselves, and we didn't donate to the community, we didn't participate in the community. My generation, we get involved in politics, like my friend worked on the McGreevey campaign, and I got to see how the Asians are more involved. I want to be more involved.

Samantha draws on a broader connection with Asian Americans and tries to create distance from her Korean immigrant parents when talking about political involvement. Samantha's friend played a key role in helping Samantha develop a political consciousness, by showing Samantha that more Asians should be concerned about legislative life and by giving her possible paths for political action.

Some of the Korean Americans I talked with have initiated new evangelical approaches to American politics. Sonia is a Korean American in her late twenties, lives in New York, works as an attorney, and is part of a multiethnic congregation.[46] She told me she and her husband, also a Korean American, joined with an African American man from their church to spearhead a group "of more moderate Democrats and Republicans to come together to kind of bridge the big stream of the right/left divide." Sonia later said she thinks her political role, as a Christian, is to "start dialogue and get involved in dialogue."

The Model of the Black Church

Given that most research on the relationship between Korean Americans and African Americans stresses conflict, it is surprising that those respondents who are most involved in American politics look to black Christians and black church models of political involvement as exemplars. Korean Americans who are actively involved in politics find more in common with black than white Christians.[47] Black Christians provide Korean Americans in both Korean and multiethnic congregations with models for political action, models that incorporate both a distinctive ethnic identity and a distinctive religious orthodoxy.[48] Korean Americans mention the important role African American Christians have in their lives, in particular through helping them to understand issues of justice and political action. Sooyoung told me she is beginning to see "solidarity" between the Korean American and African American communities: "I think it's like that for any minority," she explained. "Even at work, the closest person who I consider a friend, she's a forty-year-old black woman; she's a believer and I'm a believer and we talk about our faith."

Jim, a Korean American and one of the pastors at Manna, told me he "became a Christian" through the evangelism of an African American man he met as an undergraduate. Jim said, "I went to church with him at an African American church. He exposed me to a lot of justice issues and a heart for the poor." Jim explained that the commitment he now has to social justice influences how he sees his role as a pastor at Manna, revealing the influence that black Christians have had on his life and his approach to the connection between Christianity and social justice.

Tim is a Korean American in his early thirties, attends a multiethnic church in California, and works as a researcher for a drug company.[49] He said: "I hate to say it this way, but when it's the 'colored man' against the 'white man' then I think it's the 'colored' man who is going to band together. I think we saw that, perhaps a little bit, during the [L.A.] riots here." Tim was at first afraid of offending me with his comment about political alliances. But it is clear that when it comes to issues of social justice, he aligns more with nonwhite than white Americans.

Interestingly, although Korean Americans look to black American rather than white American Christians for ways to develop a political consciousness, they do not become involved in black congregations. Korean Americans are primarily part of second-generation, multiethnic, pan-Asian churches affiliated with largely white denominations, or involved in white congregations. This is a particularly significant finding: it shows the potential that this group of Korean Americans (those who look to black Christians for a model of political involvement) may have to influence the institution of American evangelicalism more broadly.

These narratives reveal the ability and desire of Korean Americans to become involved in the American political system when they have role models who are involved politically and/or peer support that gives them ways to connect being Christian with being an American minority. Those who are involved in politics often negotiate unique perspectives of what it means to be an evangelical, challenging the frame for politics among not only Korean American evangelicals but also the wider evangelical community. Pascal's story is especially important. As a seminary professor in a well-known evangelical seminary, he challenges future pastors to become more involved in social justice in their local communities. He provides a model for pastors at his largely white seminary, both Korean Americans and those of other ethnic groups—a model that will encourage future Christian leaders to "identify with the call to justice." All of the Korean American pastors I interviewed attended seminaries that are primarily white. If they attain leadership in seminaries and denominations, as there is evidence they are doing, they have the potential to change the relationship of American evangelicalism to social justice and civil society.

Conclusions

The relationship Korean American evangelicals have to politics is different from their relationship to local community volunteerism. Individual churches provide Korean Americans with particular models for helping individuals in their community. However, Korean Americans generally do not think their congregations are political entities. This means that across congregations, Korean Americans share similar institutional narratives of American evangelicalism when talking about political participation. Some emphasize commitment to individual relationships and evangelistic goals as reasons for not participating in political structures. Others draw on conservative evangelical political rhetoric. Some Korean Americans think Christians should be involved in politics but have difficulty locating models of involvement when their parents are not political or when they lack models of broader Asian American political participation.

The most significant stories are those that do not fit a clear existing model yet involve individuals who still find ways to meaningfully participate either in local or national politics. A distinct group of Korean Americans reject both noninvolvement and the passive adoption of a fairly uninvolved Religious Right evangelical political agenda, in favor of looking for other paradigms that will incorporate their identities as Asian Americans, ethnic minorities, and Christians. Although they do not join black churches, they do adopt aspects of black church models for political participation.

These findings also show the potential of Korean Americans and other groups of new immigrants to change the intersection of politics and American Christianity. Neither a model of conservative politics nor of noninvolvement adequately fits the narratives of these respondents. We do not yet know the particular influence Korean American evangelicals and other groups of Asian Americans will have on American evangelicalism. If they remain separatist and individualistic in their interpretation of the connection between Christianity and politics, their presence, although accepted, will not be a force for change.

Another possibility, however, is that second-generation Koreans will add more support to the liberal social justice agenda of many black churches or even create a unique Korean American or Asian American evangelical approach to politics. If they take distinctive immigrant histories that keep discrimination fresh in their minds into leadership positions in seminaries and churches, they may yet emerge as a subgroup that brings change to American evangelicalism and, by extension, the linked institution of American politics.[50]

In my conclusion, chapter 8, I draw together the themes I have discussed here about political identities and practices, as well as the other core parts of the book about larger civic models, identities, and practices for Korean Americans in ethnic and multiethnic churches, to make projections about the influence this second-generation group, and other nonwhite second-generation immigrants, may have on American evangelicalism and American religion and civic life more broadly.

8

Implications for Institutional Change

I began by telling the stories of two Korean American evangelicals, Bill and Jim. From the perspective of an outsider, Bill and Jim look very similar. Both are second-generation Korean Americans; are American citizens; have several years of higher education and work in the economic mainstream; and participate in the same religious tradition. Yet, in spite of their demographic similarities, Bill, Jim, and the other Korean Americans with whom I talked have very different ways of understanding civic responsibilities.

Through studying civic identities and practices among second-generation Korean American evangelicals, I found that involvement in American civic life is socially constructed and varies even for Korean Americans who share the same structural location in terms of race, ethnicity, class, and education. Families, workplaces, and immigrant communities are important domains in which Korean American evangelicals develop civic identities and practices. Religion, however—and specifically American evangelicalism—is the most central institution the Korean Americans I talked with draw on for developing ideas and practices of civic life. Their local churches are particular contexts where they gain cultural resources, in particular cultural schemas, for constructing civic identities and ways to relate identities to practices of local community service. Churches are not as central, however, for developing models of political involvement. Rather, Korean Americans negotiate political ideas and practices via broader institutional evangelical models of political participation. These stories have implications for how Korean Americans and other new Americans might, through their influence on American evangelicalism, reshape and influence ideas about American citizenship that are now taken for granted.

Civic Models, Identities, and Practices

Most of the Korean Americans I talked with identify more as Americans than as Koreans. Yet very few see themselves as "real" Americans in the same way they perceive someone who is of European ethnicity to be an American. Likewise, few Korean Americans think others perceive them as fully American. The awareness that they potentially will not be seen as Americans, however, does not hinder their commitment to local community service.

In particular, Korean Americans are concerned about being *good* Americans. They use religious cultural resources to develop and justify civic responsibilities. Most of the more than 90 second-generation Korean American evangelicals who participated in this study said that American evangelicalism provides them with specific models for understanding civic responsibility. Korean American evangelicals have an outward-looking focus and overwhelmingly care about broader American life outside their ethnic community and outside their specific congregation.

Researchers who study immigrant religion and those who study evangelicalism find that both groups are mainly concerned about providing for the needs of those in their own congregations. In contrast to these findings, my research shows that *second-generation* Korean American evangelicals *do* focus on service to the non-Korean and non-Christian communities. The results of this study contribute important insight into Korean Americans' motives for being outward-looking. They focus on serving those in their local communities because of connected ethnic and religious understandings. Second-generation Koreans want to be different from the first generation, which they perceive as ethnocentric—based on their perception that first-generation Koreans provide only for the needs of other Koreans. The second generation actually creates its own distinctive ethnic space by focusing on the needs of the broader non-Korean community. Yet it is also significant that Korean Americans differentiate themselves from the first generation in a distinctively religious way. They use the institutional resources of evangelical Christianity, such as a focus on sharing faith with multiple audiences, to justify reaching out to and serving the non-Korean community. Korean Americans in both second-generation and multiethnic churches focus on the importance of Korean Americans doing community service. Pastor Joseph from Grace, the second-generation church where I spent the most time, explained that it should be a uniform mission for second-generation Korean churches to serve the communities in which they are located. Pastor Simeon, also a Korean American and one of the pastors at Manna, the multiethnic church, also thinks that Korean Americans in local churches should serve the non-Koreans in their communities. However, as I have shown, the story of civic responsibility for Korean American evangelicals is significantly more complicated than one that simply says that second-generation Korean Americans are more outward-looking than the first generation.

Church-Based Models of Civic Responsibility

Ethnic and multiethnic congregations are centrally important sites in establishing different and patterned possibilities for Korean American civic identities and the consequences such identities have for civic practices. Their churches provide particular cultural schemas that mediate between larger institutional American evangelical ideas about civic responsibility and individual Korean American ethnic identities and practices of local civic responsibility. As I discussed in chapter 4, those who participate at Grace or in other second-generation Korean congregations connect church membership to a *communally obligated* approach to civic responsibility. This model is characterized by a sense of obligations to their congregation and the wider American society. Manna and the other multiethnic churches also stress obligations to serve in their local communities, but they have a more *individually negotiated* approach and do not proscribe specific kinds of participation.

Approaches to the connection between evangelical Christianity and ethnicity, class, and public religion are constituent components of these civic models. The Korean Americans at Grace and Manna and those in other second-generation and multiethnic churches make different connections between ethnicity and religion. In particular, while researchers often see the ethnic makeup of a church only as a demographic variable, church-specific attitudes toward ethnicity and ways of constructing it are also types of cultural resources.[1] Korean Americans at Grace and other second-generation congregations want to distance themselves from their Korean parents by divorcing Christianity from its connection with Korean culture and adopting a more nonethnic Christianity. Approach to class position is also reflected in how second-generation Koreans view the American Dream. Interestingly, through religious discourse, these children of immigrants *explicitly* distance themselves from the American Dream. *Implicitly*, however, they reify the idea that anyone can "make it" in American society if he or she is willing to work hard. Communal obligations also encourage participation in public life, but in a way that upholds the existing American social order rather than using Christianity to provide a means of critique.

Korean Americans at Manna and other multiethnic churches stress a more individually negotiated approach to the relationships of Christianity, ethnicity, class, and public participation. Multiethnic churches provide Korean Americans space to be different from first-generation Koreans through developing their own approach to the connection between faith and ethnicity rather than committing to one version of ethnic Christianity, that of Korean Christianity. Korean Americans at Manna, for example, use evangelical Christianity to develop narratives as American minorities. This approach has the consequence of fostering a distinctively Christian appreciation for wider American diversity within the constraints of American evangelicalism, an appreciation that is manifested both in ethnicity and the politics of lifestyle. An individually negotiated approach to civic responsibility also gives Korean Americans space, when necessary, to use Christianity for social critique and to motivate action outside of accepted social structures. Korean Americans at Manna, for example, have respect for those who are involved in alternative political movements. They also talk about God's judgment on what they see as the sinful parts of American history.

Overlapping Civic Identities

When I first began this research, I thought participation in a second-generation or multiethnic church would be evidence of degree of ethnic assimilation. I reasoned that as Korean Americans moved further from the ethnic identity of their immigrant parents, they would be less likely to participate in an ethnic-specific church. I thought those who participated in second-generation churches would be more inclined to provide services to the Korean community and those who participated in multiethnic churches might have greater loyalties to a wider multiethnic American community.

My respondents soon taught me that the concepts of "more Korean" or "more American" are largely artificial and imposed categories. It became more important to ask how Korean Americans construct identities on their own terms. Gaining distance from the first generation does not translate directly into uniform ethnic assimilation into American society. Individuals have agency, and use the approach to Christianity in their churches to reframe American categories of race, ethnicity, and class. However, while Korean Americans might have agency in constructing identities, identities do not completely vary according to individual preference. Civic identities are overlapping, with both constructed and structured aspects.

Korean Americans in these different kinds of congregations construct civic identities in specific patterned ways. Korean Americans use cultural schemas in their churches, such as approach to spirituality, to help themselves create civic identities. Christian identities structure ethnic and class identities. For example, because of their desire to break the link between Korean culture and Christianity held by their parents, the leadership of Grace talks about ethnicity or race in few overt ways in sermons and teachings. Implicitly, public discourses such as teachings and sermons reinforce the ideas that good Christians are hard-working and do not "act like victims"—ideas these second-generation individuals believe members of their parents' generation sometimes uphold.

Such cultural schemas act as lenses through which to view the larger American categorization of Asian Americans as the so-called model minority. Many of the Korean Americans at Grace and other second-generation churches have unconscious schemas that reinforce a spiritual view of the model minority. They believe that Korean Americans have primordial ethnic and spiritual characteristics that predispose them to be financially successful. At Grace, this perspective has the consequence of reinforcing boundaries between Korean Americans and the impoverished members of their local community. Korean Americans at Grace deeply desire to reach out to and help those in their local community. However, viewing themselves as hardworking and as overcomers of poverty makes it difficult for them to connect with minorities whom they perceive as less hard-working and as "acting like victims."

At Manna and other multiethnic churches, identities are also overlapping in patterned ways. A cultural schema that fosters more individually negotiated approaches to civic responsibility engenders appreciation for diversity. In particular, Korean Americans in multiethnic churches use Christianity to justify ethnic diversity. Young-Mi, a Korean American at Manna, told me her church helps her to appreciate different racial and ethnic groups because God made and cares for everyone. Those in multiethnic churches do not have to choose between being Korean or American. Rather, they negotiate dual and malleable identities as both Koreans and Americans. Perhaps most memorably, Collin, a Korean American at Manna, said that being a Christian and experiencing residence in this world and in the "kingdom of God" helps him realize how to be both Korean and American: "Because we understand that we are in America, but we are not fully American. We are different because we are Korean."

Korean Americans in multiethnic congregations use Christianity to adopt social identities as "multiethnic people." They connect an appreciation of ethnic diversity to religious morality. They believe that since God created ethnic groups, it is immoral for a church not to be committed to upholding ethnic diversity. This approach has the consequence of downplaying stereotypical Korean attributes. These include hierarchical relationships between the first and second generation, gender hierarchies, and societal images of Asian Americans as model minorities. Korean Americans in multiethnic churches see Christianity as stressing commonality between racial and ethnic groups, while retaining an appreciation for distinctive ethnic and racial group differences. In particular, Korean Americans in these kinds of religious settings say they have a lot in common and generally have positive relationships with black Americans—a significantly different attitude from that held by those who attend second-generation churches.

Connecting Civic Identities to Civic Practices

Spending extensive time in the midst of two congregations and surveying their members allowed me to develop a deeper understanding of how models of civic responsibility and consequent civic identities connect to actual civic practices. Because Grace and Manna are located near the same city, Old Town—a small city that is low income and multiracial—local community service means that Korean Americans in each church need to relate to and serve a population that is very different from them in social class and ethnicity. The surveys I did at both Grace and Manna reveal that their churches are the primary contexts where these Korean Americans learn what types of volunteer activities they should participate in. Yet the two congregations differ in how their models of civic responsibility connect with community service.

Grace's more communal orientation means that the members go together to do volunteer activities. Korean Americans there told me that, on the one hand, being a Korean American church is an asset to volunteerism. Because members come from a common ethnic group, the church has an easier time galvanizing them toward the same volunteer goal. On the other hand, being a Korean church leads to discrimination by others and creates unwanted and frustrating barriers. While Korean Americans at Grace see themselves more as Christians than specifically *Korean* Christians, the outside community might view them primarily as Asians. Joshua, one of the leaders at Grace, said the youth shelter where they volunteer "thought twice about letting the church volunteer there" when they found out the congregation was Asian, for fear that members of Grace would not be able to connect with the kids in the shelter. Joshua went on to explain that this consideration probably would not have been raised if they "were a white church."

The individually negotiated model of civic responsibility at Manna helps Korean Americans there construct civic practices differently from those at Grace. Korean Americans at Manna adopt the church's emphasis on connecting Christianity to being multiethnic. They are motivated toward community service because "God values diversity and caring for different kinds of people." Stressing acceptance of diversity in general means that the church also accepts diverse opinions about doing community service. Korean Americans at Manna told me this logic is appealing to them as a way of gaining distance from the "legalism of first-generation churches." For example, women are free to let individual "callings" determine their service activities, rather than what they see as traditional Korean gender expectations that would limit them primarily to care-taking roles.

This cultural logic also necessitates constant negotiation of individual ideas about volunteering. A focus on respect for individual ideas about volunteering means that although members think "being like Jesus" necessitates reaching out to the local community, they have a difficult time deciding to whom they should reach out or what kinds of specific actions reaching out should include. Deciding which volunteer activities to participate in takes more negotiating because activities are not specifically prescribed by the church. Korean Americans at Manna talk a lot about community service and think they have commonalties with the other ethnic minorities in Old Town, such as a common racial location and struggle to overcome poverty. However, the leadership at Manna finds it difficult to motivate members to participate in church-sponsored community service.

Manna is successful, though, in helping Korean Americans develop an "ethic of community service." This ethic is consistently reinforced in church public teachings. As a consequence, Korean Americans at Manna have access to more diverse kinds of volunteering than those sponsored by the church community and actually volunteer more. An individually negotiated ethic of civic responsibility thus emerges as a key cultural resource that fosters *more* individual volunteerism for Korean Americans at Manna than at Grace, the ethnic-specific church.

Institutional Evangelical Models of Political Involvement

While Korean Americans look to their particular congregations for ways to do community service, their ideas about the connection between politics and religion are *not* linked as tightly to congregational models of civic responsibility. Rather, political views are patterned according to larger institutional models of American evangelicalism. Korean Americans fold aspects of evangelicalism in with what it means to be an Asian American, or the broader category of an American minority, to structure political understandings. Some Korean Americans legitimate political noninvolvement through an apolitical evangelical theology. They think good Christians should focus more on people's spiritual needs by bringing others into the faith rather than being involved in community or national politics. These Korean Americans believe that, as one of my respondents explained, "We live in a country where church is church and state is state." According to this group, Christians should focus on helping individuals rather than changing political structures, seeking to improve society through spreading Christianity.

Others align with the Religious Right, the most public model of politics among American evangelicals. Identifying with the Religious Right is a common political identity for Korean Americans, and a significant group of Korean Americans have conservative political approaches to issues such as abortion, homosexuality, and economic policy. Such views, however, are not the basis for political action.

Korean Americans for whom political involvement is most important take their models of involvement from black churches and/or negotiate their own "Asian American Christian" models. Surprisingly, given the wealth of literature that stresses conflict between Korean and black Americans, a distinct group of Korean Americans borrows a model of political life from black Christians, a model that takes into account unique experiences of discrimination as nonwhite Americans while retaining a distinctive Christian identity. If this group grows among Korean Americans and Asian Americans more broadly, it may have the potential to bring changes to broader evangelicalism.

A New Approach to Identity Construction

In this book I have also provided substantial empirical findings that suggest new theoretical possibilities for the connection between individuals, organizations, and institutions. Organizational theory shows that organizations like churches—even within the same institution, such as American evangelicalism—might vary considerably in how they utilize the resources of their structural location as evangelicals. Rarely, however, do such theories explain how differences in organizations within the same institution influence identity construction for the individuals within them. As I explained in chapter 2, the findings of my research bring us one step closer to such understandings.

In particular, this research adds complexity to the debate over whether identities are individually constructed or largely primordial—socially structured by forces outside the individual.[2] In one sense, structural locations provide preconceived identity categories for Korean Americans: they are Asian Americans. They are racially nonwhite. However, and more important, I have also shown that Korean Americans use the cultural schemas from their local congregations to reinterpret these categories and to create their own identities. For example, Korean Americans at Grace and the other second-generation churches are more likely to accept constructs of Asian Americans as model minorities. However, Korean Americans at Manna and the other multiethnic churches use Christianity to renegotiate the meaning the externally imposed model-minority category has in their relationship to other Americans. In particular, they use Christianity to stress the commonality with black Americans that their racial location as nonwhite Christians gives them.

This approach to identity overlaps with that of other theorists who see identity as fluid and many-sided rather than primordial or completely structured by the environment or imposed social categories. I have shown here also that identities are not completely negotiated but are patterned according to the location of individuals in specific organizations and institutions. Institutions, like American evangelicalism, influence the content of cultural schemas generated by their component organizations. And the content of cultural schemas an organization generates matters for identity construction. It is important that these churches are located within institutional evangelicalism. Because of the evangelical location of their church context, Korean Americans in each congregation need to decide how to talk about their identities in ways that put Christianity first. Consequently, race, ethnic, and class components of identities are explained and interpreted in terms of the master-identity of being a Christian.

While scholars often leave the study of identity at the formation of abstract categories that describe individuals or groups, identities also matter for practices. The interpretive frameworks Korean Americans use to determine social belonging indicate particular sets of practices. For Korean Americans at Grace, believing that Korean American evangelicals are often inherently economically and educationally successful creates boundaries between Korean Americans and the groups they are trying to help in Old Town.[3] For Korean Americans at Manna, believing that wealth comes as a result of God's blessing and that ethnic categories should be recognized but not used to privilege some groups over others largely erases the boundaries they might have had with the residents of Old Town.

Cultural theories of institutional change focus on how institutionalized cultures, such as American evangelicalism, structure how organizations and individuals act, even if they do not appear to behave in ways that further the narrowly defined rational interests of a given organization or individual. Attention to development of schemas among individuals and organizations provides theoretical tools for developing a cultural theory institutional change. Attention to schemas problematizes the trajectory of institutional changes by opening the possibility for changes to come to institutions both from the top down as well as, under certain conditions, from the bottom up. I found through empirical work on these cases that individuals come to organizations with cultural schemas that they gain from other organizations and institutions. For example, Korean Americans brought ideas about race and ethnicity from their educational settings and families with them into congregational settings. When individuals bring new cultural schemas into organizations, these new cultural schemas might enable individuals, via their organizational memberships, to change the institutions such organizations inhabit.

Theories of institutions rarely connect the study of identity with institutional change. However, if the identity constructs I have discovered for Korean Americans at the social level, particularly among those in multiethnic churches, are also realized at the collective level, they have the potential to mobilize change in American evangelicalism. With regard to politics, the most involved Korean Americans are not members of the Religious Right; they instead look to black Christians to develop their own understandings of Korean American and Asian American Christian political participation. These particular identity constructions use Christianity to legitimate a social justice and minority consciousness. Unlike black Christians, who largely form their own denominational and church bodies, Korean Americans remain, especially among the second generation, largely involved in evangelicalism. If such identities are found at the level of the collective among a broader group of Korean Americans and even Asian Americans, they have the potential to change the way American evangelicalism understands the relationship between Christianity, race, and politics.

Institutional Changes to Civic Life

For those concerned with the future of American civic life, this research shows the importance of considering the differences between first- and second-generation immigrants. Motivated by a desire to create ethnic boundaries from the first generation, second-generation immigrants may connect religion to civic life in very different ways from their parents. Work that considers diverse types of religious participation and congregations with different ethnic compositions will help scholars of civil society gain a fuller understanding of the influence immigrants and their children are having on broader American civic life.

Specifically, by comparing Korean Americans in second-generation and multiethnic churches, I discovered that civic identity overlaps with other identities and has the potential to vary for Korean Americans in different congregational contexts. Some scholars seem to assume that civic assimilation, defined as community and political participation outside specifically ethnic contexts, will proceed in tandem with economic assimilation.[4] These theorists reason that as new Americans become part of the mainstream economy, they will also adopt more cohesive identities as Americans, becoming more uniformly integrated into American civil society. However, certain kinds of identities, such as religious ones, may be more dominant than class position in determining civic life, and may even reconstruct the meaning of class and ethnic components of civic identities. I have shown here that, even for Korean Americans in the same social class, participation in a congregation helps them create cohesive yet *different* civic identities, with different implications for civic practices. Such a finding challenges a unitary model of civic assimilation.

Scholars of civic life should also consider the importance of understanding the institutional fields and organizational contexts in which individual volunteers are embedded. American evangelical congregations are within the broader institution of American religion. Congregations are also a kind of voluntary organization in civil society. As such they are linked to other voluntary organizations within civil society. Scholars of civic life are often overly concerned with the resources and motivations that individuals bring to civic participation. I have shown here the importance of also studying the organizational contexts from which individuals volunteer.

One of the next steps in understanding civic life ought to be an examination of organizational reception. For example, although the members of Grace have a desire to volunteer, other community organizations have suspicions about whether, because of perceived racial differences, Korean Americans will be able to relate to those they want to serve. Clearly there is value in considering both the *potential* ethnic religious organizations have to mobilize community involvement and the *barriers* to involvement that being part of such an organization engenders.

These findings also bring a broader understanding of the role congregations, specifically evangelical ones, play in the lives of immigrants. Much of the research on religion and immigration examines the functional aspects of congregations in relation to immigrant adaptation, asking to what extent congregations provide networks and resources for economic advancement. Yet these are functions that any community service or ethnic cultural organization could provide. To focus exclusively on these aspects of religious participation misses what is distinctively religious about the content of what goes on in congregations as related to civic life—that they provide normative understandings, or moral meanings. Moral meanings are part of congregation-based cultural schemas, schemas that help individual members decide who is most deserving of help and which community service activities have the most spiritual value. In short, moral meanings matter for civic practices.

The specific findings about civic practices in multiethnic churches should challenge how we think about the connection of religious individualism to civic participation. Most scholars see individual understandings of religion—which focus on one's personal connection with the supernatural rather than obedience to communal authorities and structures—as inherently antithetical to building the strengths of the broader American community. I show here that the kind of religious individualism necessary to sustain a multiethnic evangelical church may actually *foster* commitment to civic participation. Multiethnic churches do this through providing members with an owned ethic of civic responsibility, which, while individually negotiated, is also transposed to civic participation in diverse arenas other than those specifically connected to local churches. This kind of individualism, which means each individual develops an ethic of care that is used in all settings to ask the question "What is my specific responsibility to provide help?" actually increases individual acts of community service for those who are part of multiethnic churches.

Religious organizations not only influence and shape civic identities and practices but are a major constituent part of civil society. As such, when they change, they have the ability to change other aspects of civil society that might not seem overtly religious. For example, if Korean Americans in multiethnic congregations more widely use Christianity to develop a minority consciousness and an active politic around such consciousness, this will potentially change not only American evangelicalism but also American political life.

Institutional Changes to American Religion

As we think about the future role of Korean Americans in American evangelicalism, my findings are particularly significant in what they say about institutional change. It is not inevitable that Korean Americans will remain separate, adapt to white Christianity, or leave Christianity all together. There is the potential for many Korean Americans to stay within American evangelicalism, while joining with other nonwhite evangelicals in bringing change to the intersection of race, civic participation, and Christianity. I have shown here that ethnic religious contexts provide Korean Americans with diverse pathways for civic adaptation.

The differences in the relationship between civic identities and practices among Korean Americans in second-generation and multiethnic evangelical churches have implications for larger issues facing Korean American evangelicals. During my discussions with Korean American leaders and congregation members in second-generation Korean congregations around the country, it was clear that they face issues similar to those faced by members of Grace, my central case study on such congregations.

A crucial tension for Korean Americans is negotiating their relationship to first-generation Korean congregations. Second-generation churches are often affiliated with and need resources from first-generation congregations. Yet second-generation churches desire a distinctive mission from the first generation. One solution to this tension may come through demographic shifts. The stream of immigration from Korea has decreased in recent years, meaning that fewer first-generation immigrant congregations are needed. As the average age of second-generation Koreans moves from young adulthood to middle adulthood and as more second-generation Koreans achieve economic and educational success, Korean Americans will be able to fully support their own congregations without the financial backing of first-generation churches. As the parent churches become smaller and fewer in number, the second generation may even be in the position of needing to provide financial support to sustain first-generation churches. This could foster significant autonomy for second-generation churches.

Many second-generation Korean leaders emphasize the necessity for the second generation to break their affiliations with first-generation Korean churches in order to broaden civic participation. However, while they may attain physical distance from the first generation, the larger issue will be how they negotiate *ethnic* cultural distance from those in their parents' generation. Second-generation Korean churches generally start because there are second-generation Koreans who have distinct needs and the first generation does not speak English well enough to minister to those needs. For example, the second generation needs independent services, so Christianity can be explained in English and made relevant to a second generation raised primarily in an American cultural context. As they increasingly want to have a broader impact on American life outside the Korean community, however, Korean Americans are beginning to ask if there are actual advantages to being part of a second-generation Korean congregation.

In their answers to this question, Korean Americans in ethnic churches create distinctions from the first generation by being more outward-looking. Although second-generation churches are mainly Korean American, ironically, these religious organizations often try to be culturally *nonethnic*. In practice, this means Korean Americans talk little about being Korean during the course of congregational life. By focusing so much on gaining ethnic distance from first-generation Korean Americans, second-generation congregations do not see how Christianity might be used to justify appreciation for Korean ethnicity or multiethnicity more generally. By trying to divorce Christianity from ethnic culture, they are really adopting an unexamined ethnic culture similar to that of white American Christianity. Korean Americans in these churches often do not recognize that Christianity and ethnicity have the ability to intertwine in a way that connects faith to appreciation for all peoples, a perspective that could strengthen their community service efforts through providing areas of commonality with non-Koreans in their local communities.

Korean American congregations also try to be distinctive from first-generation churches through their denominational affiliations. First-generation Korean congregations are part of central denominations in American society but form separate Korean-specific bodies within them. As second-generation congregations move from being the "child congregations" of adult first-generation churches to having their own self-conscious leadership and economic resources, they often join different mainline or evangelical nondenominational churches from those joined by first-generation Koreans. Unlike those of the first generation, these ethnic second-generation churches do not have separate ethnic-specific bodies within their denominations but are part of the core denominational structure and even leadership.

Through their full participation in denominations, second-generation Korean congregations may have a different influence on American Christianity than first-generation churches. In particular, if second-generation Korean churches find ways to connect Christianity to appreciation of ethnicity, they might bring discussions about ethnicity to the fore in the largely white denominations where their churches are members.

This work also has broader implications for Korean Americans who join multiethnic and pan-Asian congregations. These Korean Americans provide more insight into how new Americans are bringing and may continue to bring changes to American institutions like religion and civic life. Korean American pastors and leaders largely assume that those who leave second-generation Korean evangelical congregations leave the faith altogether. Korean Christian leaders commonly call this the "silent exodus" of the second generation.[5] Yet, rather than leaving Christianity, a significant number of Korean Americans become part of multiethnic and pan-Asian churches.

Some might view the phenomenon of Korean Americans joining multiethnic churches as reflective of a broader trend towards ethnic assimilation. It would be erroneous, however, to use this lens exclusively to interpret the identities of Korean Americans who participate in multiethnic churches. Only between 7 and 10 percent of American congregations are truly multiethnic or multiracial.[6] By participating in a multiracial congregation, Korean Americans are developing social identities outside the mainstream of American religious life and outside American evangelicalism in particular. Manna and the other multiethnic churches where I interviewed Korean Americans are not de facto multiethnic because of demographic changes in their community or because a denominational structure forced them to embrace ethnic diversity; rather, they are intentionally trying to *become* multiethnic.

Korean Americans who are part of multiethnic churches have access to a clearly articulated ideological and theological framework that supports the deliberate embrace of ethnic diversity as central to the mission of Christianity. A person attending Manna, for example, could not walk out of the church without hearing ethnic diversity talked about in sermons, receiving literature discussing the multiethnic vision of the church, or overhearing casual conversations about the struggles involved in the congregation becoming more multiethnic.

On the one hand, Korean Americans who attend Manna and other multiethnic churches have a framework available to them that affirms an ethnically diverse community as *necessary* to a full realization of the Christian mission. On the other hand, a religious individualism may be necessary to keep individuals together who come from diverse ethnic cultures. Evangelicalism makes religious individualism a possibility through valuing an individual relationship with God over commitment to communal structures and creeds. These findings show that religious individualism has the possibility to foster, as it did for Korean Americans at Manna, a commitment to civic participation.

Korean Americans in multiethnic churches will have the most impact on American evangelicalism and broader American civic life if they are able to develop a specifically ethnic version of what sociologist Christian Smith calls an "engaged orthodoxy." By this Smith means that evangelicals are both able to retain distinctively evangelical identities and not lose a sense of what it means to be evangelical, while at the same time engaging with the nonevangelical world around them. Similarly, those in multiethnic churches need to think of themselves as part of a community of nonwhite Christians who also have protean identities, that is, those who are comfortable living in between two cultures, and with whom they can form collective identity coalitions geared toward active mobilization. To be most effective in bringing change, Korean Americans in multiethnic churches must draw boundaries to separate themselves from both first-generation Korean American evangelicals and from a broader and largely white American evangelicalism. In so doing, they occupy a social space from which they have the potential to build bridges with other American evangelicals, while at the same time challenging the accepted ways both of these groups view the relationship between Christianity and ethnicity.

The "New" American Christianity

A study of how new Americans might potentially change American evangelicalism is also a study of changes in American civil society. American evangelicalism is a major movement in American society, with between 25 and 35 percent of Americans identifying as evangelicals. American evangelicals form a major political force in American society.[7] This study is reflective of underlying demographic changes in American Christianity. While scholars of religion focus on the "new religious America," it may be more demographically accurate to focus on the "new Christian America."[8] Nearly two-thirds of the new immigrants (those who came post-1965) are Christians, and many of these are conservative Protestants.[9] Demographically, these new Americans will influence American Christianity by changing its racial and ethnic composition.

It is also important, however, to look beyond demographic shifts to the more fundamental changes a new race and ethnic composition may bring to the doctrines of Christianity and the way Christianity connects with American public life. Many new Americans are more conservative on issues of sexual morality than other American Christians.[10] However, they are often more liberal on issues of economic policy, particularly public policies influencing American racial and ethnic minorities. Members of black congregations also hold this paradoxical view about the relationship of Christianity to morality and economic policy. Yet black Christians, who hold in tension a traditional Christianity with what is generally seen as a liberal ethic of social justice, are *not* often involved in mainstream American evangelical institutions such as seminaries, para–church ministries, and evangelical political coalitions. Korean Americans and Asian Americans more generally, however, *are* becoming increasingly involved as participants and leaders in these American evangelical institutions.

Changes in institutions come in different ways. They can come through new demographic populations and subsequent changes in the structuring of resources. Institutional changes also happen through specific institutional channels. Given these processes, American evangelicalism will be most likely to change evangelical ideas about race and ethnicity if, along with demographic changes, those who have the power to bring such broader changes adopt a specifically Christian theological approach that legitimates ethnic diversity. To find out the potential new Americans have to change American Christianity, we must also ask whether they have the resources to do so. Do they have a different view of race and ethnicity than other American Christians? If so, do they have a collective identity as a group that wants to bring change?

New Americans increasingly have a presence as leaders in institutional evangelicalism. For example, Asian Americans (and particularly East Asians) are beginning to enter into leadership in American evangelical seminaries. In 1995, there were 4,253 Asian Americans enrolled at member institutions of the Association of Theological Schools. This represents a 60 percent increase from 1991. A large number of Asian seminarians are Korean, and many of these are members of the second generation. Asian Americans, and Korean Americans in particular, are the fastest growing major ethnic group in evangelical seminaries, and, importantly, many of them are choosing not to join first-generation ethnic-specific churches.[11] The new categories for the relationship of religion to civic life I have presented here reveal the ways that Korean Americans are already influencing American Christianity's public relationship to race and ethnicity, as well as specific pathways for how they might continue to do so in the future.

To project the possibilities for institutional change, we should also ask if American evangelicalism is open to making ethnic diversity and a fight for the interests of specific ethnic groups part of its institutional framework. In one sense, modern American evangelicalism has not been at the forefront of championing racial and ethnic diversity and equality. When Martin Luther King Jr. talked about the most segregated hour of Christian America being 11 o'clock on Sunday morning (the time when most Christians attend church) his sentiments applied to American evangelicalism as much as or more than any other tradition.[12] Yet, at the same time that the numbers of Asian Americans are increasing in evangelical seminaries, there is also evidence that American evangelicalism is presently undergoing restructuring with respect to race, making more space for discussions of race, at least at the level of individuals. The Southern Baptist Convention, a major evangelical and demographically largely white denomination, has publicly apologized for the sins of their earlier exclusion on the basis of race. Promise Keepers, a large interdenominational evangelical organization for men, focuses on "racial reconciliation among Christians" as one of its goals.[13]

In this institutional evangelical context, the leadership of Korean Americans and other new Americans in coethnic, pan-Asian, multiethnic, and even white congregations, as well as in denominational structures, is currently influencing American evangelicalism as a movement.[14] At the beginning of this book, I mentioned a conversation I had with a white pastor of an evangelical church in northern California. When I told him I was studying Korean American evangelicals, this pastor mentioned he was part of a meeting for his denomination (Evangelical Covenant Church) in which he interacted with the pastor of a multiethnic, largely Asian American church with over 2,000 members. The Korean American pastors of that church were bringing new issues to his denomination's meetings. They sought both to change the denomination's appeal to a nonwhite population and to influence the theological approach of the denomination toward ethnic diversity. During the same period, I talked with a white pastor of a Presbyterian congregation in New York State. When I explained my research, this pastor told me a story about his experiences with the pastor of a second-generation Korean congregation (also a fellow member of the PCUSA). The Korean pastor spoke at a retreat that the white pastor also attended where they talked about the importance of congregations learning to discuss race and ethnicity and make ethnic diversity a core part of their churches' mission.

Because of demographic changes in ethnic composition as a result of recent immigration, the leadership of American Christianity may not continue to be white. In particular, Asian Americans as well as Latino Americans (one-fourth of whom currently self-identify as evangelicals) are already changing the face of American Christianity. With fluency in English and access to educational resources such as degrees from elite seminaries, their voices will not be easily marginalized. In an evangelical institutional context that is beginning to consider race, these new groups may influence institutionalized American evangelicalism's embrace of a racial and ethnic consciousness.

New Americans and American Religion

Though this book focuses on Christianity, the influence that non-Christian religions (which have become more numerous as a result of new immigration) will have in American civic life should not be dismissed. The research I present here has implications for how new Americans who participate in various traditions of Islam, Hinduism, and Buddhism might also influence American civic life. The United States, formerly a Christian nation, has become the world's most religiously diverse nation, home to a rich plurality of traditions. And although researchers have thick descriptions of these new religious traditions, we do not know if the members of non-Western religions will be institutionally incorporated in the American religious and broader civic landscapes.

History tells us there is the possibility of American public religion moving toward diversity. What was formerly a Protestant nation became what sociologist Will Herberg has called a Protestant, Catholic, and Jewish nation—denoting not only the influence of Protestant thought but also the cultural incorporation of Jewish and Catholic heritages into the public conception of American religion.

Integration, adaptation, and change, however, depend on not only the desire of immigrants and their children to become part of American civic life but also the desire of other groups of Americans to receive them and, more important, to allow them to have influence on American civic institutions. The Korean Americans whose voices we hear in these pages ultimately gained some acceptance by local community service organizations, in part, because they are part of American Christianity, a familiar American religious tradition. Second-generation immigrants who inherit a religion from their parents that seems foreign to the U.S. conception of religion may have a different experience of the intersection between religion and civic life from that of those who are part of established religions.[15] Since both race and religion structure acceptance, acceptance may occur to the extent that there are nonethnic forms of the religion in American society. For example, Buddhism is gaining wide and positive reception in American society, practiced by both immigrants and nonimmigrants.[16] Because Buddhism is gaining acceptance and credence in the United States, second-generation immigrants who are Buddhists may experience greater civic incorporation than those second-generation immigrants who are part of other non-Western religions, such as Islam.

The connection of religion to civic life among second-generation immigrants depends also on the acceptance of a religion in a broader global context. Because of the increase in global communication, Americans inherit schemas and consequent attitudes toward a religion before its adherents arrive. For example, while specific traditions of Islam have teachings that facilitate community service, isolated acts of terrorism on the part of Islamic extremists threaten the context of reception for all Islamic immigrants in the United States. This global context potentially threatens also the ability of Islamic mosques and centers to form civic ties with other organizations in the United States.[17] While religious participation may not be organizationally advantageous for civic incorporation among second-generation immigrants whose religion does not have a positive context of reception, it may still be advantageous on the individual level—to the extent that religious ideologies may motivate civic participation among individual adherents.

Recreating Categories

Census estimates tell us that, due in large part to recent immigration, by the middle of this century, nonwhite Americans will make up over 50 percent of the population.[18] In this context, it is vitally important to understand the central role religion plays in the social construction of civic responsibility among the children of new immigrants. Those who are born in the United States are citizens by birth. Yet, even among those who have citizenship, the social construction of civic responsibility varies. Individuals draw different views of what it means to be a good American from public rhetoric about who good Americans are and what they do. At the same time, local church commitments are a lens through which Korean American evangelicals interpret unique histories of immigration and discrimination as ethnic minorities. Religious identities overlap with and structure ethnic and class identities; in this process, Korean Americans adopt patterned and church-based individual ideas of local civic responsibility. These reclassifications not only are important to Korean Americans but hopefully will be important to all Americans, as "they" become "we," and we reshape together what it means to be a good American.

Appendix A: Data and Methods

This detailed description of methods will be most useful to those interested in doing research on civic life among other groups of second-generation immigrants and to those concerned generally about the intersection of theory, method, and analysis. I discuss here the methodological choices surrounding my selection of Korean Americans as the group for this study, the churches as cases, the community in which they were located, and how my approach to research guided analysis of the data.

STUDYING SECOND-GENERATION KOREANS

Several factors make Korean Americans a good group in which to examine the relationship between diverse ethnic forms of religious participation and civic life. Some of these factors I discussed in the introduction: for example, young adult second-generation Korean Americans are a distinct cohort and have a likelihood of achieving educational and economic success. Because of an interest in the relationship between religion and civic life, a more central reason for studying Korean Americans is the important role religion plays in the Korean American community.

Beyond the academic reasons for studying a particular group, research that necessitates face-to-face interaction with those being studied makes it more difficult to obscure the relationship a researcher has to the population he or she studies. When I started this research, my respondents asked me why I wanted to study Korean Americans. What they usually meant by this was not the sociological factors I discussed earlier but the deeper question: Why are you, "a white person," doing research among Korean Americans? I answered by telling them that my postcollege employment in university religious life, where I worked with Korean American students, made me curious about how religion and race intersect in American society. Many were skeptical and told me if I was really interested in issues of race and religion, studying black Americans would probably be more worthwhile because, as they explained, "American society largely thinks of race in terms of black and white." The question of why I studied Korean Americans continued to arise during the initial stages of this research. Although I did nothing to encourage such rumors, several times I overheard that someone in one of the churches believed I had a particular personal interest in studying Korean Americans because my husband was Korean or my family had adopted a Korean child. Neither of these rumors was true.

I should note here that by the end of the research I felt very much accepted by Korean Americans at both Grace and Manna. However, reflecting on my role as a researcher became an important scholarly facet of this research; their initial insistence, for example, that I must have some very personal motive for doing this research seemed to belie an underlying feeling among the Korean Americans I interviewed that they were not significant enough to be worthy of academic study. My respondents believed they were largely outside what they perceived as the "true" American racial categories of black and white. As I discussed earlier, this perception of being a new group, one exterior to current racial categories, has important implications for how Korean Americans understand civic identities and political narratives and practices.

A second question that came up often, one borne out of the necessity of their evangelical mission, was "And are you a Christian?" I answered this question with the simple reply "Yes." Researchers have different reasons for disclosing or withholding parts of their identities. Some, like myself, choose to emphasize aspects of their own history to create common ground with those among whom they are conducting research.[1] Others, for equally good reasons, stress the importance of withholding facets of their identity. My choice had advantages and disadvantages. Because I was different from my respondents in ethnic background and racial categorization, sharing a common religious identity was a way of decreasing barriers. I reasoned that if they saw me as an insider to Christianity they would probably act more "natural" around me and spend less time worrying about my salvation.

They did act more authentically. The disadvantage was that they used Christian words and lingo that they might have explained to an outsider, which might have given me greater clarity in observing how they understood their faith. However, presenting myself as a Christian meant I gained exposure to parts of their religious communities and lives that someone seen as more of an outsider might not have had access to.

GAINING ENTRÉE TO GRACE AND MANNA

Naming the Community
In deciding not to disclose the actual name of Old Town, I was fully aware of the concerns among a growing number of researchers who argue that it is important to identify communities by their actual names in order to allow other scholars to do comparison studies. Such identification also enables a larger body of researchers to hold one another accountable for conducting ethical research.[2]

In the context of this study, however, I quickly realized more anonymity was needed. I was continually surprised by the extent to which Korean American Christians are connected with one another. After a few months of field research, for example, I discovered that several of my respondents—who as adults lived on separate coasts—had been part of the same Korean church youth group as children. I soon discovered that to name the specific community would be to risk disclosing the identity of my respondents. This was coupled with the realization that, as one who did not grow up among Korean Christians, I did not have a completely accurate idea of what could be classified as personal information.

The Interviews

The bulk of analysis presented here comes from 92 interviews I conducted with second-generation Korean Americans. Forty-five of these interviewees attended either Grace or Manna. Forty-seven were Korean Americans in seven different second-generation Korean or multiethnic congregations around the United States. Forty-eight percent of my respondents were men, and 52 percent are women. All were American citizens, and self-identified as Protestant evangelicals. They were predominantly young adults between 21 and 40 years old. Nearly all had at least a four-year college degree or further graduate education, and most were working in the professional sector or attending graduate school. In addition, five interviews were done with non-Korean members of Manna, and six interviews were done for background context with first-generation Koreans and Korean nationals, resulting in a total of 103 interviews.

I started research at Grace and Manna by doing interviews with the pastors and leaders of each church. I wanted to interview Korean Americans who were fairly involved in their congregations, those who attended weekly services and participated in other activities of the church. To locate members for interviews, I initially asked the pastors of each congregation for names of those to interview in the churches. I asked specifically for names of Korean Americans who are leaders or significantly involved in the life of the congregation. At Manna, the multiethnic church, I also interviewed non-Koreans to discover their perspective about the participation of Korean Americans in the church, the interaction of Manna with the community, and its more general approach to civic life. The purpose of these interviews was to discover the perspective non-Koreans have about the participation of Korean Americans in the church, the interaction of Manna with the community, and its more general approach to civic life.

I conducted most of the interviews over a meal at a restaurant, in a local coffee shop, or in respondents' homes. At the beginning of each interview, I made time for my respondents to ask any questions they had about the study, my personal background, or what I would do with the interview materials. Each person gave me permission to tape our discussion, with the agreement that I protect confidentiality. Afterward, I made extensive notes on my insights regarding the study's central questions.

Those I interviewed at Grace and Manna mentioned geographic differences in how Korean Americans understand civic participation and the relationship of Korean Americans to other groups. For example, because of the Los Angeles riots, those at

Grace and Manna thought I might get a very different story on how African Americans and Korean Americans interact if I talked with Korean Americans on the West Coast in addition to those I interviewed on the East Coast.[3] Consequently, I initiated data collection in other areas to compare my initial results to results from Korean Americans who were also young professionals, Christians, and attended either a second-generation or multiethnic church outside of Old Town.[4]

To that end, 47 of the 92 Korean Americans were from seven different churches located in small towns, suburbs, and urban areas in California, Michigan, Illinois, New Jersey, and New York. I found these respondents through their former participation in a campus Christian organization at an elite university, through members from Grace or Manna who referred them to me, or through churches that are well known among second-generation Koreans.[5] I tried to interview some of the leaders of each of the churches that these Korean Americans attended. These national interviews were conducted either in person or over the phone. I talked in person with those who attended congregations in New Jersey, New York, or California. Additional interviews in Michigan, Illinois, California, and New York were conducted over the phone.

I was initially hesitant about doing phone interviews, concerned that without the mannerisms apparent during face-to-face discussions I would gain significantly less information. However, I found that phone interviews actually allowed me to more easily bridge the gulf of being a non-Korean researcher collecting data among a group of Korean Americans. Over the phone, my respondents more quickly forgot or never considered that I was not Korean. After several of the phone interviews, individuals even asked me if I was Korean American.

PARTICIPANT-OBSERVATION AND SURVEY AT GRACE AND MANNA

A central goal of this research was to understand how narratives and practices of civic life relate to one another. I wanted to spend time observing Korean Americans in the context of religious communities and in broader civic life. To this end, I was an active participant at both Grace and Manna during the same nine-month period, from January 2002 to September 2002. Because the churches met at different times, I was able to regularly attend services for each. In addition, I tried, whenever possible, to attend small groups and to participate in volunteer and other activities sponsored by the churches. As soon as possible after participating in services and church events, I typed extensive notes about the setting and nature of the event, as well as any mention of participation in life outside the congregation or of the connection between religion and civic life. To gain additional information about organizational life, I did a literature review of written materials from each church. This included reviewing newsletters, general mailings, and bulletins and participating in e-mail lists.

Although I was primarily interested in how Korean Americans create categories for religion and civic life, it was also important to situate those I talked with in the context of American civic practices. The pastors for Grace and Manna gave me permission to conduct, during a Sunday service, a survey of community service and political involvement. I drew the survey questions largely from the Social Capital Benchmark Survey (2000), a national public access survey and data set that includes questions about social networks, religious life, and civic participation in American communities.

TABLE A.1. Summary of Data Collection

Organizational		Individual		
Participant	Observation	Church leader interviews	Member interviews	Survey
Grace	9 months	3	19	N = 83
Manna	9 months	5	18	N = 142
National second generation	3 churches	3	23	
National Multiethnic	4 churches	4	17	

Total interviews = 92; Total survey = 225.

In appendix B, I provide a list of the questions I asked in the church surveys. Conducting a survey during a service allowed me to achieve a high response rate of 83 percent. Table A.1 provides a more detailed overview of the entire data collection.

RESEARCH FRAMEWORK AND DATA ANALYSIS

Although previous researchers provided me with insight into religion and civic life among Americans in general and among American evangelicals specifically, I wanted to make sure I was not studying this relationship among Korean Americans solely by measuring how Korean Americans compare to these other groups. To do so would be to assume a priori that Korean Americans understand the connection between religion and civic life in the same way as other groups of Americans. I wanted not only to apply concepts from other theories about religion and civic life but also to use these cases of Korean Americans in churches with different ethnic compositions to help myself understand how Korean Americans see civic life on their own terms.

My approach to data analysis resulted from this underlying conceptualization of the research process. Important to my thinking were facets of sociologist Michael Burawoy's extended case method, which suggests starting with existing theories about a phenomenon and allowing what he describes as "a running exchange between analysis and existing theory, in which the latter is reconstructed on the basis of emergent anomalies."[6] Practically, this meant that existing research about civic life for American evangelicals and Americans generally shaped my initial interview guides. Yet, as new categories emerged from the fieldwork, my interview guide periodically underwent minor changes reflecting the insight my respondents gave me about how they see civic life. For example, in my first few interviews, I asked how Korean Americans understand "citizenship." I quickly learned, however, that my respondents did not resonate with this question but really thought more about what it means to be a "good American." Consequently, I changed subsequent interview guides to ask what it meant to be a good American.

During and after the interviewing process, I began verbatim transcriptions. I personally transcribed 50 percent of the interviews and hired assistants to transcribe the other 50 percent. I then began hand-coding the data. I coded most of the interviews and field notes for themes related to civic life and the specific relationship between religion and civic life. Instead of proceeding through strict hypothesis testing, I let themes about the distinct questions I asked emerge from the data. I then tested these themes by recoding the interviews.[7]

In appendix B, I provide copies of the final interview guides I used for the research. I have also included the questions asked about civic practices in the survey conducted at both Grace and Manna. This research received approval from the Cornell University Human Subjects Review Board.

Appendix B: Interview and Survey Guides

INTERVIEW GUIDE

Script: Let me start by introducing myself. I am a researcher interested in the role that churches play in the lives of second-generation immigrants. I want to have discussions, in particular, with Korean Americans to better help me understand how Korean Americans think about their faith. Do you have any questions about the research that I might answer for you?

Work
Let me start by asking you some basic questions.

1. What kind of professional work do you do? How did you come to choose this particular work?Let's switch now to talking more about your family.
2. Could you tell me the story of why your parents came to the United States?
3. From what you remember, could you tell me about the town where you grew up and what that town or neighborhood was like?

History of Church Participation
4. If you attended church as a child, how about the church in which you grew up? How big was it? How involved were you? What kinds of things do you remember enjoying as a kid? What kinds of things didn't you like about it?
5. What about the churches you have attended since then? Ethnicity? Location?
6. Have you always attended Korean American congregations? If you have, maybe you could tell me a little about why you chose to stay part of a Korean American congregation? Or why you

chose to try other types of congregations and what that experience was like?

Religious Beliefs
7. Reflecting over your life, how did you become a Christian? (Alternative: What does it mean for you to be a Christian?)
8. How would you describe the central things you believe as part of your faith?
9. Related, what kind of things does being a Christian influence in your life?
10. Some people say that "being a good Christian necessitates helping the poor and the needy." How would you respond to that kind of statement?

Current Church
Now I am going to ask you some questions about your current church.

11. How would you describe the neighborhood where it is located? Could you tell me about the relationship your church has with the neighborhood where it's located?
12. In what ways is your congregation similar to other Korean congregations (alternative: other multiethnic churches) and what ways do you think it is different?
13. What kinds of non-Korean churches have you attended? (Alternative, if respondent attends a non-Korean church: If you have attended Korean congregations, could you describe that experience?) How would your current church compare to these churches?

Current Church Involvement
Let me ask you some more specific questions about your participation in your current congregation.

14. Could you tell me why you decided to attend this church?
15. Could you tell me about your role in the congregation? In what kind of activities do you participate regularly?
16. How do you think that you are the same or different from Korean Americans who attend multiethnic congregations/ white congregations (Alternative: Korean churches)?

Civic Life
Now, I want to ask you a few questions about your life outside your congregation.

17. What kinds of activities are you involved in that are not related to church?
18. Are you an American citizen? If so, when did you become an American citizen?
19. How would you describe what it means to be a "good American" ? By your definition, do you think of yourself as a "good American"? (If no, what kinds of things are keeping you from being a better American?)

20. How did you develop your ideas about what it means to be a good American?
21. Does your church help you to be a better American? If so, how?
22. What does it take to "fit in" to American society?
23. How do you think of your role in American politics?
24. If you were volunteering in your community, what types of people do you think you would most like to help? What draws you to these sorts of people?
25. In contrast, what kinds of people would you shy away from or find it difficult to help?

Ethnic and Civic Identities
Let me ask you a few questions about being Korean.

26. Could you start by telling me a little about the role being Korean plays in your life?
27. What is your relationship with your family like?
28. When do you think of yourself as "Asian American" and not "Korean American"?
29. When do you think of yourself as "American" and when do you think of yourself as "Korean?"
30. Do you think that others view you as an American? Why or why not?
31. What experiences do you have with discrimination? Could you tell me the story of the experience that was most significant for you?

Interethnic and Interracial Relationships
32. I am interested in knowing how you think the Korean community relates to other nonwhite communities. Could you give me some thoughts about this?
33. Could you describe the relationship of the African American community to the Korean community? How does this relationship play out in your own life, if at all?
34. Do you, for instance, ever sense increased solidarity between African Americans and Korean Americans based on a common minority status?
35. Do you think of, for example, the Japanese as being "more American" because they have been in the United States longer than Korean Americans? (Why or why not?)
36. Are there other questions that I should be asking to better understand the experience of second-generation Korean Americans in American society?

Demographics
For the sake of bookkeeping, there are some questions I would like to ask you to help me situate you among other individuals I have talked with.

37. Age:
38. Marital status/ethnicity and occupation of spouse:
39. Education:

40. Occupation:
41. Parent's Occupation:
42. How many siblings? Place in birth order?
43. Currently live where? With whom?
44. Korean language skills? (How would you describe your Korean language skills? Are you bilingual, for example?)
45. Denomination of church you currently attend:
46. Address of church/type of neighborhood of church:
47. Grew up where? (ethnic makeup/socioeconomic status of neighborhood)

CHURCH SURVEY

I am conducting a survey about the relationship between church participation and community life. I hope this questionnaire will also help the church think about its present life and future plans. Please take a few minutes to respond to these questions. In most cases, you can just circle the response that best fits you. There are no right answers. When you really cannot answer, just skip to the next question. Your individual answers will be anonymous and held in the strictest confidence. When you have completed the survey, give it me or one of the ushers as you leave. I will be standing at the back of the sanctuary. Thank-you

First, some questions about your church attendance.

1. How long have you been attending this church? (Circle one answer)
   1 Do not regularly attend this church
   2 One year or less
   3 Two to four years
   4 Five to nine years
2. What factors were *most* a part of your decision to attend Grace/Manna?
   _____(Please list)
3. Not including weddings and funerals, how often do you attend church services? (Circle one answer)
   1 Every week (or more often)
   2 Almost every week
   3 Once or twice a month
   4 A few times per year
   5 Less often than that
4. If you attend church more than once a week, please write an estimate of the number of hours you spend per week in all church activities. (Include time spent at small group, discipleship of church members, etc.)
   _____(Number of hours)
5. Approximately how much driving time (in minutes) does it take you to get to church? _____ (One-way time in minutes)
6. In the past 12 months, have you taken part in any sort of activity with people at your church other than attending Sunday morning services? (Circle one answer)
   1 Yes If yes, please list activities that you are regularly involved in
   _____

2 No

Below are some questions about the community where you live.

7. What is the name of the town where you currently live? _____(Name of town).
8. How many years have you lived in your community? (Circle one answer)
   1 Less than one year
   2 One to five years
   3 Six to ten years
   4 Eleven to twenty years
   5 More than twenty years
   6 All my life
9. Do you expect to be living in your community five years from now? (Circle one answer)
   1 Yes
   2 No
   3 Don't know
10. If you were going to volunteer, what community would you be most likely to volunteer in? (Circle one answer)
    1 The community where my church is located
    2 The community where my house is located
    3 Church and home are in same community
    4 Some other neighborhood or local community
       If 4, Please write name of town _____
    5 Would not be likely to volunteer in a local community
11. If you were volunteering, where would you be most likely to locate volunteer opportunities? (Circle one answer)
    1 A community volunteer organization (such as United Way...)
    2 Through my college or university
    3 Through my church
    4 Some other place
       If 4, please write place _____
    5 My own personal investigation
    What kind of community activities are you involved in ?
12. Any community service organization that is faith-based or church-sponsored, <u>such as but not exclusive</u> to Habitat for Humanity or a Pregnancy Center? (Circle one answer)
    1 Yes
       If yes, please write organization _____
    2 No
13. A parents' association, like the PTA or PTO, or other school support or service groups? (Circle one answer)
    1 Yes
       If yes, please write organization _____
    2 No

14. A charity or social welfare organization that provides services in such fields as health or service to the needy? (Circle one answer)
    1 Yes,
       If yes, please list organization _____
    2 No
15. Ethnic, nationality, or civil right's organization, such as the Association for Asian American students or Korean American student's association? (Circle one answer)
    1 Yes
       If yes, please write organization _____
    2 No
    3 Not applicable (less than 18 years old)
16. Other public interest groups, political action groups, political clubs, or party committees? (Circle one answer)
    1 Yes
       If yes, please write organization _____
    2 No

    The next set of questions are about public affairs.
17. How interested are you in politics and national affairs? (Circle one answer)
    1 Very interested
    2 Somewhat interested
    3 Not at all interested
18. Are you currently registered to vote? (Circle one answer)
    1 Yes
    2 No
    3 Not eligible to vote
19. Did you vote in the presidential election in 2000 when George Bush ran against Al Gore? (Circle one answer)
    1 Yes, voted
    2 No
    3 Less than 18 years old in 2000
       Which of the following things have you done in the PAST 12 MONTHS?
20. Have you signed a petition? (Circle one answer)
    1 Yes
    2 No
21. Attended a political meeting or rally? (Circle one answer)
    1 Yes
    2 No
22. Worked on a community project? (Circle one answer)
    1 Yes
    2 No
23. Donated blood? (Circle one answer)
    1 Yes
    2 No
    3 Can't give blood

24. Helped out a stranger? (Circle one answer)
    1 Yes
    2 No
25. How many times during the PAST 12 MONTHS have you volunteered? (By volunteering, I mean any unpaid work you've done to help people besides your family and friends or people you work with.)
    _____ (Number of times)
26. Thinking POLITICALLY and SOCIALLY, how would you describe your own general outlook? (Circle one answer)
    1 Very conservative
    2 Moderately conservative
    3 Middle-of-the-road
    4 Moderately liberal
    5 Very liberal
    6 Something else. If you circled number 6, please describe
    _____
27. What is your primary occupation? (Circle one answer)
    1 College student
    2 Graduate student
      If 2, please write area of study_____
    3 Work full-time
      If 3, please write occupation _____
    4 Not applicable (under 18 years old)
28. If you work full-time, how many hours do you work per week?
    _____ (Hours per week).
29. If you work full-time, how long does it take you to get to your workplace (one-way trip) on a typical day? _____ (Answer in minutes, time one-way)
30. What is your marital status? (Circle one answer)
    1 Currently married
    2 Separated
    3 Divorced
    4 Widowed
    5 Never married
31. Including yourself, how many adults (those over 18 years old) live in your household? _____ (Persons-people)
32. When choosing a church, how important is it that the church have other people of your ethnicity? (Circle one answer)
    1 Very important
    2 Somewhat important
    3 Not at all important
    4 Not applicable

Now a few questions about where you fit within the American population as a whole?

33. How old are you? _____(Years)

34. Are you: (Circle one answer)
    1 Male
    2 Female
35. What is the highest level of school you have completed or the highest degree you have received? (Circle one number)
    1 Less than high school
    2 High school graduate
    3 Some college
    4 Associate's degree
    5 Bachelor's degree
    6 Graduate degree
36. Do you consider yourself to be: (Circle ALL numbers that apply)
    Caucasian-American?   1 Yes   2 No
    African-American?   1 Yes   2 No
    Asian-American?   1 Yes   2 No
    Hispanic-American?   1 Yes   2 No
    Native-American?   1 Yes   2 No
    Other   1 Yes   2 No
        → If Other, please write _____
37. Would you say your background is Chinese, Korean, Japanese, Filipino, or something else? (Circle one answer)
    1 Chinese
    2 Korean
    3 Japanese
    4 Filipino
    5 Asian Indian
    6 Vietnamese
    7 Cambodian
    8 Other
    If 8, please specify_____
38. Are you an American citizen? (Circle one answer)
    1 Yes
    2 No
39. If under 18 years old, what is the occupation of your parents?
    Mother _____(Please write occupation)
    Father _____(Please write occupation)
    Could you please give your exact address?
    _____

   (Note: This information will only be used to determine demographic information for the area where you live and otherwise will be kept confidential)

   Thank-you for filling out this survey.
   Please write any additional comments on the back of this sheet.

Notes

CHAPTER 1

1. The names of the two central churches in this study and the name of the community in which they were located have been changed. In addition, I changed the names of all individuals I interviewed.

2. See Smith, Emerson, Gallagher, Kennedy, and Sikkink 1998, for example, which provides an overview of the place of American evangelicalism in American society.

3. I discuss the notion of "schema" further in chapter 2. See also DiMaggio 1997, Sewell 1996.

4. According to the National Center for Health Statistics Annual Reports, during the 1990s births to immigrants accounted for 54 percent of population growth. According to the 2000 Current Population Survey, pg. 9, currently, about 12 percent of the 281.4 million Americans were foreign-born. This statistic includes naturalized citizens, resident legal aliens, and resident illegal aliens (2000 Current Population Survey, U.S. Census Bureau).

5. Here I am referring to the Hart-Celler reforms of 1965. See Hirschman, Kasinitz, and DeWind 1999.

6. In *Immigrant America*, sociologists Alejandro Portes and Ruben Rumbaut write: "never before has the United States received immigrants from so many countries, from such different social and economic backgrounds, and for so many reasons. Although pre–World War I European immigration was by no means homogenous, the differences between successive waves of Irish, Italians, Jews, Greeks, Poles often pale by comparison with the current diversity." Portes and Rumbaut 1996, p. 7.

7. At the time of the 2000 U.S. census, there were 1,076,872 Koreans in the United States. Those who were born in Korea but came to the United

States as young children often become naturalized citizens and refer to themselves as second-generation. Most statistics describing the number of second-generation immigrants do not take into account the latter group.

8. See Kitano and Daniels 2000.

9. See Eck 2001, who discusses the increasing religious diversity of American society, as well as Wuthnow and Hackett 2003.

10. See, in particular, Lee 1996.

11. See Wuthnow 1991.

12. Source: 1997 and 1998 Gallup Polls (as reported in Gallup and Lindsay, 1999). Some researchers have challenged these church attendance figures. See, for example, Hadaway, Marler, and Chaves 1993.

13. See Putnam 2000; Verba, Schlozman, and Brady 1995; Wuthnow 1999.

14. See Tocqueville 1969 [1835, 1840].

15. How the number of evangelicals is classified depends on whether surveys examine core beliefs or just ask for self-classification as "evangelical." See Smith et al. 1998.

16. See, for example, recent articles about American evangelicals and their influence on American public life: Goodstein 2005; Leland 2004; Luo 2005; Mahler 2005.

17. See Wuthnow 1988.

18. See Lincoln and Mamiya 1990.

19. See Wuthnow 1988. Perhaps the evangelical religious Left is best characterized by theologian Ron Sider's book *Rich Christians in an Age of Hunger* 1997, which currently has over 350,000 copies in print.

20. Both Bellah, Madsen, Sullivan, Swidler, and Tipton 1985 and Wuthnow 1999 explore the role of individualism in American religion and its connection to religion's influence on civic life. See Marsden 1991 for an overview of American evangelicalism.

21. See Regnerus, Smith, and Sikkink 1998, who discuss historical changes in financial giving among American evangelicals.

22. See Gordon 1964, p. 67.

23. See Ebaugh and Chafetz 2000; Min 1992.

24. See Alumkal 2001; Cha 2001; Chong 1998.

25. See Ecklund and Park 2005, who also make this point. Carolyn Chen (2002) provides one of the few studies of immigrant religion and civic life.

26. See Herberg 1955.

27. See Lee 1996.

28. At the time I began this study, there were 239,228 second-generation Korean Americans living in the United States. The number of Korean Americans is from the 2000 census and refers to those born in the United States, with parents who were from Korea.

29. See Alba and Nee 2003 for a further discussion of recent immigration.

30. According to the former Immigration Naturalization Service, Korean Immigration had the following pattern For 1970–80, 271,956; for 1981–90, 338,800; and for 1991–96, 113,667.

31. See Verba, Schlozman, and Brady 1995, who explain that increases in class and education generally increase participation in a local community. According to 1999 census data on household income, all Korean Americans, both first- and second-generation, have a median household income of $40,037. The median household income for the U.S. population was $41,994. Scholars of Korean Americans estimate that this number is much higher for adult second-generation Koreans and far surpasses that of the U.S. population as a whole; Kitano and Daniels 2000.

32. See Zhou 2004.

33. See Chai 1998, whose respondents also used this saying.

34. This is not to say that there was no recorded presence of Christianity in Korea before the twentieth century. See the website of the Catholic Bishops' Conference of Korea at: www.cbck.or.kr/eng/ccik/history_03.htm, for a brief history of Catholicism's presence in Korea as early as the early eighteenth century.

35. See Kim 2000 for a more extensive discussion of South Korea's unique affinity to Protestant Christianity. See, in particular, pp. 117–118.

36. See Hunt 1980.

37. Space limitations do not allow me to do justice to the vast and detailed history of Korean Christianity. For more extensive discussions, see Chung 1995; Clark 1986; Hunt 1980. And for a discussion of more general aspects of Korean history, which includes a discussion of Christianity's introduction to Korea, see Cummings 1997.

38. See Portes and Rumbaut 1996, who discuss the professional class status of some groups of post-1965 immigrants.

39. See Hurh and Kim 1990.

40. See Warner 2001.

41. In addition to Min 1992, see also Kwon, Kim, and Warner 2001 for references to studies on first-generation Korean churches.

42. Min 1992 also makes this point.

43. Warner 2001 also makes this point.

44. See Lee 1996, an important article in *Christianity Today*, a widely circulated evangelical Christian publication, for a discussion of the "silent exodus" of not only second-generation Koreans but also other second-generation Asian Americans from the immigrant churches of their parents. Chai 2001 also mentions that Korean church leaders talk about the "silent exodus" of Korean Americans.

45. See Min and Kim 2005, who show that 54 percent of those born in Korea who came to the United States at a young age and second-generation Koreans identified as Protestants. This study was based on a small number of respondents (N=200). However, it is the only known random-sample survey of religiosity among second-generation Korean Americans.

46. See Warner 2001.

47. Min and Kim 2002 discuss the growing number of pan-Asian congregations in their introduction. Emerson and Chai Kim 2003 provide typologies for multiracial and multiethnic congregations.

48. See Alumkal 1999 and Chai 2001 for discussions of the role of coethnic Korean fellowships and churches in the formation of Korean and Christian identities.

49. See Edgell 2005, who stresses the importance of studying local community ecology for the fullest understanding of congregational life.

50. See Hart 1992 and Wuthnow 1991 for a further discussion of resources for civic participation as including the motivations and meanings that foster civic participation.

51. See Min 1992.

52. See Allahyari 2000; Tipton 1982.

53. Emerson and Smith 2000 argue this. See also Ammerman 1997; Becker 1998; Swidler 1986 for broader discussions of organizational culture.

54. This is a quotation taken from the Holy Bible, Luke 10 (1978). The popular story is one of Jesus speaking with an expert on the Jewish law who asks Jesus the question "Who is my neighbor?" that is, "For whom do I have a responsibility to provide care?"

CHAPTER 2

1. Swidler 1986 describes cultural "tool-kits" and Wuthnow 1996 describes cultural "rag bags" as the collections of resources individuals bring to certain situations and use in situation-dependent ways to make sense of their lives. See Geertz 1973, who views culture as shared systems of symbols and as more coherent than these previous views.

2. See Swidler 1986; Wuthnow 1987, 1996 for a discussion of this view of culture in greater detail.

3. See, for example, Swidler 1986, 2000; Wuthnow 1987, which bring in the importance of understanding nonmaterial aspects of culture.

4. See Griswold 2005.

5. For example, see Bourdieu 1973, 1984, examining how individuals' actions and propensities are constrained by the various forms of capital they have access to. See also, for example, Friedland and Alford 1991, who see institutions as providing cultural realities that constrain the behavior of individuals and organizations.

6. Here I draw on the work of Sewell 1992 and others who use his ideas in their empirical work (Edgell 2005; Gallagher 2003). Sewell argues, as I do in this book, that culture can be both constraining and enabling.

7. For example, see Geertz 1973.

8. See Swidler 1986, 2000, who is generally linked with this view. See also Martin 1992.

9. See Jepperson and Swidler 1994.

10. See DiMaggio 1997, p. 269, for context of this quotation.

11. See Edgell 2005; Sewell 1996.

12. See Meyer and Rowan 1977.

13. The backdrop for this way of understanding an institutional approach to culture is found in Wuthnow 1987.

14. See, for example, D'Aunno, Succi, and Alexander 2000. See also Jepperson and Meyer 1991, who, while they discuss change, do so primarily at the level of variation in organizational forms between nation-states.

15. See, for example, Wilde 2004. The work of sociologist Melissa Wilde, while not directly comparing Catholicism to other religious institutions, does show how highly codified Catholicism is as a religious institution and how difficult it would be to bring change to the institutional level.

16. See Edgell 2005 for an elaborate discussion of different approaches to ministry. See also Becker 1999 for a discussion of how different congregations adopt approaches to organizational problems surrounding race based on factors other than their denomination or faith tradition.

17. See Cerulo 1997 for an overview of recent sociological research on identities. Some social theorists think the word "identity" should be replaced with other more conceptually useful terms. See, for example, Brubaker and Cooper 2000. I think these criticisms are overcome by specifying identity at different levels. See Owens 2003.

18. See primarily Owens 2003, p. 214. See also Park 2004, who uses Owen's framework to interpret the identities of young Asian American leaders.

19. See Owens 2003, p. 224.

20. See Lamont 1992.

21. See also Lamont and Molnar 2002 for a discussion of boundaries across the social sciences.

22. Gamson 1992, for example, thinks that a common collective consciousness is a crucial underpinning for the development of a social movement.

23. See Cerulo 1997.

24. See Smith 1998, p. 118.

25. For examples of scholarship that appropriates Smith's theory of subcultural identity in the realm of gender, see Denton 2004; Gallagher 2003.

26. See Ignatiev 1995 for a further discussion of the whiteness framework.

27. See Bartkowski 2004, p. 112. In programs such as Promise Keepers, an influential national evangelical ministry for men, the "race problem" has been about creating better individuals who will have more black friends but very little about changing the American institutions of education or work. According to sociologist John Bartkowski (2004, p. 113), this means that "defining racism as a personal sin enables men to confront their hidden racial animus and to develop interracial friendships that were previously absent in their lives.... Yet, despite these admirable developments, the Promise Keepers' commitments to eradicating prejudice 'one man at a time' generally forestalls discussions about the social character of racial stratification in American society."

CHAPTER 3

1. As I mentioned in chapter 1, a first-generation church provides financial support and a building space to Grace. This congregation has a Korean name, and I have given it a Korean pseudonym.

2. The Westminster Confession of Faith is an explanation of Christian doctrine from the reform tradition of Christianity. For more information and a reprint of the confession, see the website of the Presbyterian Church in America, at: www.pcanet.org/general/cof_contents.htm.

3. The flag has a white field, representing the purity of Christ. There is a blue canton, with a red cross in the middle, to symbolize the crucifixion of Christ.

4. Field notes from 4/21/02.

5. See appendix A for a further explanation of demographics and other information about Old Town.

6. Ideally Grace would have been located closer to Old Town; but in an urban area, being 10 miles away from a city is considered close.

7. From U.S. Department of the Census 2000.

8. From U.S. Department of the Census 2000.

9. See appendix A for a further discussion of how I presented myself when studying these two churches.

10. "English ministry" refers to a service held in English. An English ministry is generally the English-speaking service of a first-generation immigrant congregation. They vary in the extent to which they are separate congregations or merely a service for a first-generation church.

11. Information about history of church compiled from interviews with church leaders.

12. Min and Kim 2002 contend that most second-generation Korean congregations are located within or affiliated with first-generation congregations.

13. A term used by evangelical Christians to mean keeping one another focused on obeying the commands of Christ.

14. The survey resulted in over 80 participants (N = 83).

15. I use Michele Lamont's (1992, p. 14) definition of upper middle class as "college-educated professionals, managers, and businessmen."

16. During the time I was there, I met only one person who was outside of these categories, a young person of college age who was enrolled in a practical program, and not planning to attend a prestigious four-year university.

17. Interview conducted 3/14/02.

18. See Smith, Emerson, Gallagher, Kennedy, and Sikkink 1998, p. 242.

19. Interview conducted 3/14/02. Joshua also described the congregation as "evangelical" in an interview conducted 4/10/02.

20. For a broader discussion of varieties of evangelicalism and its distinctions from Christian fundamentalism, see Marsden 1991.

21. Stott is currently rector emeritus of All Souls, Langham Place, London. He is mentioned often in world evangelism conferences as a global evangelical leader who has a great impact on world evangelism. See the website of AD2000 and Beyond, at: www.ad2000.org/celebrate/ezemandu.htm. See also the website of the 1999 conference of the International Fellowship of Evangelical Students held in Seoul, Korea (at: www.e-n.org.uk/ifes.htm), which specifically references Stott as a mentor for Korean churches and student evangelism. I attended this conference, at which Stott was one of the main speakers. Throughout the conference, I noticed that participants from Korea and from African nations affectionately called him "Papa John," a gendered term reflecting Stott's position as a "father" within evangelicalism. Stott, an elderly man, needed to have informal Korean "bodyguards" surround him to keep Christian leaders from the more than 180 different nations present at the conference from constantly approaching him to ask for a moment of spiritual

insight or an autograph. The previous observation attests to Stott's influence as a global evangelical leader.

22. A stole is a liturgical garment worn over the black robe that covers street clothing for liturgical services.

23. In my long interviews, I asked questions about the respondent's Korean language skills.

24. Communion is a ritual in Christian churches where members drink and eat juice or wine and bread or crackers to commemorate the death and resurrection of Jesus Christ. The juice or wine symbolizes the blood of Christ, and the bread symbolizes the body of Christ, which Christians believe was given as a substitutionary offering to pay for their human wrongdoing or sins against God.

25. Field notes from 3/31/02.

26. The specific biblical passage Pastor Chung referred to was from John 51.

27. Quotation from "Two Becoming One," a brochure that discusses the history of the church.

28. Interview conducted 4/18/02.

29. Interview conducted 5/14/02.

30. Field notes from 3/5/02.

31. See Deuteronomy 32–Joshua 7.

32. Survey completed at Manna main congregation, 10/26/02. Survey of Manna City Church, conducted 11/16/02.

33. See Min and Kim 2002.

34. Russell Jung examined 44 pan-Asian congregations in the San Francisco Bay Area. A specific mission of these congregations was to target Asian American ethnic groups, whereas targeting this specific group was *not* a part of Manna's mission (Jeung 2002).

35. See Emerson and Chai Kim 2003.

36. Emerson and Chai Kim 2003

37. Specifically, the church sent two of its pastoral staff, a Chinese American man and a second-generation Korean American man, to form a fellowship about two miles from Manna: Manna City Church. Thirty people were at the service when I visited the church during the fall of 2002. Field notes from 11/16/02.

38. Although the church was primarily young professionals and students, these "notable exceptions" included several people who came to church dressed in worn, old clothing out of necessity rather than fashion choice, something I never saw at Grace.

39. Interview conducted 4/18/02.

40. See Poloma 1982.

41. Willow Creek is an evangelical megachurch in a suburb of Chicago known for disseminating its resources about approaches to ministry, particularly via small groups, to other congregations. See their website for more information, at: www.willowcreek.org/.

42. Interview conducted 4/18/02.

43. See also appendix A.

44. Interview conducted 5/22/02.

45. Interview conducted 4/29/02.

46. Interview conducted 4/17/02.
47. Interview conducted 5/01/02.
48. Interview conducted 6/19/02.
49. Interview conducted 5/19/02.
50. Interview conducted 5/21/02.
51. Interview conducted 7/16/02.

52. I asked for information about fluency in Korean language in the long interview, not the survey. Because I spoke a little Korean, it was easier to determine the level of Korean language fluency through a discussion with a respondent rather than through a survey, where individual understandings of any scale chosen to represent language fluency would have an influence on the validity of the responses.

CHAPTER 4

1. See 2000 Census Report, "Profile of the Foreign-Born Population in the United States: 2000."

2. The term "socially constructed" reflects a tradition in sociology that recognizes the importance of social interactions in constructing identities with practical implications in social life (Goffman 1963). Sociologists of religion argue that congregations are important places for the construction of moral identities (Becker 1999; Wuthnow 1995; Warner 1988).

3. Douglas 1973; Bergesen 1977, 1984 examine the influence ideologies and practices of groups have on the formation of collective ideas and practices of moral order for individuals.

4. Although Korean can be a racial category, here I primarily use the term *ethnic group* to characterize Korean Americans, by which I mean those who self-consciously share a distinctive history and descent from a common homeland (Cornell and Hartmann 1998).

5. See Min 1992.
6. See Lamont 1992, especially pp. 57–58.
7. Interview conducted 3/14/02.
8. Interview conducted 4/10/02.
9. See Lamont 2000.
10. Lamont 2000, pp. 60–61.
11. Interview conducted 7/01/02.
12. Interview conducted 8/08/02.
13. See Wuthnow 1996 for a discussion of the "American Dream."
14. See Swidler 2000. See also Bernstein 1975 for a discussion of how individuals use class-specific speech codes.
15. Interview conducted 4/10/02.
16. Interview conducted 4/01/03.
17. See Bellah 1975.
18. Field observation notes 4/21/02.
19. Interview conducted 6/23/02.
20. Interview conducted 4/12/02.

21. Sociologist Pyong Gap Min (1992) finds first-generation immigrant congregations mainly provide social services to their own members.

22. See Garfinkel 1984 [1967].

23. See Wuthnow 1994 for a further discussion of small groups in other religious contexts.

24. Focus group conducted 3/05/02.

25. Interview conducted 7/16/02.

26. Interview conducted 5/29/02.

27. Multiracial and multiethnic congregations comprise between eight and ten percent of American congregations. (Chaves 1998; Emerson and Smith 2000).

28. Interview conducted 5/21/02.

29. Interview conducted 7/16/02.

30. Interview conducted 8/26/02.

31. See Meeks 2001.

32. See Putnam 2000.

33. Interview conducted 11/16/02.

34. Participant observation conducted 4/01/02.

35. The views of a guest speaker may not always correspond exactly to those of a given congregation. In this instance, however, the speaker was well known by the leadership of the congregation and many of its members.

36. Interview conducted 5/02/02.

37. Interview conducted 5/21/02.

38. See Lamont 1992; Lamont and Molnar 2002 for discussions about how group boundaries are created.

39. Both John Stott and J. I. Packer are important evangelical leaders. See Brooks 2004. Packer is perhaps best known for his book *Knowing God*, which has sold over 500,000 copies. See Packer 1993. Korean evangelicalism has certainly gained worldwide prominence. The largest Protestant church in the world is now in Korea; the Yoido Full Gospel Church in Seoul, South Korea, with over 750,000 members. The pastor of this church, David Yonggi Cho, is now having an influence on U.S. evangelicalism. See the website of National Public Radio, at: www.npr.org/templates/story/story.php?storyId=4815908.

40. See Bellah 1967, who draws on Max Weber's prophetic view of religion and sees the possibility for religion to be used to challenge the social order (Weber 1963 [1922]).

41. See Lamont 1992, 2000; Lamont and Molnar 2002.

CHAPTER 5

1. See Schudson 1998.
2. Interview conducted 8/19/02.
3. See Andreas 2001; Kennedy 1996; Shklar 1991.
4. See Shklar 1991.
5. See Kennedy 1996.

6. See also Kluegel and Bobo 1995, who examine different approaches to understanding white's' beliefs about the black-white socioeconomic gap and argue against a symbolic racism perspective.

7. See Omi and Winant 1994, pp. 55–56.

8. See Ignatiev 1995; Loewen 1988.

9. See Ignatiev 1995, p. 148–176, for a discussion of religion's role in helping the Irish assimilate in to the American racial system.

10. See Loewen 1988.

11. See Portes 1996; Waters 1999.

12. See Harris and Sim 2002; Espiritu 1992; Portes 2001.

13. See Nobles 2000; Harris and Sim 2002 for discussions of census categories for race and ethnicity.

14. See Espiritu 1992; Nobles 2000.

15. See, for example, Lee and Bean 2004.

16. See Lifton 1993 for a discussion of the protean self.

17. See Osajima 1988; Okihiro 1994; Herrnstein and Murray 1994.

18. See Takaki 1989; Zhou and Gatewood 2000; Hurh and Kim 1989.

19. See Abelman and Lie 1995; Kibria 2002.

20. Interview conducted 5/19/02.

21. See Chai 1998, 2001; Chong 1998.

22. See Busto 1996.

23. Interview conducted 3/14/02.

24. Interview conducted 4/10/02.

25. See Swidler 1986.

26. Participant-observation of Sunday service conducted 4/21/02.

27. I should note here that although Grace members are more involved in church-sponsored social service activities, Manna members are more involved overall in social service activities. I discuss this finding further in chapter 5.

28. Participant-observation of Sunday service conducted 2/24/02.

29. Interview conducted 5/29/02.

30. Interview conducted 7/16/02.

31. See Abelman and Lie 1995; Min 1996.

32. See Min 1996. In chap. 5, "Hostility toward Korean Merchants in Black Neighborhoods," pp. 73–95, Min examines the conflict between black Americans and Korean American store owners. Min is referring entirely to *first*-generation Korean store owners in his work.

33. Interview conducted 5/12/02.

34. Interview conducted 4/12/02.

35. Interview conducted 5/16/02.

36. Interview conducted 8/10/02.

37. Interview conducted 4/10/02.

38. Interview conducted 4/10/02.

39. Interview conducted 8/06/02.

40. See Yang 1999.

41. See Lifton 1993.

42. Interview conducted 7/18/02.

43. Interview conducted 6/20/02.
44. Interview conducted 5/16/02.
45. See Nevins 2002 for a discussion of how citizenship is constructed for those who do not have access to legal citizenship status.
46. See Ecklund 2005b.
47. See Kanter 1977; Pettigrew 1987.
48. See Emerson and Smith 2000; DeYoung, Paul, Emerson, Yancey, and Kim 2003.
49. See Cornell 1996.
50. See Lifton 1993.

CHAPTER 6

1. Participant-observation from 3/22/02.
2. Participant-observation from 11/16/02.
3. Manna City Church is an arm of Manna Fellowship that was established during the last few weeks of my time observing the churches. Manna's central congregation sent a group of about 30 members to start a fellowship closer to the center of Old Town. Although this group meets on Sunday afternoons, during the same time as the central congregation, it retains membership with Manna, and both groups are seen as members of the same congregation.
4. See Verba, Schlozman, and Brady 1995, who argue that family political participation is an important indicator of individual political participation.
5. Min 1992 finds that Korean immigrant congregations often provide social services for other Korean immigrants, particularly those in their congregations.
6. See Allahyari 2000, who examines the "moral self," or ideas individuals have about how they ought to act in the world.
7. E.g. Bankston and Zhou 1996; Min 1992; Nee and Sanders 2001.
8. See Ebaugh and Chafetz 2000.
9. See, in particular, Putnam 2000; Verba, Schlozman, and Brady 1995; Wilson and Musick 1997. Other research also examines individual motivations to volunteer based on the "meaning" of volunteer activities (Becker and Dhingra 2001; Ecklund 2005b). See Foley 2002 for a discussion of how some forms of religious participation provide social capital for civic incorporation.
10. For example, see the work of anthropologist Mary Douglas (1966, 1973), as well as that of Clifford Geertz (1973).
11. See Tipton 1982, who discusses moral meaning in this way.
12. See Ammerman 1997; Becker 1999.
13. See Ammerman 1997; Wuthnow 1994.
14. Survey questions are included in appendix B.
15. Interview conducted 3/14/02.
16. Interview conducted 4/10/02.
17. See also work by Ebaugh and Chafetz 2000 that examines immigrant religion in the Houston area.
18. E-mail communication to the members of Grace 4/20/03.
19. Field notes from 5/19/02.

20. According to Mary Douglas, groups with better defined social boundaries exercise more control over their members (Douglas 1973).
21. E-mail communication to the members of Grace, 6/15/02.
22. Interview conducted 4/29/02.
23. Interview conducted 5/22/02.
24. See Gallagher 2003; Lakoff 2002.
25. See Gallagher 2003, p. 151, where Gallagher discusses this further. See also Denton 2004, who uses Smith's "subcultural identity" framework to compare understandings of gender between liberal and conservative Protestants.
26. Question wording taken from Social Capital Benchmark Survey 2000.
27. Interview conducted 8/10/02.
28. See Eckstein 2001.
29. See Wuthnow 1991, p. 152.
30. Interview conducted 5/2/02.
31. Interview conducted 7/16/02.
32. Interview conducted 5/16/02.
33. Interview conducted 5/21/02.
34. Additional comments individuals wrote in on the survey also reveal the personal, individually negotiated approach to community service at Manna. Next to the question "How big an impact do you think you can make on your community?" a respondent from Manna wrote in the margin "Does it matter? I will do what God tells me to do or where to go. I don't need to 'make a big impact,' and if I do, cool." When I asked "If you were volunteering, where would you be most likely to locate volunteer opportunities, another person circled both "through personal investigation" and "through my church" and then wrote in at the bottom, "dependent on God's calling."
35. Interview conducted 6/23/02.
36. Interview conducted 5/19/02.
37. Interview conducted 6/19/02.
38. Interview conducted 5/21/02.
39. Interview conducted 7/16/02.
40. Interview conducted 7/09/02.
41. Field notes from 11/16/02.
42. See Cnaan 1997 and Ebaugh and Chafetz 2000, in particular pp. 71–79.
43. See Bellah, Madsen, Sullivan, Swidler, and Tipton 1985, pp. 221.
44. See Wilson and Musick 1997 for a discussion of "informal" volunteering.
45. See Ecklund 2003, 2005a, examining how individually negotiated ideas of spirituality are connected to communal commitments among Catholic women.

CHAPTER 7

1. Interview conducted 6/18/02.
2. See Gamson 1992.
3. See Fowler, Hertzke, and Olson 1999; Guth, Green, Smidt, Kellstedt, and Poloma 1997; Leege and Kellstedt 1993; Verba, Schlozman, and Brady 1995.
4. See Harris 2003; Putnam 2000; Verba, Schlozman, and Brady 1995.

5. See Hart 1992.
6. See Wuthnow 1991, 1995.
7. See Eliasoph 1990, 1996; Gamson 1992; Lichterman 1996.
8. See Wilcox 1992; Wuthnow 1988.
9. See Keller 2003; Krugman 2002; Lee 2002.
10. See Wilcox 1996, p. 5.
11. See Green 1995; Wilcox 1992.
12. See Smith, Emerson, Gallagher, Kennedy, and Sikkink 1998, pp. 195.
13. See Fowler, Hertzke, and Olson 1999, pp. 15, 37–41. See Smith 2000, pp. 115–128.
14. See Emerson and Smith 2000; Lincoln and Mamiya 1990; Wilcox and Gomez 1990.
15. See Fowler, Hertzke, and Olson 1999, pp. 166.
16. In addition, it is important to note that according to historical analysis of the United States census, voter registration is higher for presidential election years than other years. See the website of the U.S. Census Bureau, www.census.gov/population/www/socdemo/voting.html.
17. Interview conducted 4/17/02.
18. Interview conducted 5/14/02.
19. Interview conducted 7/04/02.
20. Interview conducted 3/25/03.
21. See Gamson 1992.
22. Interview conducted 8/10/02.
23. Interview conducted 10/06/02.
24. See Verba, Schlozman, and Brady 1995, pp. 422, 437–439.
25. See Levitt 2001, in particular pp. 127–158.
26. Interview conducted 7/19/02.
27. Interview conducted 8/10/02.
28. Interview conducted 5/30/02.
29. Interview conducted 5/16/02.
30. Interview conducted 7/17/02.
31. Interview conducted 5/30/02.
32. See Espiritu 1992 for a discussion of "Asian American" as a political category.
33. Shiao 1998.
34. Interview conducted 4/23/03.
35. Interview conducted 7/09/02.
36. Interview conducted 7/05/02.
37. See Wilcox 1992, 1996 for a discussion of conservative politics among American evangelicals, and the Religious Right.
38. Interview conducted 4/28/02.
39. Interview conducted 1/16/03.
40. Interview conducted 7/03/02.
41. I attended Mi-Young's congregation on several different occasions and took participant observation notes of services. The congregation was "multiethnic," in that whites did not comprise more than 80 percent of the church (Emerson and Chai Kim 2003).

42. The conference was held at Wheaton College, Wheaton, Illinois, a well-known evangelical undergraduate college.

43. In 1999, Paull Shin was elected U.S. senator from the state of Washington.

44. Interview conducted 4/16/03.

45. Interview conducted 8/07/02.

46. Interview conducted 6/03/02.

47. For research on conflicts between black Americans and Korean Americans, and particularly between Korean store owners in urban areas and their customers, see Abelman and Lie 1995; Min 1996.

48. See Lincoln and Mamiya 1990; Morris 1984; Wilcox and Gomez 1990.

49. Interview conducted 6/20/02.

50. See Edgell 2005 for a further explanation of how religion is often linked with other central American institutions.

CHAPTER 8

1. See Swidler 1986; Wuthnow 1996.

2. See, for example, Brubaker and Cooper 2000; Cerulo 1997.

3. See Lamont 1992 for a broader discussion of boundary construction in identity formation.

4. See Gordon 1964.

5. See Lee 1996 for a specific discussion of the "silent exodus."

6. See Emerson and Chai Kim 2003.

7. Fowler, Hertzke, and Olson 1999; Lakoff 1996; Wilcox 1996 provide different overviews of evangelical Christian perspectives on politics.

8. See Eck 2001, who discusses the "new" religious America.

9. See Warner 2004.

10. See Espinosa, Virgilio, and Miranda 2003 for a discussion of Latino American evangelical Christians.

11. See Lee 1996. Statistics compiled from Association of Theological Schools member institutions.

12. See King 1992.

13. See Bartkowski 2004; Emerson and Smith 2000; Gallagher 2003.

14. See Jeung 2002; Kim, Warner, and Kwon 2001.

15. See, for example, Wuthnow 2005, who also makes this point.

16. See Cadge 2004.

17. See Goodstein and Niebuhr 2001.

18. Currently, about 12 percent of the 281.4 million Americans are foreign-born. This statistic includes naturalized citizens, resident legal aliens, and resident illegal aliens; 2000 Current Population Survey, United States Census Bureau, pp. 2-9.

APPENDIX A

1. See Ammerman 1987.

2. See Becker 1999; Eiesland 1998.

3. See Abelman and Lie 1995.

4. See Barker 1984, pp. 12–37, giving precedent for situating local groups in the midst of research among those who are in the same social location but outside the central groups that are the focus of a study.

5. Examples of elite universities include Ivy League colleges and universities and prominent small liberal arts schools or state universities.

6. See Burawoy, Burton, Furguson, Fox, Gamson, Gartrell, Hurt, Kurtzman, Salzinger, Schiffman, and Ui 1991, p. 11.

7. See Strauss and Corbin 1990 for a further description of this approach to analyzing qualitative data.

References

Abelman, Nancy, and John Lie. *Blue Dreams: Korean Americans and the Los Angeles Riots*. Cambridge: Harvard University Press, 1995.

Alba, Richard, and Victor Nee. *Remaking the American Mainstream: Assimilation and Contemporary Immigration*. Cambridge: Harvard University Press, 2003.

Allahyari, Rebecca Anne. *Visions of Charity: Volunteer Workers and Moral Community*. Berkeley: University of California Press, 2000.

Alumkal, Antony W. "Preserving Patriarchy: Assimilation, Gender Norms, and Second-Generation Korean American Evangelicals." *Qualitative Sociology* 22 (1999): 127–139.

——. "Being Korean, Being Christian: Particularism and Universalism in a Second-Generation Congregation." In *Korean Americans and Their Religions*, ed. Ho-Youn Kwon, Kwang Chung Kim, and R. Stephen Warner, 181–192. University Park: Pennsylvania State University Press, 2001.

Ammerman, Nancy Tatom. *Bible Believers: Fundamentalists in the Modern World*. New Brunswick: Rutgers University Press, 1987.

——. *Congregation and Community*. New Brunswick: Rutgers University Press, 1997.

Andreas, Peter. "The United States Immigration Control Offensive: Constructing an Image of Order on the Southwest Border." In *Crossings: Mexican Immigration in Interdisciplinary Perspectives*, ed. Marcelo M. Suárez-Orozco, 343–356. Cambridge: Harvard University Press, 2001.

Bankston, Carl L., and Min Zhou. "The Ethnic Church, Ethnic Identification, and the Social Adjustment of Vietnamese Adolescents." *Review of Religious Research* 38 (1996): 18–37.

Barker, Eileen. *The Making of a Moonie: Choice or Brainwashing?* Oxford: Blackwell, 1984.

Bartkowski, John P. *The Promise Keepers: Servants, Soldiers, and Godly Men.* New Brunswick: Rutgers University Press, 2004.
Becker, Penny Edgell. "Making Inclusive Communities: Congregations and the 'Problem' of Race." *Social Problems* 45 (1998): 451–472.
———. *Congregations in Conflict: Cultural Models of Local Religious Life.* Cambridge, England: Cambridge University Press, 1999.
Becker, Penny Edgell, and Pawan H. Dhingra. "Religious Involvement and Volunteering: Implications for Civil Society." *Sociology of Religion* 62 (2001): 315–335.
Bellah, Robert. "Civil Religion in America." *Daedalus* 96 (1967): 1–21.
———. *The Broken Covenant: American Civil Religion in Time of Trial.* New York: Seabury Press, 1975.
Bellah, Robert, Richard Madsen, William M. Sullivan, Ann Swidler, and Steven M. Tipton. *Habits of the Heart: Individualism and Commitment in American Life.* New York: Harper and Row, 1985.
Bergesen, Albert James. "Political Witch Hunts: The Sacred and the Subversive in Cross-National Perspective." *American Sociological Review* 42 (1977): 220–233.
———. *The Sacred and the Subversive: Political Witch-Hunts as National Rituals.* Monograph series. Storrs, Conn.: Society for the Scientific Study of Religion, 1984.
Bernstein, Basil. *Class, Codes, and Control: Theoretical Studies towards a Sociology of Language.* New York: Schocken Books, 1975.
Bourdieu, Pierre. "Cultural Reproduction and Social Reproduction." In *Knowledge, Education, and Cultural Change*, ed. Richard Brown, 71–112. London: Tavistock, 1973.
———. *Distinction: A Social Critique of the Judgment of Taste.* Cambridge: Harvard University Press, 1984.
Brooks, David. "Who Is John Stott?" *New York Times*, November 30, 2004, p. A23.
Brubaker, Rogers, and Frederick Cooper. "Beyond 'Identity.'" *Theory and Society* 29 (2000): 1–29.
Burawoy, Michael, Alice Burton, Ann Arnett Furguson, Kathryn J. Fox, Joshua Gamson, Nadine Gartrell, Leslie Hurt, Charles Kurtzman, Leslie Salzinger, Josepha Schiffman, and Shiori Ui, eds. *Ethnography Unbound.* Berkeley: University of California Press, 1991.
Busto, Rudy V. "The Gospel According to the Model Minority? Hazarding an Interpretation of Asian American Evangelical College Students." *Amerasia Journal* 22 (1996): 133–147.
Cadge, Wendy. *Heartwood: The First Generation of Theravada Buddhists in America.* Chicago: University of Chicago Press, 2004.
Cerulo, Karen A. "Identity Construction: New Issues, New Directions." *Annual Review of Sociology* 23 (1997): 385–409.
Cha, Peter T. "Ethnic Identity Formation and Participation in Immigrant Churches: Second-Generation Korean American Experiences." In *Korean Americans and Their Religions: Pilgrims and Missionaries from a Different Shore*, ed. Ho-Youn Kwon, Kwang Chung Kim, R. Stephen Warner, 141–156. University Park: Pennsylvania State University Press, 2001.

Chai, Karen J. "Competing for the Second Generation: English-Language Ministry at the Korean Protestant Church." In *Gatherings in Diaspora: Religious Communities and the New Immigration*, ed. R. Stephen Warner and Judith Wittner, 295–331. Philadelphia: Temple University Press, 1998.

———. "Beyond 'Strictness' to Distinctiveness: Generational Transition in Korean Protestant Churches." In *Korean Americans and Their Religions: Pilgrims and Missionaries from a Different Shore*, ed. Ho-Youn Kwon, Kwang Chung Kim, and R. Stephen Warner, 157–180. University Park: Pennsylvania State University Press, 2001.

Chaves, Mark. *National Congregations Study Data File and Code Book*. Tucson: University of Arizona, Department of Sociology, 1998.

———. *Congregations in America*. Cambridge: Harvard University Press, 2004.

Chen, Carolyn. "The Religious Varieties of Ethnic Presence." *Sociology of Religion* 63 (2002): 215–238.

Chong, Kelly. "What It Means to Be Christian: The Role of Religion in the Construction of Ethnic Identity and Boundary among Second-Generation Koreans." *Sociology of Religion* 59 (1998): 259–286.

Chung, Jun Ki. "Christian Contextualization in Korea." In *Korean Cultural Roots: Religion and Social Thoughts*, ed. Ho-Youn Kwon, 81–104. Chicago: North Park College and Seminary, 1995.

Clark, Donald. *Christianity in Modern Korea*. Lanham, Md.: University Press of America, 1986.

Cnaan, Ram A. *Social and Community Involvement of Religious Congregations Housed in Historic Religious Properties: Findings from a Six-City Study*. Report. Philadelphia: University of Pennsylvania School of Social Work, 1997.

Cornell, Stephen. "The Variable Ties That Bind: Content and Circumstance in Ethnic Processes." *Ethnic and Racial Studies* 19 (1996): 265–289.

Cornell, Stephen, and Douglas Hartmann. *Ethnicity and Race: Making Identities in a Changing World*. Thousand Oaks, Calif.: Pine Forge Press, 1998.

Cummings, Bruce. *Korea's Place in the Sun: A Modern History*. New York: Norton, 1997.

D'Aunno, Thomas, Melissa Succi, and Jeffrey A. Alexander. "The Role of Institutional and Market Forces in Divergent Organizational Change." *Administrative Science Quarterly* 45 (2000): 679–703.

Denton, Melinda Lundquist. "Gender and Marital Decision Making: Negotiating Religious Ideology and Practice." *Social Forces* 82 (2004): 1151–1180.

DeYoung, Curtiss Paul, Michael O. Emerson, George Yancey, and Karen Chai Kim. *United by Faith: The Multiracial Congregation as an Answer to the Problem of Race*. New York: Oxford University Press, 2003.

DiMaggio, Paul J. "Culture and Cognition." *Annual Review of Sociology* 23 (1997): 263–287.

Douglas, Mary. *Purity and Danger: An Analysis of the Concepts of Pollution and Taboo*. New York: Routledge, 1966.

———. *Natural Symbols: Explorations in Cosmology*. New York: Pantheon Books, 1973.

Ebaugh, Helen Rose, and Janet Saltzman Chafetz. *Religion and the New Immigrants: Continuities and Adaptations in Immigrant Congregations*. New York: Alta Mira Press, 2000.

Eck, Diana. *A New Religious America: How a "Christian Country" Has Now Become the World's Most Religiously Diverse Nation.* New York: HarperCollins, 2001.

Ecklund, Elaine Howard. "Catholic Women Negotiate Feminism: A Research Note." *Sociology of Religion* 64 (2003): 515–524.

———. "Different Identity Accounts for Catholic Women." *Review of Religious Research* 47 (2005a): 135–149.

———. "'Us' and 'Them': The Role of Religion in Mediating and Challenging the 'Model Minority' and Other Civic Boundaries." *Ethnic and Racial Studies* 28 (2005b): 132–150.

Ecklund, Elaine Howard, and Jerry Z. Park. "Asian American Community Participation and Religion: Civic 'Model Minorities'?" *Journal of Asian American Studies* 8 (2005): 1–22.

Eckstein, Susan. "Community as Gift-Giving: Collectivistic Roots of Volunteerism." *American Sociological Review* 66 (2001): 829–851.

Edgell, Penny. *Religion and Family in a Changing Society.* Series in Cultural Sociology. Paul DiMaggio, Michèle Lamont, Robert Wuthnow, and Viviana Zelizer, eds. Princeton: Princeton University Press, 2005.

Eiesland, Nancy. *A Particular Place: Exurbanization and Religious Response.* New Brunswick: Rutgers University Press, 1998.

Eliasoph, Nina. "Political Culture and the Presentation of a Political Self." *Theory and Society* 19 (1990): 465–494.

———. "Making a Fragile Public: A Talk-Centered Study of Citizenship and Power." *Sociological Theory* 14 (1996): 261–289.

Emerson, Michael O. and Karen Chai Kim. "Multiracial Congregations: An Analysis of Their Development and a Typology." *Journal for the Scientific Study of Religion* 42 (2003): 217–228.

Emerson, Michael O., and Christian Smith. *Divided by Faith: Evangelical Religion and the Problem of Race in America.* New York: Oxford University Press, 2000.

Espinosa, Gastón, Elizondo Virgilio, and Jesse Miranda. "Hispanic Churches in American Public Life: Summary of Findings." Notre Dame, Ind.: University of Notre Dame, 2003.

Espiritu, Yen Le. *Asian American Panethnicity: Bridging Institutions and Identities.* Philadelphia: Temple University Press, 1992.

Foley, Michael W. "Religious Institutions as Agents for Civic Incorporation: A Preliminary Report on Research on Religion and New Immigrants," paper presented at *The Annual Meeting of the American Political Science Association.* San Francisco: 2002.

Fowler, Robert Booth, Allen D. Hertzke, and Laura R. Olson. *Religion and Politics in America: Faith, Culture, and Strategic Choices.* Boulder, Colo.: Westview Press, 1999.

Friedland, Roger, and Robert R. Alford. "Bringing Society Back In: Symbols, Practices, and Institutional Contradictions." In *New Institutionalism in Organizational Analysis,* ed. Walter W. Powell and Paul J. DiMaggio, 232–266. London: University of Chicago Press, 1991.

Gallagher, Sally. *Evangelical Identity and Gendered Family Life.* New Brunswick: Rutgers University Press, 2003.

Gamson, William A. *Talking Politics.* New York: Cambridge University Press, 1992.
Garfinkel, Harold. "Studies of the Routine Groups of Everyday Activities." In *Studies in Ethnomethodology,* ed. Harold Garfinkel, 35–75. Cambridge, England: Polity Press, 1984.
Geertz, Clifford. *The Interpretation of Cultures.* New York: Basic Books, 1973.
Goffman, Erving. *Stigma: Notes on the Management of Spoiled Identity.* New York: Simon and Schuster, 1963.
Goodstein, Laurie. "Evangelicals Open Debate on Widening Policy Questions." *New York Times,* March 11, 2005, p. A16.
Goodstein, Laurie, and Gustav Niebuhr. "Attacks and Harassment of Middle-Eastern Americans Rising." *New York Times,* September 14, 2001, p. A1.
Gordon, Milton. *Assimilation in American Life: The Role of Race, Religion, and National Origins.* New York: Oxford University Press, 1964.
Green, John. "The Christian Right and the 1994 Elections: An Overview." In *God at the Grassroots: The Christian Right in the 1994 Elections,* ed. Mark J. Rozell and Clyde Wilcox, pp. 1–18. Lanham, Md.: Rowman and Littlefield, 1995.
Griswold, Wendy. "The Sociology of Culture." In *The Sage Handbook of Sociology,* ed. Craig Calhoun, Chris Rojek, and Bryan S. Turner, New York: Sage, 2005.
Guth, James L., John C. Green, Corwin E. Smidt, Lyman A. Kellstedt, and Margaret M. Poloma. *The Bully Pulpit: The Politics of Protestant Clergy.* Lawrence: University Press of Kansas, 1997.
Hadaway, C. Kirk, Penny Long Marler, and Mark Chaves. "What the Polls Don't Show: A Closer Look at U.S. Church Attendance." *American Sociological Review* 58 (1993): 741–752.
Harris, David R., and Jeremiah Joseph Sim. "Who Is Multiracial? Assessing the Complexity of Lived Race." *American Sociological Review* 67 (2002): 614–627.
Harris, Fredrick. "Ties That Bind and Flourish: Religion as Social Capital in African-American Politics and Society." In *Religion as Social Capital: Producing the Common Good,* ed. Corwin Smidt, 121–137. Waco, Tex.: Baylor University Press, 2003.
Hart, Stephen. *What Does the Lord Require? How Americans Think about Economic Justice.* New York: Oxford University Press, 1992.
Herberg, Will. *Protestant, Catholic, Jew.* Garden City, N.Y.: Doubleday, 1955.
Herrnstein, Richard J., and Charles Murray. *The Bell Curve: Intelligence and Class Structure in American Life.* New York: Free Press, 1994.
Hirschman, Charles, Philip Kasinitz, and Josh DeWind, eds. *The Handbook of International Migration: The American Experience.* New York: Russell Sage Foundation, 1999.
Holy Bible, The: New International Version. Grand Rapids, Mich.: Zondervan Bible, 1978.
Hunt, Everett, Jr. *Protestant Pioneers in Korea.* Maryknoll, N.Y.: Orbis Books, 1980.
Hurh, Won Moo, and Kwang Chung Kim. "The 'Success' Image of Asian Americans: Its Validity, and Its Practical and Theoretical Implications." *Ethnic and Racial Studies* 12 (1989): 512–538.
———. "Religious Participation of Korean Immigrants in the United States." *Journal for the Scientific Study of Religion* 29 (1990): 19–34.

Ignatiev, Noel. *How the Irish Became White*. New York: Routledge, 1995.
Jepperson, Ronald L., and John W. Meyer. "The Public Order and the Construction of Formal Organizations." In *The New Institutionalism in Organizational Analysis*, ed. Walter W. Powell and Paul J. DiMaggio, 204–231. Chicago: University of Chicago Press, 1991.
Jepperson, Ronald L., and Ann Swidler. "What Properties of Culture Should We Measure?" *Poetics* 22 (1994): 359–371.
Jeung, Russell. "Asian American Pan-Ethnic Formation and Congregational Culture." In *Religions in Asian America: Building Faith Communities*, ed. Pyong Gap Min and Jung Ha Kim, 215–243. Walnut Creek, Calif.: AltaMira Press, 2002.
———. *Faithful Generations: Race and New Asian American Churches*. New Brunswick: Rutgers University Press, 2005.
Kanter, Rosabeth Moss. *Men and Women of the Corporation*. New York: Basic Books, 1977.
Keller, Bill. "God and George W. Bush." *New York Times*, May 17, 2003, p. A17.
Kennedy, Randall. "Dred Scott and African American Citizenship." In *Diversity and Citizenship: Discovering American Nationhood*, ed. Gary Jacobson and Susan Dunn, 101–102. New York: Rowman and Littlefield, 1996.
Kibria, Nazli. *Becoming Asian American: Second-Generation Chinese and Korean American Identities*. Baltimore: Johns Hopkins University Press, 2002.
Kim, Andrew. "Korean Religious Culture and Its Affinity to Christianity: The Rise of Protestant Christianity in Korea." *Sociology of Religion* 61 (2000): 117–133.
Kim, Kwang Chung, R. Stephen Warner, and Ho-Youn Kwon, "Korean American Religion in International Perspective." In *Korean Americans and Their Religions: Pilgrims and Missionaries from a Different Shore*, ed. Ho-Youn Kwon, Kwang Chung Kim, and R. Stephen Warner, 3–24. University Park: Pennsylvania State University Press, 2001.
King, Martin Luther, Jr. *I Have a Dream: Writings and Speeches That Changed the World*. Edited by James M. Washington. New York: HarperCollins, 1992.
Kitano, Harry H. L., and Roger Daniels. *Asian Americans: Emerging Minorities*. Englewood Cliffs, N.J: Prentice Hall, 2000.
Kluegel, James R., and Lawrence Bobo. "Prejudice, Politics, and the American Dilemma." In *Prejudice, Politics, and the American Dilemma*, ed. Paul M. Sniderman, Philip E. Tetlock, and Edward G. Carmines, 127–147. Stanford: Stanford University Press, 1995.
Krugman, Paul. "Gotta Have Faith." *New York Times*, December 17, 2002, p. A35.
Kwon, Ho-Youn, Kwang Chung Kim, and R. Stephen Warner, eds. *Korean Americans and Their Religions: Pilgrims and Missionaries from a Different Shore*. University Park: Pennsylvania State University Press, 2001.
Lakoff, George. *Moral Politics: What Conservatives Know That Liberals Don't*. Chicago: University of Chicago Press, 1996.
———. *Moral Politics: How Liberals and Conservatives Think*. Chicago: University of Chicago Press, 2002.
Lamont, Michèle. *Money, Morals, and Manners: The Culture of the French and the American Upper-Middle Class*. Chicago: University of Chicago Press, 1992.

———. *The Dignity of Working Men: Morality and the Boundaries of Race, Class, and Immigration.* Cambridge: Harvard University Press, 2000.

Lamont, Michèle, and Virag Molnar. "The Study of Boundaries across the Social Sciences." *Annual Review of Sociology* 28 (2002): 167–195.

Lee, Felicia R. "The Secular Society Gets Religion." *New York Times*, August 24, 2002, p. B7.

Lee, Helen. "Silent Exodus—Can the East Asian Church in America Reverse Flight of Its Next Generation?" *Christianity Today*, August 1996, 50–53.

Lee, Jennifer, and Frank D. Bean. "America's Changing Color Lines: Immigration, Race/Ethnicity, and Multiracial Identification." *Annual Review of Sociology* 30 (2004): 221–242.

Leege, David C., and Lyman A. Kellstedt, eds. *Rediscovering the Religious Factor in American Politics.* Armonk, N.Y.: Sharpe, 1993.

Leland, John. "Hip New Churches Pray to a Different Drummer." *New York Times*, February 18, 2004, pp. A1, A17.

Levitt, Peggy. *The Transnational Villagers.* Berkeley: University of California Press, 2001.

Lichterman, Paul. *The Search for Political Community: American Activists Reinventing Commitment.* Cambridge, England: Cambridge University Press, 1996.

Lifton, Robert Jay. *The Protean Self: Human Resilience in an Age of Fragmentation.* New York: Basic Books, 1993.

Lincoln, C. Eric, and Lawrence H. Mamiya. *The Black Church in the African American Experience.* Durham, N.C.: Duke University Press, 1990.

Loewen, James W. *The Mississippi Chinese: Between Black and White.* Prospect Heights, Ill.: Waveland Press, 1988.

Luo, Michael. "Billy Graham Returns, to Find Evangelical Force in New York." *New York Times*, June, 21, 2005, pp. B1, B6.

Mahler, Jonathan. "The Soul of the New Exurb." *New York Times Magazine*, March 27, 2005, pp. 30–37, 46, 50, 54, 57.

Marsden, George M. *Understanding Fundamentalism and Evangelicalism.* Grand Rapids, Mich.: Eerdmans, 1991.

Martin, Joanne. *Cultures in Organizations: Three Perspectives.* New York: Oxford University Press, 1992.

Meeks, Chet. "Civil Society and the Sexual Politics of Difference." *Sociological Theory* 19 (2001): 325–343.

Meyer, John W., and Brian Rowan. "Institutionalized Organizations: Formal Structure as Myth and Ceremony." *American Journal of Sociology* 83 (1977): 340–363.

Min, Pyong Gap. "The Structure and Social Functions of Korean Immigrant Churches in the United States." *International Migration Review* 26 (1992): 1370–1394.

———. *Caught in the Middle: Korean Communities in New York and Los Angeles.* Berkeley: University of California Press, 1996.

Min, Pyong Gap, and Dae Young Kim. "Intergenerational Transmission of Religion and Culture: Korean Protestants in the US." *Sociology of Religion* 66 (2005): 263–282.

Min, Pyong Gap, and Jung Ha Kim, eds. *Religions in Asian America: Building Faith Communities.* New York: Alta Mira Press, 2002.

Morris, Aldon. *The Origins of the Civil Rights Movement: Black Communities Organizing for Change*. New York: Free Press, 1984.

Nee, Victor, and Jimy M. Sanders. "Understanding the Diversity of Immigrant Incorporation: A Forms-of-Capital Model." *Ethnic and Racial Studies* 24 (2001): 386–411.

Nevins, Joseph. *Operation Gatekeeper: The Rise of the "Illegal Alien" and the Making of the United States–Mexico Boundary*. New York: Routledge, 2002.

Nobles, Melissa. *Shades of Citizenship: Race and the Census in Modern Politics*. Stanford: Stanford University Press, 2000.

Okihiro, Gary. *Margins and Mainstreams: Asians in American History and Culture*. Seattle: University of Washington Press, 1994.

Omi, Michael, and Howard Winant. *Racial Formation in the United States: From the 1960s to the 1990s*. New York: Routledge, 1994.

Osajima, Keith. "Asian Americans as the Model Minority: An Analysis of the Popular Press Image in the 1960s and 1980s." In *Reflections on Shattered Windows: Promises and Prospects for Asian American Studies*, ed. Gary Y. Okihiro, Shirley Hune, Arthur A. Hansen, and John M. Lui, 165–174. Pullman: Washington State University Press, 1988.

Owens, Timothy J. "Self and Identity." In *Handbook of Social Psychology*, ed. John Delamater, 205–232. New York: Kluwer Academic, 2003.

Packer, J. I. *Knowing God*. Downers Grove, Ill.: InterVarsity Press, 1993.

Park, Jerry Z. "The Ethnic and Religious Identities of Young Asian Americans." Ph.D. diss., University of Notre Dame, 2004.

Pettigrew, Thomas F., and Joanne Martin. "Shaping the Organizational Context for Black American Inclusion." *Journal of Social Issues* 43 (1987): 41–78.

Poloma, Margaret. *The Charismatic Movement: Is There a New Pentecost?* Boston: Hall, 1982.

Portes, Alejandro. *The New Second Generation*. New York: Russell Sage Foundation, 1996.

Portes, Alejandro, and Rubén Rumbaut. *Immigrant America: A Portrait*. Berkeley: University of California Press, 1996.

———. *Legacies: The Story of the Immigrant Second Generation*. Berkeley: University of California Press, 2001.

Putnam, Robert. *Bowling Alone: The Collapse and Revival of American Community*. New York: Simon and Schuster, 2000.

Regnerus, Mark C., Christian Smith, and David Sikkink. "Who Gives to the Poor? The Influence of Religious Tradition and Political Location on the Personal Generosity of Americans towards the Poor." *Journal for the Scientific Study of Religion* 37 (1998): 481–493.

Schudson, Michael. *The Good Citizen: A History of American Civic Life*. New York: Free Press, 1998.

Schmidley, A. Diane, U.S. Census Bureau, Current Population Reports, Series P23-206, Profile of the Foreign-Born Population in the United States: 2000, U.S. Government Printing Office, Washington, D.C., 2001.

Sewell, William. "A Theory of Structure: Duality, Agency, and Transformation." *American Journal of Sociology* 98 (1992): 1–29.

———. "Historical Events as Transformations of Structures." *Theory and Society* 25 (1996): 841–881.
Shiao, Jiannbin Lee. "The Nature of the Nonprofit Sector: Professionalism versus Identity Politics in Private Policy Definitions of Asian Pacific Americans." *Asian American Policy Review* 8 (1998): 17–43.
Shklar, Judith N. *American Citizenship: The Quest for Inclusion.* Cambridge: Harvard University Press, 1991.
Sider, Ronald J. *Rich Christians in an Age of Hunger.* Nashville: Word, 1997.
Smith, Christian. *Christian America? What Evangelicals Really Want.* Berkeley: University of California Press, 2000.
Smith, Christian, Michael Emerson, Sally Gallagher, Paul Kennedy, and David Sikkink. *American Evangelicalism: Embattled and Thriving.* Chicago: University of Chicago Press, 1998.
Strauss, Anselm, and Juliet Corbin. *Basics of Qualitative Research: Grounded Theory Procedures and Techniques.* Newbury Park, Calif.: Sage, 1990.
Swidler, Ann. "Culture in Action: Symbols and Strategies." *American Sociological Review* 51 (1986): 273–286.
———. *Talk of Love.* Chicago: University of Chicago Press, 2000.
Takaki, Ron. *Strangers from a Different Shore: A History of Asian Americans.* New York: Penguin, 1989.
Tipton, Steven M. *Getting Saved from the Sixties: Moral Meaning in Conversion and Cultural Change.* Berkeley: University of California Press, 1982.
Tocqueville, Alexis de. *Democracy in America.* Translated by George Lawrence. Edited by J. P. Mayer. New York: HarperCollins, 1969. Originally published 1835.
Verba, Sidney, Kay Lehman Schlozman, and Henry E. Brady. *Voice and Equality: Civic Volunteerism in American Politics.* Cambridge: Harvard University Press, 1995.
Warner, R. Stephen. *New Wine in Old Wineskins: Evangelicals and Liberals in a Small-Town Church.* Berkeley: University of California Press, 1988.
———. "The Korean Immigrant Church as Case and Model." In *Korean Americans and Their Religions: Pilgrims and Missionaries from a Different Shore,* ed. Ho-Youn Kwon, Kwang Chung Kim, and R. Stephen Warner, 25–52. University Park: Pennsylvania State University Press, 2001.
———. "Coming to America: Immigrants and the Faith They Bring." *Christian Century,* February 10, 2004, pp. 20–23.
Waters, Mary C. *Black Identities: West Indian Immigrant Dreams and American Realities.* Cambridge: Harvard University Press, 1999.
Weber, Max. *The Sociology of Religion.* Boston: Beacon Press, 1963. Originally published 1922.
Wilcox, Clyde. *Gods Warriors: The Christian Right in Twentieth Century America.* Baltimore: Johns Hopkins University Press, 1992.
———. *Onward Christian Soldiers: The Religious Right in American Politics.* Boulder, Colo.: Westview Press, 1996.
Wilcox, Clyde, and Leopoldo Gomez. "Religion, Group Identification, and Politics among Black Americans." *Sociological Analysis* 51 (1990): 271–285.

Wilde, Melissa J. "How Culture Mattered at Vatican II: Collegiality Trumps Authority in the Council's Social Movement Organizations." *American Sociological Review* 69 (2004): 576–602.

Wilson, John, and Marc Musick. "Who Cares? Toward an Integrated Theory of Volunteer Work." *American Sociological Review* 62 (1997): 694–713.

Wuthnow, Robert. *Meaning and Moral Order: Explorations in Cultural Analysis.* Berkeley: University of California Press, 1987.

———. *The Restructuring of American Religion.* Princeton: Princeton University Press, 1988.

———. *Acts of Compassion: Caring for Others and Helping Ourselves.* Princeton: Princeton University Press, 1991.

———. *Sharing the Journey: Support Groups and America's New Quest for Community* New York: Free Press, 1994.

———. *Learning to Care: Elementary Kindness in an Age of Indifference.* New York: Oxford University Press, 1995.

———. *Poor Richards Principle: Recovering the American Dream through the Moral Dimension of Work, Business, and Money.* Princeton: Princeton University Press, 1996.

———. "Mobilizing Civic Engagement: The Changing Impact of Religious Involvement." In *Civic Engagement in American Democracy*, ed. Theda Skocpol and Morris P. Fiorina, 331–363. Washington, D.C.: Brookings Institute Press, 1999.

———. *America and the Challenges of Religious Diversity.* Princeton: Princeton University Press, 2005.

Wuthnow, Robert, and Conrad Hackett. "The Social Integration of Practitioners of Non-Western Religions in the United States." *Journal for the Scientific Study of Religion* 42 (2003): 651–667.

Yang, Fenggang. *Chinese Christians in America: Conversion, Assimilation, and Adhesive Identities.* University Park: Pennsylvania State University Press, 1999.

Zhou, Min. "Are Asian Americans Becoming 'White'?" *Contexts: Understanding People in Their Social Worlds* 3 (2004): 29–37.

Zhou, Min, and James V. Gatewood. "Mapping the Terrain: Asian American Diversity and the Challenges of the Twenty-First Century." *Asian American Policy Review* 9 (2000): 5–29.

Index

Action strategies, individuals, group membership and, 52–53
Agency, personal, 91
  greater, in American evangelicism, 22, 23
  identity construction and, 24–25, 142
All-Korean second-generation churches, 10
American,
  "good,", 70, 140, 157, 163, 166
  identity as, 73–74, 92
  "real," 86, 87, 140
American Christianity, new, 153–55
American civic life, 14–15
American Dream, 57, 58, 65, 141
  Christianized version of, 61–62
  as cultural script, 58
  immigrants and, 57–58
  second-generation Korean Americans and, 57–58, 59
American Evangelicalism, vi
  as cultural schema development resource, 17, 23
  Korean Americans influence on, vi
American religion, new Americans and, 155

American social order
  Christian ideal of upholding, 60–61
  Manna's space for negative views about, 65–66, 142
Asian Americans, 77, 78, 137, 154, 155
  politics and, 128, 129, 130, 134, 185*n*32
Assimilation, 142
  civic, 4
  ethnic negotiation v. ethnic, 50
  not multiethnic church participation cause, 152
  religious participation and cultural, 7
Attendance. *See* Motives for attendance

Bacon, Jean, 56
Bellah, Robert, 60
Black Americans, 75, 76, 77, 82–85
  Korean Americans conflict with, 83, 182*n*32, 186*n*47
  Korean-American multiethnic churches and, 84–85
  multiethnic v. ethnic-specific church relationship to, 77, 143

200   INDEX

Black Christians
   new Americans and, 153
   as political models for Korean
      Americans, 122, 135–37, 146, 147
Black churches, cultural schemas
   from, 69
Black-white continuum, 86
Bobo, Lawrence, 75
Boundaries, 55, 90, 91, 147, 177n21
   Grace and organizational, 104, 184n20
   identity formation and, 147, 186n3
   with moral dimensions, 56
   second-generation Korean Americans
      and, 52–63, 88, 140, 148, 151
Boundary creation, model-minority
   image and, 78, 143, 147
Boundary ideology, 54
Boundary work, 24, 71
Bowling Alone (Putnam), 67
Bu-Hual congregation, 34–38, 177n1,
   179n22
   Grace beginnings as English ministry
      of, 33, 178n10
   speaking Korean and, 38
Burawoy, Michael, extended case method
   of, 163
Bush, George W., 60, 128

Career decisions
   Christianity interpretation and, 59–60
   identity creation as spiritual pursuit
      and, 88–89
Caring, 14
Categories, 73–77, 80, 86, 87, 88,
   90, 92
   recreating, 142, 146, 156–57
Catholicism, institutional change and,
   22, 177n15
Cell groups, Manna, ethnic diversity and,
   63–64
Change, evangelicalism openness to,
   22–23, 147
Cho, David Yonggi, 181n39
Christian, 3, 4, 89, 90, 166
Christian identity, vi, 3, 146–47
   race/ethnicity and, 4, 13, 151

Christian left, 7, 174n19
Christian right, 121
Christianity
   career decisions and interpretation of,
      59–60
   church demography and interpretation
      of, 52
   Grace, ethnicity and, 55
   Grace's problems focus and, 62
   Korean, 9–10, 175n34, 175n35, 175n37,
      181n39
   Korean American, 9–10
   Korean American civic identity
      negotiation and, 71
   in Korean culture, 9
   Manna's ethnic diversity focus and, 43,
      64, 144
   multiethnic church schema for, 92
   new American, 153–55
   "spiritual" v. "ethnic," 52–63
Christianity Today, 175n44
Church choice, ethnic negotiation v.
   ethnic assimilation in, 50
Church, current, 166
Church involvement, current, 166
Church participation history, 165–66
Church-based models of civic
   responsibility, 141–42
Citizenship, 91, 183n45
Civic assimilation, 4
Civic identity, 73–93
   Christianity and creation of, 11–13
   civic practices and, 144–45
   Grace's distinct categories for, 86
   individual construction of, 74
   Manna, ethnic minority America and,
      84–85
   Manna's overlapping categories
      for, 90
   model-minority stereotype and
      creation of, 78, 84–85
   overlapping, 90, 142–43, 148
   race and, 85–88
   religion's role in, 12–13
Civic integration, religion fostering,
   vi, 7

Civic life, 6, 166–67
　broader issues of, 14–15
　institutional changes to, 148–50
　religion and, 3–15
　religiously motivated model of, 13, 14
Civic models
　community service and, 95–118
　identities, practices and, 140–46
Civic participation
　Christianity-based personal ethic and, 5, 149
　professional/economic success and, 8, 175n31
　religion-guided, 4, 7–8
Civic practices
　civic identities and, 144–45
　congregation-provided moral meanings and, 149
Civic programs, church-based, 5
Civic responsibility
　church-based models of, 141–42
　congregational models of, 52–54, 70
　evangelical resources for, 68–69
　Grace's communal obligations model of, 62, 102
　individually negotiated civic practices and, 66–68, 98, 99
　individually negotiated model of, 52, 63, 98, 99, 113, 116, 141, 184n34
　Manna's diversity of schemas for, 65
　models of, 51–71, 52–54, 54t, 70, 95–118, 98, 116, 140, 141–42
　origins of organizational schemas for, 68–69
　prioritizing community service and models of, 52, 53
　as reaching out, 61–63
　second-generation Korean-Americans construction of, 51, 69, 139
　as upholding American social order, 60–61
Civil religion
　defined by Bellah, 60
　Grace and Christian, 60–61
Civil Rights Movement, 76, 121
Class, Grace and indicators of, 36

Class distinctions in ethnic-specific churches, racial boundaries and, 77
Cnaan, Ram, 117
Commonality, 91, 143, 146
　Manna focus on, 81, 84–85, 145
Communal model of civic life, 52
Communal obligation, 105
　church-sponsored community service as, 104
　as Grace volunteerism model, 57, 98, 101–9, 116, 141
Communally focused church service, 62
Communion, 38, 179n24
Community service, 3–4, 182n27
　being like Jesus and, 112, 113
　Christianity/ethnicity connection and, 151
　civic models and, 95–118
　consequences of individually negotiating, 115–16
　evangelicals and, 7
　Grace, evangelism, and, 99, 103
　Grace, Old Town residents and, 63, 144
　Grace v. Manna evangelism views and, 95–99
　Grace/Manna civic responsibility models prioritizing, 52, 53
　Grace's distancing spiritual categories v., 80
　individually negotiated ethic and, 67, 98, 99, 113, 115, 145, 184n34
　individually negotiated v. obligation motivated, 112
　motivational challenges and individually negotiated, 113, 115, 145
　multiethnic v. ethnic-specific attitudes to, 20
　second-generation, 140–41
Community service practices
　moral-meaning shaped preferencing of, 100, 101
　resources for constructing, 98, 183n4

202   INDEX

Congregations
  Christianity-based moral narratives
    and, 116
  ethnic-specific, 23, 108, 109, 141
  "forms of capital" v. moral meanings
    view of, 99–100, 183n9
  in immigrant life, 149
  Korean only, 17
  as lacking political-involvement
    models, 119
  studying community and, 11, 176n49
Construction
  of civic responsibility, 51, 139
  of identity, 17, 24–25, 74, 91, 146–48,
    180n2
  of identity, new approach to, 146–48
  of individual identity and cultural le-
    vels of analysis, 17
  social, 180n2
  of whiteness, social, 75–76, 182n9
Cultural assimilation, religious
  participation and, 7
Cultural levels of analysis, individual
  identity construction and, 17
Cultural resources, interpretive
  frameworks as, 5, 19
Cultural schema, 19–20, 25, 70, 71, 90,
  100, 142, 143, 147. See also Schema
  of American evangelicalism, 17, 23
  example of, 20–21
  Grace, borrowed from white
    church, 69
  individual identities and, 23–25
  institutional constraints and, 21
  within institutional, 21–22
  Manna, borrowed from Black
    churches, 69
  for model-minority stereotype, 78
  transference of, 20
Cultural script, American Dream as, 58
Cultural tools for interpreting
  wealth, 80
Culture, 176n, 176n1, 176n2, 176n3
  approach to, 18–19
  as constraining and enabling, 18,
    176n5, 176n6

  individual identity and malleability
    of, 19
  as resources/meanings collection, 18

Data analysis and research framework,
  163–64
Data and methods, 159–64, 187n4,
  187n5, 187n7
Data collection, summary of, 163t
Demographics, 167–68, 172
  Christian interpretation of, 52
  diversity in, 76
  of Manna, 40–41, 179n38
  New Christian America and, 153
  racial changes in, 17, 153, 154, 155
Denominational affiliation. See also
  Silent exodus
  as generational distinctiveness
    attempt, 151–52
DiMaggio, Paul, 19
Diversity, 14, 43, 53, 141, 142, 144, 155
  American Christianity's racial/ethnic,
    v, 174n9
  American civic life influenced by
    religious/ethnic, 5–8
  America's religious, 155, 156, 174n9
  demographic, 76
  Manna and appreciation of, 63–68, 145
  Manna's cell groups and ethnic, 63–64
  Manna's discourse embracing, 53
  Manna's goal of racial, 41
  Manna's spiritual lens view of, 81
  Manna's support of political, 64
Divided by Faith (Emerson and Smith), 26

Economic mobility, explicit rejection/
  implicit acceptance of, 57–60, 61
Emerson, Michael, 26, 27, 41
Engaged orthodoxy, 152–53
English language, 33, 34, 49
Ethic
  civic participation and Christianity-
    based personal, 5, 149
  community service and individually
    negotiated, 67, 98, 99, 113, 115, 145,
    184n34

Manna and life, 66
Manna and volunteerism, 116
volunteerism and individualist v.
    collectivist, 13, 98–99
Ethnic minority, 91, 157
Ethnic negotiation, ethnic assimilation
    v., 50
Ethnic religious organizations, reception
    of, 149
Ethnicity, vi, 92, 180n4
    Christianity and interpreting, 11–13
    Grace discouraging focus on, 62
    Grace, religion and, 31–38, 44–46
    Manna, religion and, 38–44, 46–49
Ethnic-specific church, 108, 109, 141.
    See also Grace
    Black Americans and multiethnic
        church v., 77, 143
    racial boundaries/class distinctions
        and, 77
    schema-creation and, 23
Evangelical Covenant Church, 155
Evangelical cultural schemas, racial v.
    Christian identity and, 13
*Evangelical Identity and Gendered Family
Life* (Gallagher), 106
Evangelical Korean Americans, civic
    responsibility and, 8
Evangelicalism, vi, 20, 22, 36, 95–99,
    178n20
    core beliefs of, 6
    cultural resources and institutional,
        21–22
    cultural schema within institutional,
        21–23
    ethnicity/class/public-participation
        connection and, 141–42
    institutional elasticity of, 22, 23
    institutional models of political
        involvement and, 145–46
    Korean Americans influence on, 8,
        154, 155
    as major American social/political
        group, 6, 153, 174n15
    new American leadership in
        institutional, 154, 155

political action models for Korean
    Americans and, 121–23, 140, 145–46
politics linked to, 137, 186n50
possibilities for change within, 22–23,
    147
practice v. ideology in family
    life and, 106
racial demographic change and, 17,
    153, 154, 155
racial/ethnic institutional change
    possibilities and, 154–55
racial-relations interpretation and,
    76–77
religious individualism made possible
    by, 152
second-generation Korean Americans
    and change in, 10, 137, 140,
    147, 148
structural-location interpretation
    and, 53
as subculture, 25
Evangelicals
    giving to poor and, 7
    Korean American, 8–9, 11, 130–32, 155
    public issues and, 7
    public models of, 6–7, 174n16
Evangelism
    as church community service
        priority, 52
    differing ideas of practicing, 22
    Grace's community service vignette
        and, 95–96
    Grace's coupling volunteering
        with, 103
    Grace's volunteer activities and, 98
    Manna vignette about community
        service and, 96–97
Extended case method, of Michael
    Burawoy, 163

First-generation Korean American
    church, 181n21
    in second-generation view, 56–57
First-generation Korean Americans
    Black Americans conflict with, 83,
        182n32, 186n47

First-generation Korean Americans (*continued*)
   Christianity/economic mobility link and, 58
   political noninvolvement and, 124–30
   second-generation boundaries from, 52–63, 88, 140, 148, 151
   second-generation church ethnic distance from, 150–51
Forms of capital approach, limitations of, 99–100

Gallagher, Sally, 106, 184n25
Gamson, William, 120
Garfinkel, Harold, 61
Gender, 106–7, 113–15, 143, 177n25, 184n25
Gendered volunteerism, 106–7, 114–15
Good American, as meaning to second-generation immigrants, 51
Good citizen, Korean American cultural understandings about, 11
The Good Citizen: A History of American Civic Life (Schudson), 73
Grace Church (Grace), 29, 101, 177n1
   American/Korean culture negotiation and, 37
   America's founding/Christian values connection and, 60
   approach to Christianity at, 36–37
   author's self-presentation at, 33, 34, 38, 159–60
   as autonomous congregation, 34
   Black Americans' victim mentality perception and, 83
   building of, 29
   Christian civil religion and, 60–61
   Christianity/economic mobility link rejected at, 58–59
   civic model consequences at, 107–9
   class/age/ethnic homogeneity of, 36
   class/professional status indicators at, 36
   committees of, 35
   communal obligations model and, 57, 62, 98, 101–9
   communally focused church service and, 62
   data analysis at, 163–64
   data gathering at, 11
   as distinctive second-generation congregation, 33–34, 68–69
   ethnicity at, 37–39, 54–57
   as evangelical, 36
   explicit rejection/implicit acceptance of economic mobility at, 57–60, 61
   financial attainment viewed as cultural trait at, 79
   first/second generation culture negotiation at, 37–38
   gaining entree to, 160–62
   good Christian/good American connection and, 60, 61
   group-based Volunteerism and, 105
   helping other minorities and, 53, 63
   history and organization of, 34–36
   implicit affirmation of model-minority image and, 79–80
   leadership team at, 34
   Manna's models of civic responsibility v., 54t
   Manna's similarities and differences with, 31, 68–69
   membership, 34
   motivational pressure for congregational participation and, 104, 105
   nonethnic Christianity of, 54–57, 68
   non-Korean organizations view of, 109
   participant-observation and survey at, 162–63
   Pastor Joseph and, 34
   people of, 36
   prioritizing difference from first generation and, 52–63, 68–69
   problems focus discouraged by, 61–62
   race/religion/ethnicity at, 29–49
   as reformed, 36
   relationship to Bu-Hual, 34–38
   religion/race/ethnicity and, 31–38, 44–46
   religious rituals, at, 37

research framework at, 163–64
speaking Korean, and, 37
spirituality/wealth connection interpretation and, 79
Sunday service at, 29–30
survey at, 35, 162–63, 168–72, 178n14, 178n15, 178n16
volunteer activities of, where respondent locates, 108t
volunteerism coupled with evangelism at, 98, 103
women's roles at, 35, 106, 107
Grace, motivation for attending, 44–46, 49–50, 104, 105
  exclusively ethnic, 44, 46
  mainly spiritual, 44, 45–46
  nonreflective, 44, 45
  varied, 49–50
Group memberships, as institutional framework/individual actions mediators, 52, 180n3

Hart-Celler reforms, 173n5
Herberg, Will, 156
Holy Spirit, Manna emphasis on, 42

Identity, 3, 74–77, 175n48, 177n17. See also Civic identity
  adhesive, 88
  agency and construction of, 24–25, 142
  boundaries and, 147, 186n3
  career decisions and creation of, 88–89
  Christian, vi, 3, 4, 13, 146–47
  Christian reordering of racial/ethnic, 13
  civic life and religious, 148, 157
  cultural schemas within individual, 23–25
  either-or categories for, 88
  ethnic, 3, 4, 142, 157
  ethnic/civic, 142, 167
  fluid, 88, 92
  formation of, 74–78, 147, 186n3
  individually constructed v. socially structured, 146

  Korean, 92, 143
  Manna categories for civic, 89
  model-minority stereotype and, 78, 84–85
  multiethnic churches and protean, 77, 88, 92, 143, 146
  multiple, 77, 88–90, 143, 146, 147
  new approach to construction of, 146–48
  overlapping civic, 142–43
  Owens on personal, 24, 177n18
  Owens on social, 24
  protean, 77, 88, 92, 143, 146
  racial and civic, 74–77, 85–88
  racial and religious, 26–27
  religious, 26–27
  second-generation Korean Americans and, 14, 142
  social movements and collective, 24, 76, 177n22
  spiritualized sense of ethnic, 90
  subcultural, 25–26, 27, 177n25
Ignatiev, Noel, 75–76
Immigrant generation, gender, and volunteerism at Manna, 113–15
Immigrants, 116, 153, 156–57, 173n4, 173n6, 174n30, 175n38, 186n18
  American Dream and, 57–58
  congregation and, 99, 149
  religion/civic life connection and second-generation, 156
Immigration, 5, 17, 99, 150, 156, 157
Immigration reforms, 5, 76, 173n5
Income Characteristics of Old Town Compared to U.S. Population, 32t
Individualism
  civic commitment fostered by religious, 149, 152, 174n20
  Manna volunteerism and religious, 110
Individually negotiated model of civic responsibility, 52, 63, 98, 99, 113, 116, 141, 184n34
Institutional change
  to American religion, 150–56
  to civic life, 148–50
  cultural schemas and, 21

Institutional change (*continued*)
  cultural theory of, 147
  evangelicalism v. Catholicism and, 22
  implications for, 139–57
Institutions
  Black v. Asian-American participation in mainstream evangelical, 153
  defined, 21
  organizations changing, 22, 147
Integration, religion and civic, vi, 7
Interethnic relationships, 167
Interpretive framework, 90. *See also* Cultural schema
  cultural levels of analysis and, 5, 19
  multiethnic Christianity, Manna and, 110
Interracial relationships, 91, 167
Interview questions
  on church participation history, 165–66
  on civic life, 166–67
  on current church, 166
  on current church involvement, 166
  on demographics, 167–68
  on ethnic and civil identities, 167
  on interethnic and interracial relationships, 167
  on religious beliefs, 166
  on work, 165
Interview script/guide, 165–68
Interviews, conduct and method of, 161–62, 180*n*52
Irish Americans, social construction of whiteness and, 75–76, 182*n*9
Islam, 156

Jesus, being like, at Manna, 98, 112

Kim, Karen Chai, 41
King, Martin Luther, 66, 84, 121
King, Martin Luther, Jr., 154
Kluegel, James, 75
Korean American evangelicals, 8–9, 155
  factors favoring civic involvement of, 8
  as foreigners, 8
  in local congregations, 11
  Religious Right model and, 130–32
Korean American political noninvolvement, lack of agency as frame for, 126
Korean Americans
  cultural schemas and, 27
  ethnic identity and, 4
  evangelicalism influenced by, 8, 154, 155
  multiethnic churches, Black Americans and, 84–85
  as "other," 73–74, 144
  religion/civic life relationship and, 3–15
Korean Americans in second-generation churches, relationship to Black Americans of, 83–84
Korean Americans political noninvolvement
  lack of models as frame for, 126–30
  local soul-saving work as frame for, 124–26
Korean Christianity, 175*n*34, 175*n*35, 175*n*37, 181*n*39
  as distinctively Korean, 9
  Protestant missionary influence on, 9
Korean identity, 92, 143
Korean immigrant church
  becoming part of American Protestantism, 9–10
  nonreligious functions of, 10, 54
Korean language skills, 37, 52, 168, 179*n*23, 180*n*52
Korean-only congregations, 17

Lamont, Michèle, 24, 54, 56, 75, 178*n*15
Larson, Sheila, 117
Levels of analysis. *See* Cultural levels of analysis
Levitt, Peggy, 127
Lifton, Robert Jay, 88, 92
Local civic responsibility, as individually negotiated civic practices, 66–68
Loewen, James W., 76

Malcolm X, 84
Manna Church (Manna), 101
  approach to Christianity at, 42–43
  author's self-presentation at, 38, 159–60
  as charismatic but not Pentecostal, 42
  Christian flag at, 30, 178n3
  Christianity/multiethnicity connection at, 39, 43, 64, 144, 152
  church building of, 30
  community service focus v. group-based civic involvement discourse at, 67–68
  data analysis at, 163–64
  demography of, 40–41, 179n38
  diversity appreciation and, 63–68, 145
  ethic of volunteerism and, 116
  ethnic minorities commonality and, 81, 84–85, 145
  ethnicity at, 38–44
  evangelical distinctive approach of, 42–43, 68–69
  gaining entree to, 160–62
  Grace's models of civic responsibility v., 54
  history and organization of, 38–42
  Holy Spirit emphasis at, 42
  individually negotiated community service and, 52, 54, 63, 98, 99, 109–10, 113, 144, 145, 184n34
  individually negotiated volunteering motivations and, 111–13
  Korean Americans at, 46–49
  Korean v. American identity tension and, 89
  larger Christian community and, 43–44
  leadership of, 40
  life ethic of caring for all and, 66
  member resistance to multiethnicity at, 39
  model-minority image rejected by, 80–82
  multiethnic self-definition and, 52
  multiethnicity of, 38–44, 46–49, 52, 143, 152
  participant-observation and survey at, 162–63
  pastors of, 40
  race/religion/ethnicity at, 29–49
  relaxed approach of, 42
  research framework at, 163–64
  schema challenging model-minority stereotype and, 85
  similarities/differences with Grace and, 31, 68–69
  space for social critics at, 65
  spiritual ethnic-conflict framework provided by, 85
  Sunday service at, 30–31
  survey at, 40–41, 162–63
  women's roles at, 114–15, 144
Manna City Church, 96, 179n37, 183n3
Manna City Fellowship, 41
Manna Fellowship, 11
  data gathering at, 11
Manna, motivation for attending, 46–50
  ministry pressure as, 47, 48–49
  socioeconomic distance as, 47, 49
  spirituality as, 47, 48
  varied, 49–50
Meyer, John, 21
Min, Pyong Gap, 41, 54, 181n21, 183n5
Ministry to the Poor, 67, 181n35
Model(s)
  Black Christians as political, 122, 135–37, 146, 147
  church based civic responsibility, 141–42
  of civic responsibility, 54t
  community service and civic, 95–118
  evangelicals and public, 6–7, 174n16
  noninvolvement and lack of, 126–30
  political action and evangelical, 121–23, 140, 145–46
  political involvement and institutional evangelical, 145
  political involvement and lack of, 119

Model-minority stereotype, 53, 77, 78–82, 91, 143, 146
  civic identity creation and, 78, 84–85
  cultural schema for, 78
  Grace and implicit affirmation of, 79–80
  Manna rejection of, 80–82
Moral dimensions, boundaries with, 56
Moral meanings, 183n11
  community service and, 99, 100
Moral self, 12, 183n6
  Manna and unique, 99
Motivation
  for attending Grace, 44–46, 104–5
  for attending Manna, 46–50
  community service and vision v. obligation based, 112
  Grace participation pressure and, 104–5
  individually negotiated community service approach and, 113, 115, 145
  Manna's individual negotiation of volunteering, 111–13
Motives for attendance
  at Korean American church, 44–46
  at multiethnic church, 46–49
  variety of, 49–50
Multiethnic church, v, 4, 10, 17, 64, 92, 134, 141, 149, 150, 153, 155, 175n47, 181n27, 185n41. *See also* Manna; Multiethnicity
  Black Americans and ethnic specific v., 77, 143
  Christian mission and Manna vision of, 39, 152
  civic life frameworks developed by, 23
  defined, 43
  individually negotiated model of civic responsibility and, 52, 98–99, 102
  racial reconciliation and, 82
  religion/civic life relationship and ethnic-specific v., 77
  second-generation Korean Americans and, 10, 142
Multiethnicity, 143
  Manna and, 38–44, 46–49, 143
  Manna and resistance to, 39
  at Manna as mission and interpretive framework, 43
  Manna, Christianity and, 43, 64, 144
  Manna's core spiritual value of, 81
  Manna's sanctions upholding, 63
Multiple identities, 89–90, 147
  adhesive, 88
  protean, 77, 88, 143, 146

Names, changed, 160–61, 173n1, 177n1
Narratives
  congregations and Christianity-based moral, 61–63
  of Korean-American politics as future participation key, 120
  of local civic responsibility, 61–63
National civic responsibility
  as religiously motivated social critics, 64–66
  as upholding American social order, 60
New American Christianity, 153
New Americans
  Black Christians and, 153
  possibly changing evangelicalism, 153
New Christian America, demography and, 153
Non-Christian religion, civic incorporation of, 156
Nonethnic Christianity, in second-generation churches, 54–57, 68, 151

Old Town, 11, 30–31, 144, 147, 178n6
  Grace outward focus and community service in, 62
  real name concealed of, 160–61
  as study choice, 33
  urban nature of, 33
Omi, Michael, 75, 87
Organizational schemas, for civic responsibility, 68–69, 70, 71
Organizations
  changing institutions, 22, 147
  nation states and, 176n14
Owens, Timothy, 24

Packer, J. I., 37, 69, 181n39
Pan-Asian churches, 10, 175n47, 179n34
Participant observation, 162–63
Pastor Joseph, 35, 36, 55, 60, 62, 79, 80, 101, 104
Pastor Phil, 39, 42, 43, 81
  broad evangelical knowledge of, 42, 43
  on Manna's theological perspective, 42
Personal ethic, 5
Political involvement, institutional evangelical models of, 145–46
Politics, for Korean Americans
  Black Christians as model for, 122, 135–37, 146, 147
  congregation-imparted models lacking in, 119
  congregation-provided resources for, 120–21
  evangelical political action models and, 121–23, 140, 145–46
  evangelicalism and, 119–38, 186n7
  evangelically influenced noninvolvement and, 122
  first-generation noninvolvement in, 124–30
  future participation and narratives of, 120
  moral frameworks for action and, 121
  new models for, 132–35
  noninvolvement in, 124–30
  political/national affairs interest percentages and, 123
  political/social thinking self-description and, 130t
  Presbyterian-sponsored conference on, 134, 186n42
  Religious Right model and, 130–32, 147
  as secondary to local soul-saving, 124–26
  voter registration percentages and, 124t
Presbyterian Church (USA), 134
Professional success, second-generation view and true Christianity v., 59
Promise Keepers, 154
  racism and, 27
Protean identity, 77, 88, 92, 143, 146
Protestantism, and Korean Americans, 10, 175n45
Putnam, Robert, 67

Race, 92
  Christianity and interpretation of, 11–13
  civic identity and, 74–78, 85–88
  evangelicalism and, 17, 76–77, 153, 154, 155
  ministry programs and, 23, 177n16
  religion/ethnicity at Grace and Manna, 29–49
  theory, 75
Racial categories, 73–77, 86, 87, 88
  census and, 76, 182n13
Racial formation, 75
Racial identity, 26–27, 74–78, 84–85
Racial location, cultural schema and, 26
Racialization, of new immigrant groups, 76
Racism
  symbolic, 75, 182n6
  white v. black evangelical views, on, 26–27
Reaching out, 12
Reformed evangelicalism, Grace congregation and, 36
Relationships, interethnic and interracial, 167
Religion
  America and importance of, 6
  America and non-Christian, 155, 156
  civic life and, 3–15
  civic participation fostering, 4, 7–8
  identity and, 26–27
  institutional changes to American, 150–56
  Manna, race/ethnicity and, 38–44, 46–49
  new Americans and American, 155
  race/ethnicity, Grace and, 31–38, 44–46

Religious beliefs, 166
Religious communities, forming civic identity and, 6
Religious organizations, immigrants and, 7
Religious right, 7, 130–32, 145, 147, 185n37
Research framework, and data analysis, 163–64
Resources
  civic responsibility and evangelical, 68–69
  for constructing community service practices, 98, 183n4
  cultural, 18
  cultural, congregation-provided, 11, 176n50
Rights-regarding citizen, 73
Rowan, Brian, 21

Sanctions, upholding Manna multiethnic focus, 63
Schema, 12
  civic responsibility and organizational, 68–69
  DiMaggio on, 19
  evangelicalism and organizational/individual, 19–20
  interpretation of race/ethnicity and, 12
  for Korean American civic responsibility, 51
  social location and, 20
Schudson, Michael, 73, 74
Second-generation immigrants, "good American," meaning for, 51
Second-generation Korean American churches, 155. *See also* Grace Church; Second-generation Korean Americans
  aligned with American "white" evangelicalism, 61
  America viewed as Christian nation by, 60
  culturally nonethnic attempt of, 151
  ethnic distance from first generation by, 150–51
  first-generation church relation to, 150–51, 178n12
  white churches' ethnicity awareness possibly influenced by, 151
Second-generation Korean Americans, vi, 5, 83–84, 159–60, 173n7, 174n28
  American Dream and, 57–58, 59
  Black Americans and, 82–85
  boundaries from first generation, 52–63, 88, 140, 148, 150–51
  civic responsibility construction by, 51, 69, 139, 189n2
  evangelicalism change from, 10, 137, 140, 147, 148
  outward-looking community service of, 140–41
  religious involvement of, 10
  studying, 159–60
Self
  -definition through definition of other, 82–85
  Manna's focus on, 67
Seminaries, Asian/Korean Americans in, 153, 154
Shin, Senator Paull, 134, 186n43
Silent exodus, 10, 152, 175n44, 186n5
Smith, Christian, 25, 26, 27, 106, 121–22, 152–53
  on subcultural identities, 25, 177n25
Social Capital Benchmark Survey (2000), 100
Social construction
  of second-generation civic responsibility, 157
  of whiteness, 75–76, 182n9
Social critics, Manna space for, 65
Social location, 19, 20, 25
  racial, 26
Social movements, 120
Sociology of culture, theoretical interlude on, 17–27
Soul-saving, politics secondary to local, 124–26
Southern Baptist Convention, 154
Spiritual accountability, 34, 178n13

Spirituality
    as Grace's attendance motive, 45, 46
    Grace's interpretation of wealth
        connection to, 79
    individually negotiated approach to
        community service and, 118,
        184n45
    as Manna attendance motive, 47, 48
Stott, John, 37, 69, 178n21, 181n39
Structural location, 52, 53, 116, 139
Subcultural identities, 25–26, 106,
    185n25
Subculture, 25
Sunday service
    at Grace, 29–30
    at Manna, 30–31
Survey questions, 168–72
    church related, 169
    community service related, 169–70
    personal data and demographic, 172
    public affairs related, 170–71
Swidler, Ann, 58, 80

Talk of Love (Swidler), 58
Tocqueville, Alexis de, 6

Victim mentality
    Grace perception of Black Americans
        and, 83
    sermons at Grace discouraging, 62
Volunteer activities
    all Manna, 111t
    Korean American members of Manna,
        111t
Volunteerism, 95–118, 100
    gender and, 106–7, 114–15
    Grace, as primarily through church,
        107, 108
    Grace communal obligations model of,
        101–9
    Grace, immigrant generation and, 102

Grace/Manna similarities/differences
    in, 97–101
Grace's communal control v. Manna's
    individual development approach
    and, 109
Grace's coupling evangelism with,
    98, 103
Grace's obligatory and group
    based, 105
immigrant generation and, 114
individualistic v. collectivist ethic and,
    13, 98–99
Manna, relative meaning of helping
    poor and, 113, 115
Manna, religious individualism
    and, 110
Manna's unique "moral self" for, 99
organizational contexts and, 148
Voter registration, 123, 124t, 185n16

Waters, Mary, 76
Westminster Confession of Faith, 30,
    177n2
White churches, Grace borrowed cultural
    schemas from, 69
Whiteness, 26, 177n26
    social construction of, 75–76,
        182n9
"Who is my neighbor?", 14, 176n54
Wilcox, Clyde, 121
Wilde, Melissa, 177n15
Willow Creek, 42–43, 179n41
Winant, Howard, 75, 87
Women
    Grace and roles of, 35, 106, 107
    Manna and roles of, 114–15, 144
Work, 165

Yang, Fenggang, 88
Yoido Full Gospel Church, 181n39
Yuppie mentality, 59

Breinigsville, PA USA
11 March 2010
234017BV00003B/6/P